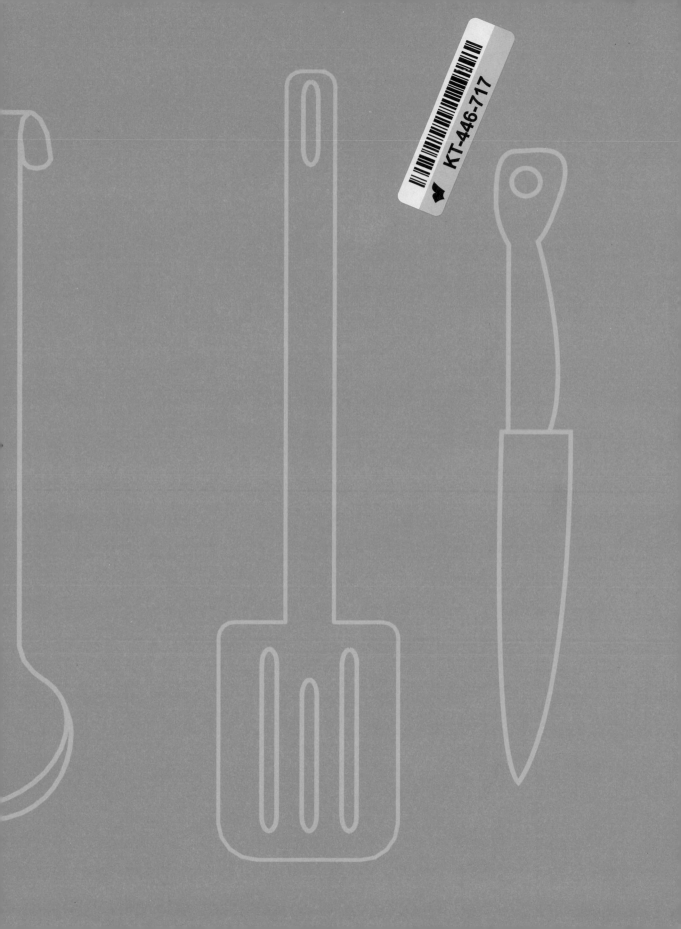

Good Housekeeping
THE FAMILY
COOK
BOOK

Good Housekeeping

THE FAMILY COOK BOOK

CONSULTANT EDITOR BARBARA DIXON

COLLINS & BROWN

First published in United Kingdom in 2006 by
Collins & Brown Limited
151 Freston Road
London W10 6TH

An imprint of Anova Books Company Ltd.

The Good Housekeeping website address is
www.goodhousekeeping.co.uk

3 4 5 6 7 8 9

ISBN 978-1-84340-357-9

A catalogue record for this book is available from the British
Library.

Reproduction by Anorax Imaging Ltd, Leeds
Printed and bound by WKT Co Ltd, China

This book can be ordered direct from the publisher. Contact
the marketing department, but try your bookshop first.

www.anovabooks.com

NOTES

Both metric and imperial measures are given for the
recipes. Follow either set of measures, not a mixture
of both, as they are not interchangeable.

- All spoon measures are level.
  1 tsp = 5ml spoon; 1 tbsp = 15ml spoon.
- Ovens and grills must be preheated to the specified
  temperature.
- Use sea salt and freshly ground black pepper unless
  otherwise suggested.
- Fresh herbs should be used unless dried herbs are
  specified in a recipe.
- Medium eggs should be used except where otherwise
  specified. Free-range eggs are recommended.
- Calorie, fat (including saturates) and carbohydrate
  counts per serving are provided for the recipes.
  Where a recipe serves a variable number, these
  counts range from a larger to a smaller figure
  according to the portion size, which is determined
  by the number you are serving.

DIETARY GUIDELINES

- Note that certain recipes, including mayonnaise,
  lemon curd and some cold desserts, contain raw or
  lightly cooked eggs. The young, elderly, pregnant
  women and anyone with an immune-deficiency
  disease should avoid these, because of the slight
  risk of salmonella.
- Note that some recipes contain alcohol. Check
  the ingredient list before serving to children.
- For all vegetarian recipes (V = vegetarian) containing
  cheese, ensure you buy a vegetarian version (available
  from supermarkets) which should contain vegetable
  derived rennet.

CONTENTS

INTRODUCTION

My mother is a list maker and I've picked up on this now I run my own home. Routine and planning are what keep me going through the week when, even after a day of tasting the recipes cooked in the *Good Housekeeping* kitchens, I still have to prepare supper at home.

With so many women juggling work and home commitments, the emphasis on knowing how to cook with fresh ingredients – and passing on those skills to our children – is as important now as it was in 1924 when the Good Housekeeping Institute was set up to help women around the home. This is what works for me: I do my weekly shop on a Sunday when we have a Sunday roast, usually shared with my sister and her daughters. If the oven's on anyway, I might make a stew to cook at the same time as the meat, to freeze or eat later in the week. I'll write a brief menu plan to make sure everything I've bought is used up and nothing is wasted. Monday is usually leftovers, Tuesday might be pasta, another night it's a stir-fry with rice and another night wraps, with a meaty salad and hummus.

This book includes everything you'll need for family cooking – inspirational recipes to shake up the weekday staples and classics to cook at the weekend – it will last for years and years in the kitchen and become a firm favourite. Happy cooking!

Emma

Emma Marsden
Cookery Editor
Good Housekeeping

1

GETTING STARTED

KITCHEN KNOW-HOW

The family kitchen is also frequently the family dining room and meeting place, but as well as making it a comfortable room, you also need to ensure that it is practical. Cleanliness and hygiene are very important, but with the family traipsing in and out it's bound to be hard to keep the kitchen spotless; below are some basic rules of food hygiene that, if followed, will keep you and your family safe.

KEEPING THE KITCHEN CLEAN

- It's best and safest to give worksurfaces, cupboards, sink and floor a daily clean to get rid of dirt and germs. This is especially important if you own pets that have access to the kitchen.
- Keep all utensils and equipment clean. Check those that are used infrequently – they become dust-gatherers.
- Replace washing-up cloths and brushes frequently. Change teatowels regularly and wash them at a high temperature.

PREPARING FOOD

- Always wash your hands with soap before and after handling food, and when handling different types of food (see below).

- To avoid cross-contamination, keep separate chopping boards for raw meat, fish or poultry and vegetables and cooked food – buy them in different colours to help you remember.
- After each use and in between handling raw meat, fish or poultry, scrub the board with hot, soapy water, then rinse with very hot, clean water.
- Never put cooked or ready-to-eat food on a surface that has just had raw meat, chicken or fish on it – wash the surface thoroughly first.

STORING RAW FOOD
(see also How to Shop, page 17)

- Check the 'best-before' or 'use-by' dates and any other storage instructions on the label.
- All perishable food should be put in the fridge or freezer as soon as possible after purchase.
- Store food in the fridge in the correct place (see page 12) and check that the fridge is at the correct temperature.
- To prevent one food from contaminating another, store each in plastic food bags, freezer bags or in rigid polythene containers, or wrap in aluminium foil or clingfilm. Store eggs in their box to stop them absorbing odours from other food.

STORING COOKED FOOD IN THE FRIDGE

- Cool cooked food as quickly as possible before storing it in the fridge. If convenient, divide it among several shallow containers – it will cool faster.
- Store cooked food on a higher shelf than raw food.
- Wrap and store leftovers immediately and use up as soon as possible.

REHEATING COOKED FOOD

- To kill any bacteria, food should be reheated until piping hot throughout, so check before serving.
- Reheat food once only.

STORING FISH, CHICKEN AND MEAT IN THE FRIDGE AND FREEZER

FISH

- Although fish tastes best when it's cooked and eaten on the day it's caught, most varieties can be stored for a day or two. Always check the use-by date on packaged fish, or ask the fishmonger's advice if buying from the counter.
- To store fish, remove it from its original wrapping, rinse in cold water and pat dry, then cover and place towards the bottom of the fridge.
- Frozen fish should be stored in the freezer at a minimum temperature of −18°C. White and smoked fish can be frozen for up to three months, oil-rich fish and shellfish for two months.
- To defrost fish and shellfish, leave it in the fridge overnight to thaw. Thawing fish in water leads to loss of texture, flavour and nutrients. Never refreeze it once it has defrosted. You can cook fish straight from the freezer – just add a couple of extra minutes to the cooking time.

CHICKEN

- To avoid the potential risk of food poisoning, particular care must be taken when handling raw poultry because bacteria that can cause food poisoning may be present.
- Remove the fresh chicken from its wrapping and make a note of the use-by date instructions on the label. Take out any giblets, then place on a plate, cover and store on a low shelf in the fridge. Store the giblets in a separate covered bowl in the fridge. Cook thoroughly within two days.
- Freeze chicken on the day it is purchased. Remove from its original wrapping and take out the giblets, then re-wrap in a strong freezer bag, seal and date. It will keep for up to six months. Freeze the giblets separately.
- To defrost a whole chicken, leave it in its wrapping, place on a plate and put in the refrigerator for a minimum of 12 hours. Chicken joints will take less time. Use as soon as it has defrosted. Never refreeze it once it has defrosted.

MEAT

- Remove the fresh meat from its original wrapping and make a note of the use-by date and instructions on the label. Place the meat on a plate or dish and cover loosely, then put on a low shelf in the fridge.
- Joints, steaks and chops will keep for up to three days, depending on the use-by date. Minced or cubed meat should be used within one to two days.
- Freeze meat on the day it is purchased. Wrap in a strong freezer bag, seal and date. Refer to your freezer's instructions for the keeping times of the various cuts.
- To defrost frozen meat, leave it in its wrapping, place on a plate and put in the refrigerator. Use as soon as it has defrosted. Never refreeze it once it has defrosted.

BASIC EQUIPMENT

Having the right equipment can make life so much easier in the kitchen, so always buy the best-quality equipment you can afford – it will last longer and give better results.

Consider the practicality of a separate fridge and freezer, and the size of each. Whether you cook with gas or electricity will depend on where you live, but consider a combination gas hob and electric oven; and perhaps you need a double oven. There are also various types of microwave oven available. It all depends on how and what you cook most often.

Consider the weight and balance of knives and the comfort of their handles. Always keep your knives sharp – a blunt knife will not only cause frustration, but is also more likely to slip and cut you.

Check that the pans you buy are suitable for your hob (i.e. gas or electric). The bases should be thick enough to ensure maximum heat conduction.

Select kitchen scales that can weigh both small and large amounts, and that show the weight in both imperial and metric measurements.

THE FRIDGE

The fridge is a vital piece of equipment, which keepS food fresh for longer. However, it is the main culprit for waste, and the bigger it is the more it becomes a repository for out-of-date condiments and bags of wilted salad leaves that lurk in its depths. Check the shelves and salad drawer regularly and rotate foods as you buy fresh supplies.

To ensure that you can rustle up something simple and satisfying to eat at short notice, try always to have the following ingredients in the fridge:

- Fresh produce: celery, tomatoes, garlic, onions, carrots and lemons.
- Dairy produce: cheese, eggs, butter, milk.
- Cured meats: vacuum-packed salami, chorizo and Parma ham.

How to store food in the fridge

- Cool cooked food to room temperature before putting in the fridge.
- Wrap or cover all food except fruit and vegetables.
- Practise fridge discipline. The coldest shelves are at bottom – store raw meat, fish and poultry there.
- Separate cooked foods from raw foods – put the cooked foods towards the top of the fridge.
- Use the salad drawer for leafy and salad vegetables and other vegetables such as leeks and cauliflower. Don't store potatoes or bananas in the fridge.

To make sure the fridge works properly

- Don't overfill it.
- Don't put hot foods in it.
- Don't open the door more than necessary.
- Do clean it regularly.

THE FREEZER

The freezer is an invaluable storage tool and if you use your freezer properly – particularly with batch-cooking (see page 11) – you can save precious family time and prevent a lot of wastage.

Basic freezer standbys

HERBS Frozen herbs are great timesavers. There's no wastage and the flavour is a lot better than dried herbs.
SPICES Chillies, lemongrass and ginger freeze well and can be used directly from the freezer. Grate ginger unpeeled; lemongrass and chillies can be chopped while frozen.
STOCKS There's nothing like a good home-made stock to transform the flavour of a soup, sauce or savoury dish. Boil until very reduced and concentrated in flavour, then freeze in 300ml/10fl oz quantities. Allow room for expansion in the container.
SOUPS Freeze in usable portions or buy fresh soups in cartons – these also freeze well and can be cooked from frozen. Allow room for expansion in the container.
BACON Pack in single layers between sheets of greaseproof paper, so it's easy to remove the right amount.
PASTRY Ready-made bought puff, filo and sweet dessert pastry freeze well. Make your own shortcrust, wrap in clingfilm and seal in freezer bags.
CREAM Lightly whip double cream and freeze in usable amounts in sealed containers.
FRUIT Bags of summer and tropical fruit are great for purées and quick desserts.
BREAD, CAKES AND SCONES Slice bread and cakes before freezing so that it is easy to remove just as much as you need. Sliced bread can be toasted from frozen.

How to store food in the freezer

- Freeze food as soon as possible after purchase.
- Freeze food in portions – pack in freezer bags or rigid plastic containers and label with name and date.
- Never put foods that are still warm into the freezer.
- Check the manufacturer's instructions for maximum freezing times.
- Do not refreeze food once it has thawed.

What not to store in the freezer

Some of the foods that don't store well are:

WHOLE EGGS Freeze whites and yolks separately.

FRIED FOODS These lose their crispness and can go soggy.

POTATOES In stews and casseroles potatoes lose their texture.

VEGETABLES Cucumber, lettuce and celery, and fruit such as bananas have too high a water content.

OTHER VEGETABLES Blanch first or they will lose their colour, flavour and texture.

CHEESE Hard cheeses will become crumbly once defrosted, but can be used for grating or in cooking.

SAUCES Mayonnaise and similar sauces will separate when defrosted.

To make sure the freezer works properly

- Defrost it regularly.
- Never put foods that are still warm into the freezer.
- Keep the freezer as full as possible.

Defrosting and reheating food

- Some foods, such as vegetables, soups and sauces, can be cooked from frozen – dropped into boiling water, or heated gently in a pan until thawed. Defrost other food in the refrigerator or a cold larder; never leave out in a warm room. Place food on a plate to collect any drips.
- Ensure the food is thoroughly defrosted before cooking.
- Cook food as soon as possible after defrosting.
- Ensure the food is piping hot all the way through after cooking.

THE HOB AND OVEN

These can be freestanding, integral or two separate units. Gas hobs are more easily controlled than electric, where residual heat is retained in the plates. This is an important factor if the temperature of what's being cooked is critical. It s down to personal choice and availability.

Whether your oven is gas or electric, fan-assisted, multi-functional or conventional, you'll invariably have to cook with it for a while to get to know its idiosyncrasies, since all ovens vary. Fan ovens produce a more even distribution of heat and so cook more quickly than conventional ovens. When following a recipe, you can either adjust the temperature or the cooking time – check the manufacturer's instructions.

A self-cleaning oven will certainly make spills easier to clean, but otherwise, to prevent smoke and fumes,

clean the oven regularly, not forgetting to clean the inside of the door.

To cope with spills in the oven, line the bottom with aluminium foil (keep away from any electric element), or line a baking sheet with foil and place on the shelf underneath the item being cooked.

THE MICROWAVE

A conventional microwave oven cooks by microwaves that pass through glass, paper, china and plastic and are absorbed by moisture molecules in the food. They penetrate the food to a depth of about 5cm/2in, where they cause the molecules to vibrate and create heat within the food, which in turn cooks it.

Metal deflects microwaves and so nothing metallic or containing metal decoration should be used in the oven.

The manufacturer's instruction booklet will tell you all you need to know to get the best out of the microwave oven, but below are a few handy tips.

Microwave safety

- The oven will work only if the door is closed.
- The door has a special seal to prevent microwaves from escaping.
- Never switch on the microwave oven when there is nothing inside – the waves will bounce off the walls of the oven and could damage the magnetron (the device that converts electricity into microwaves).
- Allow sufficient space around the microwave oven for ventilation through the air vents.
- If using plastic containers, use only microwave-proof plastic – ordinary plastics can buckle.

What to use a microwave for

- Cooking ready-prepared meals.
- Cooking vegetables and fish.
- Reheating cooked foods and drinks.
- Softening butter and melting chocolate.
- Drying herbs.
- Toasting nuts.
- Scrambling eggs.

What not to use a microwave for

- Browning meat (unless the oven comes with a browning unit).
- Soufflés.
- Puff pastry.
- Breaded or battered foods.

Containers for microwaving

- Any microwave-proof containers, or ovenproof glass and ceramic dishes. Choose shallow, oval or round dishes with straight sides, so that the microwaves are unable to concentrate in any corners and cook food unevenly. Choose light-coloured cookware – dark containers tend to absorb too much heat, preventing the food from cooking properly.
- Special cooking bags (pierce the bag to allow steam to escape).

Microwave tips

- Consult the manufacturer's handbook before you use the microwave for the first time.
- Use a plastic trivet so that the microwaves can penetrate the underside of the food.
- Put food around the perimeter of the turntable, leaving a gap in the middle, so that the microwaves can penetrate from all sides.
- Cover fatty foods such as bacon and sausages with kitchen paper to soak up any fat.
- If covering foods with a lid or clingfilm, leave a gap or pierce the film to allow steam to escape.
- Stir liquids at intervals during microwaving.
- Turn over large items of food, such as joints, during cooking so that the top and bottom cook evenly.
- Clean the interior and exterior of the oven regularly.

Other electrical items

Although a food processor isn't essential, it's undoubtedly the best investment a busy cook can make. It cuts out the slog in food preparation such as chopping, grating, slicing and kneading.

Other handy electrical devices are a stick blender, blender and juicer, coffee grinder and slow-cooker.

KITCHEN EQUIPMENT

These are the items that you'll need for everyday cooking, and you've probably got a good many of them already. You can add specialist equipment as and when you need it.

POTS AND PANS

Pans: large, 20cm (8in) diameter with lid; medium, 18cm (7in) diameter with lid; small, 16cm (6½in) diameter with lid

Frying pan with 24cm (9½in) diameter

Heavy-based griddle pan

Large stockpot

Steamer

Wok

MEASURING WEIGHT, VOLUME, TIME AND TEMPERATURE

Kitchen scales

Measuring spoons

Measuring jug

Kitchen timer

Thermometers: meat, oven, deep-frying, fridge

SIFTING, SIEVING, DRAINING AND STRAINING

Sieve

Colander

Salad spinner

CUTTING, CHOPPING AND PEELING

Cook's knives, one with 19cm (7½in) blade, one with 8cm (3⅛in) blade; small serrated knife

Two-pronged carving fork

Vegetable peeler

Knife sharpener

Boards: one for vegetables or cooked food, one for raw meat, fish or poultry

Kitchen scissors

STIRRING AND TRANSFERRING

Wooden spoons

Whisks

Large metal spoon

Ladle

Rubber spatula

Fish slice

Palette knife

Tongs

Salad servers

BOWLS

Salad bowls and heatproof mixing bowls in various sizes

OVEN-COOKING

Two roasting tins

Two heavy baking trays

Large, flameproof casserole dish

Pie dish

Gratin dish

Loose-based cake tin

Springform cake tin

Swiss roll tin

Wire rack

HANDY UTENSILS AND OTHER ITEMS

Oven gloves

Corkscrew and tin opener

Skewers

Grater

Pestle and mortar

Potato masher

Rolling pin

Pastry brush

Grater

Juice squeezer and fruit zester

Kitchen paper, aluminuim foil, clingfilm, greaseproof paper, baking paper or parchment, cocktail sticks, kitchen string

Kettle and toaster

STOCKING YOUR STORECUPBOARD

Once you've got a well-stocked cupboard, you can avoid the frustration of not having the right basic ingredients when you want to rustle up a meal. However, resist the urge to get carried away. It's easy to fill the cupboard with interesting bottles you 'might use one day' and before you realize it, they're well past their use-by date. Only keep essential ingredients for everyday cooking and buy herbs and spices in tiny amounts – they lose their flavour and aroma within a couple of months. Buy small jars of sauces, otherwise you'll have numerous half-used jars and bottles. Don't be put off by the size of the chart below. Once you have the basics, you can build up your stocks as and when you need to.

THE STORECUPBOARD

DRIED

Pasta and noodles

Rice: long grain, arborio and carnaroli, Thai, easy-cook, basmati, pudding

Pulses

Nuts: pinenuts, walnuts, almonds

Dried fruit: apricots, dates, sultanas, raisins

Stock cubes: chicken, beef, vegetable bouillon

Spices and herbs

Salt: table, sea, rock

Pepper: ground and peppercorns

Flour: plain, self-raising, wholemeal, cornflour

Dried yeast

Gelatine

Baking powder, cream of tartar, bicarbonate of soda

Sugar: white granulated, brown, caster, icing, demerara

Tea

Instant coffee

Real coffee (once opened, store in fridge or freezer)

Cocoa powder

BOTTLES/JARS

Mayonnaise

Tomato ketchup and purée

Anchovy essence

Tabasco sauce

Worcestershire sauce

Good-quality pasta sauce

Oriental sauces: soy, hoisin, oyster, nam pla (fish), tamari, ketjap manis, chilli

Curry paste

Chutneys

Pickles

Olives

Capers

Mustard: Dijon, English, wholegrain

Oils: olive, vegetable, corn, groundnut, sunflower, sesame

Vinegar: wine, malt, balsamic, sherry, cider

Jam

Marmalade

Honey

CANS

Chopped and whole tomatoes

Fish: tuna, salmon, anchovies

Beans and pulses: cannellini, haricot, kidney, flageolet, chickpeas

Coconut milk/cream

Fruit

A few rules on storage

- Keep food cupboards cool and dry. Line shelves for easy cleaning and clean regularly. Organize shelves – put new goods to the back and use up those in front first.
- Canned food, once opened, should be transferred to a bowl and, if not used at once, be covered and kept in the fridge.
- Some food in jars, once opened, can be kept in the cupboard, but other foods will need to be kept in the fridge – read the labels.
- Store dried pulses, herbs, beans and spices in sealed containers, preferably in the cupboard. Light can affect, for example, dried herbs and cause them to deteriorate.
- Check use-by dates regularly.

HOW TO SHOP

The way you shop will depend on your family's individual needs and your proximity to the shops, but whether it's once a week or more frequently, it's always best to make a list. This will not only help you stick to a budget – no impulse buying – but will also ensure that you buy everything you need and don't get home and find a vital ingredient for supper is missing.

Supermarkets now provide all manner of produce all year round – fresh strawberries at Christmas, asparagus way before June – so it's easy to forget where food comes from and when it is in season. Food bought in its true season will taste vastly different from forced produce, and you'll benefit from lower prices.

Only buy perishables that you'll be able to cook/eat before the use-by date. Select food wisely and buy it in optimum condition. Check that the packaging is undamaged, and that cans are not dented or bulging.

CHOOSING BEEF

- A light red meat doesn't necessarily indicate quality. Look for a meat that is dark red.
- Fat should be creamy white.
- A fair amount of fat should be distributed through the meat as fine marbling – this tenderizes the meat during cooking.
- Look for neat cuts; there should be no splinters of bone or ragged edges, and the cut should be trimmed of sinew.
- The thickness of the piece of meat should be uniform for even cooking.
- Look for the Quality Standard Mark as an assurance of quality.
- Select the cut of beef as follows:
  - **Roasting and braising**: rib, top rump, topside, silverside.
  - **Stews, casseroles and mince**: neck or clod, chuck steak, thin flank, shin.
  - **Grilling and frying**: rump, fillet, sirloin, entrecôte.

CHOOSING LAMB

- Meat from young English lambs is pale with a small amount of creamy white fat. There should be a light marbling of fat within the flesh.
- Joints and chops are smaller than those of imported lamb.
- Imported lamb tends to be slightly darker and coarser.
- The bones should be cleanly cut, with no splinters.
- Look for the Quality Standard Mark as an assurance of quality.
- Select the cut of lamb as follows:
  - **Roasting, grilling and frying**: all lamb cuts except middle neck and scrag.
  - **Stews and casseroles**: middle neck, scrag, shoulder, chump chops.
  - **Mince**: leg.

CHOOSING PORK

- Look for pale pink, firm, smooth-textured flesh.
- The fat should be white.
- The rind/skin should be smooth and hairless.
- Look for neat cuts; there should be no splinters of bone or ragged edges, and the cut should be trimmed evenly.
- Ask the butcher to score the rind/skin for you – with his large, super-sharp knives he can do it much quicker than you'll be able to at home.
- Select the cut of pork as follows:
  - **Roasting**: most cuts are good for roasting.
  - **Stews, casseroles and mince**: diced shoulder, spare ribs, belly, neck.
  - **Frying and grilling**: tenderloin or fillet, chops, escalopes.

CHOOSING FRUIT AND VEGETABLES

- Buy from a shop with a high turnover to get the freshest produce.
- Buy in season.
- Look for bright, fresh colours and crisp leaves.
- Avoid bruised, discoloured or damaged produce.
- Don't prod fruit and vegetables with your fingers – weigh in the palm of your hand.
- Buy unripe as well as ripe fruit to ensure that you'll have fruit to eat throughout the week.
- Don't buy more than you need for a week.

CHOOSING CHICKEN

- Birds should have a neat shape, an even colour and no blemishes or tears on the skin.
- The body should look meaty and plump.
- Chicken is available as poussins (baby), spring chicken (slightly older), boiling fowl, corn-fed (yellow) and as portions. To save money, joint a chicken (see page 22).
- Types of chicken:
  - ∗ **Organic**: These birds are allowed to roam free, which means they get plenty of exercise. They are reared without drugs, and eat feed that's mostly organic. This all helps to make a good, well-flavoured bird, but at a premium price.
  - ∗ **Free-range**: These birds must have access to the outside environment, but this doesn't necessarily mean having a free run – many farms make do with holes in the huts, so if the birds have been reared inside they are used to it and have no incentive to stray outside. As a result, their limbs are unexercised, making the meat less muscly and more watery. Drugs may be used routinely. In some cases you may be buying a bird that's had as many disadvantages as one that's been intensively reared. These birds are cheaper than organic birds, but more expensive than intensively reared birds.
  - ∗ **Intensively reared**: These birds are raised in overcrowded conditions. This leads to infections and the birds, feeling stressed, tend to peck each other because they don't have enough room. Since they can't move around easily, they tend to have weak legs, take less exercise and so end up fatter. Drugs and beak trimming can be used as a matter of course

CHOOSING FISH

- Try to buy fish and seafood on the day you want to eat it, as it spoils very quickly.
- Use your nose and your eyes when buying fish – it must be absolutely fresh and smell of the sea. The eyes must be bright and clear, the gills bright pink or red and the flesh firm.
- When you press the fish with your finger it should not leave an indentation, and when you pick it up it should not flop.
- The fishmonger will scale, clean, fillet or skin fish if you ask him.
- When choosing molluscs (scallops, mussels, clams, oysters), look for those with tightly closed, undamaged shells.
- Fish stocks need to be protected, so go for line-caught fish and those from sustainable sources – Icelandic or Norwegian cod, for example.
- Types of fish:
  - ∗ **White fish**: large fish such as cod and coley, are usually sold as steaks, fillets or cutlets. Smaller fish, such as whiting and haddock are sold in fillets.
  - ∗ **Flat fish**: halibut and turbot are sold in fillets or as steaks. Smaller flat fish such as plaice, lemon and Dover sole are usually sold whole, trimmed and filleted.
  - ∗ **Oily fish**: mackerel, herrings and sardines, are usually sold whole. Salmon are sold whole or in steaks.
  - ∗ **Shellfish**: these are divided into two groups – those with legs (crustaceans) and those without (molluscs). Most are available all year round.

False economies

When buying fresh food, don't be seduced by low prices for bulk purchasing or by reduced stickers, unless you're sure you can use the food before it deteriorates, or there's room in your freezer. The same goes for the BOGOF offers (buy one, get one free) – you may find you're throwing away not just food, but money.

What the labels really mean

LOW FAT Product must contain no more than 5g fat per 100g.
REDUCED FAT Must contain 25% less fat than the full-fat version.
LOW CALORIE Product must contain less than 40 calories per 100g.
REDUCED CALORIE Product must contain 25% fewer calories than a similar product.
LITE Can refer to the product's taste, colour – anything. It doesn't mean it contains less fat or fewer calories.

Fairtrade

Selecting just a few 'Fairtrade' items when you do your weekly shop can improve people's lives in the developing world. If the fruit, tea, coffee and marmalade you choose have been fairly traded, the people who produce them will have been paid a proper price, plus extra to invest in the community. Look for the 'Fairtrade' logo on products.

Make ready-made foods work for you

Sometimes you are just short of time and it's unrealistic to cook the family a whole meal from scratch. But the deli counters and canned goods shelves can provide you with the ingredients to whip up instant meals.

- Buy some good-quality Oriental stir-fry or cook-in sauces. You just need to pop the meat, chicken or prawns in the pan with it and cook it through.
- Ditto good-quality pasta sauces – for a meal in minutes.
- Use ready-baked pastry cases.
- Top bought pizza bases with your own healthy ingredients.
- Raid the deli counter for marinated vegetables, cold meats, cured fish and cheeses and add the finishing touches at home.

A NOTE ON FARMERS' MARKETS

Supermarkets are fine for doing the big once-a-week shop, but using farmers' markets, farm shops, vegetable box schemes, local butchers, greengrocers and bakers can often reap rewards in terms of quality and variety. You'll find all you need and more at a farmers' market. Take your pick of seasonal fruit and vegetables, unusual meat, cheeses and artisan bread. There are strict guidelines set out by the National Association of Farmers' Markets, so, for example, when you buy cheese know the farmer will have reared the cow or goat, milked it, then made the cheese himself.

Why is it a good idea to buy from one?

- It's a great chance to try before you buy – many suppliers will have samples for you to taste, and you can ask how the produce is grown or made.
- You're buying fresh local produce that has been recently harvested or sourced.
- It cuts down on packaging and removes the middleman, so more of the profits go direct to the supplier.
- It's generally cheaper than buying from supermarkets (their prices usually include costs such as transport).
- There is greater variety. The produce doesn't go through lots of handling stages, where each vegetable has to conform to a set standard.
- Produce often tastes better because it hasn't travelled miles in controlled conditions.

ORGANIC OR NON-ORGANIC?

Organic is big business. Visit any supermarket and you'll find not just one or two organic products, but dedicated sections. And it's not just about vegetables and meat any more – supermarket shelves are now packed with products as diverse as organic biscuits and pasta sauces. But does organic food really taste better?

The pros

THE ENVIRONMENT Organic farming is better for wildlife, causes less pollution, produces less carbon dioxide, generates less dangerous waste, improves animal welfare and provides employment in rural areas.

PESTICIDES The Soil Association allows organic farmers to use just one pesticide (rotenone) and the farmer has to justify its use. As a comparison, the non-organic industry regularly uses more than 200 pesticides.

TASTE Organic food nearly always tastes better than non-organic. For example, organic eggs have richer, more intensely flavoured yolks than non-organic; organic carrots are sweeter and vibrantly coloured; meat is fuller flavoured.

The cons

PRICE Organic food is more expensive than non-organic, but there are many more costs involved in producing it.

SOURCE Just because produce has been labelled organic doesn't mean that it's local – or even grown in Britain. Over half of organic food sold in the UK has come from abroad, with over three-quarters of that being sold through supermarkets nationwide.

TECHNIQUES

BE A CONFIDENT COOK

To enjoy cooking requires, firstly, getting organised:

■ Read the recipe to make sure you understand it and have sufficient time to make it. Find out whether you have all the necessary ingredients, then make a list of anything that you need to buy.

■ Check that you have the necessary pots, pans and other equipment.

■ Before you start cooking, clear the decks in the kitchen to give yourself room to work, and put on an apron to protect your clothes and the food.

■ Check whether the oven needs to be preheated.

■ The ingredients in a recipe are listed in order of use, so weigh and measure everything that you need, and do as much advance preparation of ingredients as possible – peeling, chopping and slicing, for example.

■ The recipe method will take you through each stage step by step. Don't rush – take your time at each step before moving on to the next one.

■ Use a kitchen timer – once something is in the oven or bubbling away on the hob, it's easy to get distracted and lose track of time.

COOKING METHODS

There are various methods of cooking – here is a quick guide to the ones most commonly used, as well as which foods are best suited to each method.

Grilling

A quick process suitable for tender cuts such as chops, steaks, bacon, oily fish and poultry joints. To ensure even cooking, food should be of even size. Always preheat the grill. The food can be placed on a rack in a grill pan directly under the heat source for a short, intense burst of heat to brown the exterior, and then moved further away from the heat to a lower level to cook the interior. Turn the food over during the grilling. To save on washing up, line the grill pan with foil – this will collect any fat or juices and can be thrown away after cooking.

Frying

There are various methods of frying, but essentially (with the exception of dry-frying), they all involve cooking in hot fat in an uncovered pan. The pan should have a thick base to conduct heat evenly, and a heatproof handle. A variety of fats can be used, depending on what is being cooked, from olive oil and vegetable oils to butter, margarine or lard. Check the recipe for the recommended fat. If you use butter for frying, add a little oil to prevent the butter from burning.

DRY-FRYING This is cooking in a hot pan without any fat. It is used for fatty foods such as sausages, hamburgers or duck, where the skin releases its own fat, or to brown nuts and spices. In some cases, the base of the pan should be smeared with a tiny amount of fat to prevent sticking.

SHALLOW-FRYING This process uses a small amount of fat – about 1 cm (½in) – which is heated in the pan over a medium heat. Food should be of even size and at room temperature. Don't crowd the pan – cook food in batches to avoid lowering the temperature of the fat. Shallow-fried food is often coated first, such as fish fillets or escalopes. Foods suitable for shallow-frying include eggs, bacon, fish, steaks, liver, sausages and potato slices.

DEEP-FRYING This uses a large amount of oil (usually vegetable), which is heated in a deep pan or deep-fat fryer to a specified temperature (a deep-frying thermometer is a useful aid to gauging the heat). The pan should be no more than half-full and the oil should be brought to temperature gradually. Foods to be deep-fried are usually coated with batter or breadcrumbs, which protects them and seals in their juices or moisture during cooking. A wire frying basket makes it easier to lower food into the oil and remove it when cooked. Cook food in small quantities to avoid lowering the temperature of the oil. Food cooks very quickly by this method and a variety of foods are suitable for deep-frying, such as fish, chicken, chips and vegetable and fruit fritters. Never leave a pan unattended when deep-fat frying.

STIR-FRYING A super-quick method, traditional in the Far East, but now popular in many countries. Before you start cooking, make sure that all the food is cut into even-sized pieces. Heat a wok or large frying pan and then add small amount of oil. Once it is hot, put in the food and keep it moving in the pan while it cooks. Don't overcrowd the pan or the food will stew rather than fry. Stir-frying can be used to cook almost any vegetable, tender cuts of meat and poultry, and fish and shellfish.

Poaching

This is a gentle method, where foods are submerged in a liquid, which is usually flavoured, and cooked on the hob. Except in the case of fish, the liquid should be heated until barely moving before the food is placed in it: it should not boil or simmer. The pan is left uncovered. Fish is added to cold liquid, which is then heated until the surface just trembles. The pan is usually covered. Foods suitable for poaching include eggs, fish (whole or cuts), shellfish, chicken, gnocchi and fruit.

Boiling

This is a fast method of cooking in liquid at a high temperature. It involves immersing the food in liquid, heating it until it comes to the boil, and then reducing the heat to either a slow, rolling boil (agitated bubbles all over the surface), or a simmer (bubbles appearing on one or two parts of the surface only). A gentle boil can be used in an uncovered pan to reduce stocks and other liquids so that they become thicker or more concentrated. Foods suitable for boiling include vegetables, eggs, rice, pasta, grains and cereals, dumplings, boiling fowl, gammon, bacon, mutton and silverside of beef.

Steaming

Steaming cooks food in a hot vapour rather than in liquid. The food has no contact with the liquid, but is put in a metal or bamboo steamer, covered with a lid and set over a pan of boiling water or a flavoured stock. There are various steamers available, the most common of which are two- or three-tier pans, the second and third tiers having holes in their base to allow steam from the lower pan to rise and cook the food. Food to be cooked by steaming has to rely on quality since there is no browning or fat involved. Foods suitable for steaming include vegetables, fish, shellfish, poultry, dumplings and wontons, and steamed puddings, both sweet and savoury.

Braising and stewing

Both are methods of cooking slowly in liquid.
BRAISING This involves cooking meat slowly on a bed of diced vegetables with the addition of a little stock. The meat is cooked whole or in large pieces and is browned over a high heat on the hob first. The stock is added, then the pan is covered with a tight-fitting lid and the meat cooks in the heat of the steam, either in the oven or on the hob. Braising is suitable for less tender cuts of meat, or those with less fat, and older poultry. Vegetables can be cooked in a similar way.

STEWING The process is similar to braising, but is used for tough cuts of meat, which are cut into small pieces and may be browned first, or not, as required. More liquid is added to the pan than for braising.

Roasting

This is a method where food is cooked in the oven by direct heat with no liquid, although a little fat is sometimes used. The food is usually put in a roasting tin (or on a rack in the tin) and, from time to time during cooking, fat and juices from the tin are spooned over the food (this is called basting). If a long roasting time is required – for a turkey, for example – the meat may be covered with foil for part of the cooking time; otherwise it is left uncovered. A skewer or meat thermometer should be used to check that the food is cooked. If using a skewer, insert it into the thickest part of the meat – the juices should run clear. See the manufacturer's instructions for using a meat thermometer. When roast meats come out of the oven, they should be left to 'rest' for about 15 minutes to allow the juices within the meat to settle and distribute evenly. The juices left in the roasting tin can be used to make gravy. Foods suitable for roasting include poultry, game, joints and fillets of beef, lamb, pork and veal, whole large fish and vegetables. (See page 262 for roasting chart)

Pot-roasting

This is a one-pot method of cooking large pieces of meat, whole birds and fish. The food is browned in hot fat first and then removed from the pan while chopped vegetables are added and browned. The food is then put on top of the vegetables and a little liquid is added, the pan is tightly covered and the food is cooked slowly in the oven or on the hob over a low heat. Foods suitable for pot-roasting include chicken, game, beef brisket or topside, stuffed and rolled breast of lamb and joints of pork.

Baking

Baked foods are cooked by dry heat in the oven, with no additional liquid. Cakes, biscuits, bread, potatoes and soufflés are cooked this way.

HOW TO COOK PERFECT PASTA

1 Allow 125g (4oz) dried pasta or 175g (6oz) fresh pasta per person.
2 Use a large pan with plenty of water so that the pasta can move around while cooking. Allow at least 1.2 litres (2 pints) water for every 125g (4oz) pasta. Add 1 tsp salt for every 1.2 litre (2 pints) water for fresh pasta; 2 tsp for dried. Although many people add a little oil to the cooking water, it's only necessary when cooking large, flat pieces of pasta, such as lasagne.
3 Bring the water to a fast boil then gradually add the pasta, unravelling any that may be clumped together. Filled pasta should be cooked over a gentle simmer, otherwise it will burst; flat pasta can be cooked at a rolling boil.
4 Fresh pasta will rise to the surface when it is cooked (2–4 minutes). For dried, follow the manufacturer's instructions as cooking times can vary. When cooked, pasta should be *al dente* (it should still have some bite rather than being completely soft). Remove it from the cooking water or it will continue to cook and become too soft.
5 Drain it immediately in a large colander (it is not necessary to rinse it) and turn it into a hot serving dish.

DRIED OR FRESH?

Although dried pasta still accounts for two-thirds of the pasta market, fresh chilled pasta sales have increased by almost half. Fresh pasta cooks in minutes – in supermarkets you can even buy freshly cooked pasta that simply needs to be reheated in the microwave.

HOW TO COOK RICE

Long grain rice is the cheapest variety. It's versatile and easy to cook, provided you follow these instructions closely. Remember this rule: double the volume of water to rice, and you won't go far wrong. Bunging a handful of rice and an unknown quantity of water into a pan just won't work.

1 Measure 150ml (5fl oz) long grain rice into a jug. Pour into a pan with ½ tsp of salt. Pour over 300ml (10fl oz) boiling water. Cover with a tight-fitting lid, bring to the boil again, reduce the heat to its lowest setting and simmer gently for 15 minutes.
2 Remove from the heat and lift the lid – the rice grains should be tender, all the liquid should have been absorbed and the surface should be covered in regularly spaced holes. It won't need draining. Fork through the rice to separate the grains. Serves 2.

CHICKEN

Buying a whole chicken is cheaper than buying individual joints, so if the family budget is stretched, it's worth knowing how to cut a chicken into six or eight pieces.

Jointing poultry

Chickens and turkeys are treated in much the same way, size being the only difference.

1 Put the bird breast-side down and, with the tip of a knife, cut round the two portions of oyster meat (which lie against the backbone) so they remain attached to the thigh joint.
2 Turn the bird over and cut through the skin where the thigh joins the body. Cut right down between the ball and socket joint, being careful to keep the oyster meat attached to the thigh. Repeat with the other leg.
3 If liked, separate the thighs from the drumsticks by cutting through at the joints. Trim off the bone end from the drumsticks.
4 Turn the chicken over again, so it is breast-side down. Using poultry shears, cut firmly through the back into the body cavity between the backbone and one shoulder blade, leaving the wing attached to the breast.
5 Repeat on the other side. Then cut right the way through the ribcage, parallel to the backbone on both sides. Pull the back section away.
6 Turn the breast, with the wings still attached, skin-side up. Remove the wing portions by cutting through at a slight diagonal so that some breast is attached to the wing. Cut the breast into two or four portions.

Testing whether a chicken or turkey is cooked

There are two good ways of testing whether a bird is cooked. Pierce the leg with a fine skewer: the juices that run out should be golden and clear with no traces of pink. Or try pulling the leg gently away from the body: it should give very easily.

Carving a cooked chicken or turkey

Don't be tempted to carve the bird as soon as it's cooked. It's best to lift it out of the roasting tin, carefully letting any juices within its body run back into the tin, and then put it on a warm serving dish. Cover with foil and leave it to 'rest' for 10–15 minutes. This resting time will allow the flesh to relax and makes carving easier.

The secret to successful carving is to use a sharp knife. Hold the bird with a strong fork and cut the legs from the body, then cut through the joint to separate the thigh from the drumstick. Hold the wing with a fork and cut through the outer layer of breast and wing joint. Ease the wing away from the body. Repeat with the other wing. To carve the breast, use the fork to secure the bird. Starting at the neck cavity and keeping the knife parallel to the breastbone, slice the meat into long, thin slices.

FISH

Ready-prepared fish comes at a price premium, but it's not difficult to gut and fillet fish yourself. You'll need a sharp filleting knife with a long blade. Round fish, such as sardines, mackerel or trout, and very large flat fish, such as turbot and halibut, are easier to skin after they have been filleted or cooked.

REMOVE THE SCALES Hold the fish firmly by the tail and, using the back of a knife or a fish scaler, scrape off the scales from tail to head – the opposite way to the direction the scales lie. This can be a messy business, so do it in the sink.

TO GUT ROUND FISH Using a sharp knife, slit the belly open from the gills to the tail vent. Using your fingers, carefully loosen the soft innards from the belly and behind the gills, then pull them out and discard. Rinse the fish thoroughly under cold running water to remove all traces of blood.

TO GUT FLAT FISH The entrails of sole or plaice, are in the cavity that lies behind the gills. Open it up, clean out the entrails and rinse the fish thoroughly.

TO FILLET A ROUND FISH Lay the fish on its side, tail towards you. Cut along the backbone from head to tail, then cut through behind the gills to separate the fillet from the head. Starting at the head end, insert the knife between the flesh and bones, keeping it close to the bones. Skim the knife over the bones to detach the fillet. Holding the fish by the exposed bones, cut the other fillet from the ribs. Check over the fillets with your fingers for any small bones and remove them with tweezers.

TO SKIN FILLETS Lay them skin-side down with the tail towards you. Make a cut at the tail end so the fillet can be lifted slightly from the skin. With salted fingers, press on the exposed skin to hold it down. Insert the knife at an angle below the fillet and cut away from you to separate it from the skin.

COOKING A FLAT FISH WHOLE Remove the dark skin only; the white skin will help keep the fish in one piece during cooking. To skin the fish, lay it on a board, dark side uppermost. Make an incision across the skin where the tail joins the body. Starting at the cut, use the point of the knife to lift a flap of skin away from the flesh until you can get a firm grip on it. Grasping the flap of skin with salted fingers

and holding down the tail in the other hand, pull the skin cleanly away in one piece. If you are filleting a flat fish, you should also remove the white skin. Once the dark skin has been removed, turn the fish over and remove the white skin in the same way.

TO FILLET A FLAT FISH Lay it on a board with the tail pointing towards you and the eyes facing up. With the tip of the filleting knife, cut from head to tail along the backbone. At the head end, insert the knife blade between the flesh and bones. Aiming to skim the blade over the bones, cut down along the flesh. When the head end of the fillet is detached, lift it and continue cutting until you have removed the fillet. Remove the second fillet from this side in the same way. Turn the fish over and cut the two fillets from this side, leaving a skeleton.

BASIC RECIPES

Below are some frequently used basic recipes.

STOCK

VEGETABLE STOCK

✋ HANDS-ON TIME: 10 MINUTES
🍲 COOKING TIME: 35 MINUTES
✗ MAKES 1.2 litres (2 pints)

225g (8oz) onions, peeled and roughly chopped
225g (8oz) celery sticks, trimmed and roughly chopped
225g (8oz) leeks, trimmed and roughly chopped
225g (8oz) carrots, peeled and roughly chopped
1.7 litres (3 pints) cold water
2 bay leaves
a few thyme sprigs
a small bunch of parsley
10 black peppercorns
½ tsp sea salt

Per 100ml (3½fl oz): 5 cals; trace fat; 1g carbohydrate

1 Put the onions, celery, leeks and carrots into a large pan. Add the water, herbs, black peppercorns and salt. Bring slowly to the boil and skim the surface. Partially cover the pan and simmer for 30 minutes. Adjust the seasoning.

2 Sieve the stock through a fine sieve into a bowl and leave to cool. Cover and keep in the fridge for up to three days. Use as required.

MEAT STOCK

✋ HANDS-ON TIME: 10 MINUTES
🍲 COOKING TIME: 4–5 HOURS
✗ MAKES 900ml (1½ pints)

450g (1lb) stewing meat, cut into pieces
450g (1lb) meat bones (see Note)
1 large onion, peeled and sliced
1 large carrot, peeled and sliced
2 celery sticks, trimmed and sliced
2 litres (3½ pints) cold water
bouquet garni (2 bay leaves, few thyme sprigs, small bunch of parsley)
1 tsp black peppercorns
½ tsp sea salt

Per 100ml (3½fl oz): 10 cals; 1g fat (of which trace saturates); 1g carbohydrate

1 Preheat the oven to 220°C (200°C fan oven) mark 7.
To impart flavour and colour, first brown the meat and bones. Put them into a roasting tin and roast for 30–40 minutes until well browned, turning occasionally.

2 Put the meat and bones into a large pan with the vegetables, water, bouquet garni, peppercorns and salt. Bring slowly to the boil and skim the surface. Partially cover the pan and simmer gently for 4–5 hours. Adjust the seasoning.

3 Sieve the stock through a fine sieve into a bowl and cool quickly. Cover and keep in the fridge for up to three days. Remove the fat layer from the surface and use the stock as required.

COOK'S TIP: According to the flavour required, use veal, beef, lamb or pork bones.

CHICKEN STOCK

✋ HANDS-ON TIME: 10 MINUTES
🍲 COOKING TIME: ABOUT 2 HOURS
✗ MAKES 1.2 litres (2 pints)

225g (8oz) onions, peeled and roughly chopped
150g (5oz) leeks, trimmed and roughly chopped
225g (8oz) celery sticks, trimmed and roughly chopped
1.6kg (3½lb) raw chicken bones (see Note)
3 litres (5 pints) cold water
bouquet garni (2 bay leaves, few thyme sprigs, small bunch of parsley)
1 tsp black peppercorns
½ tsp sea salt

Per 100ml (3½fl oz): 10 cals; 1g fat (of which trace saturates); 1g carbohydrate

1 Put the vegetables into a large pan with the chicken bones, water, bouquet garni, peppercorns and salt. Bring slowly to the boil and skim the surface. Partially cover the pan and simmer gently for 2 hours. Adjust the seasoning.

2 Sieve the stock through a fine sieve into a bowl and cool quickly. Cover and keep in the fridge for up to three days. Remove the fat from the surface and use the stock as required.

COOK'S TIP: Instead of chicken bones, you can use a large boiling chicken – obtainable from selected butchers and poulterers.

TURKEY STOCK

✋ HANDS-ON TIME: 10 MINUTES
🍲 COOKING TIME: 40 MINUTES
✗ MAKES 500ml (1 pint)

fresh turkey giblets
1 onion, peeled and quartered
1 small carrot, peeled and sliced
1 celery stick, trimmed and chopped
8 peppercorns
2 bay leaves
600ml (1 pint) cold water

Per 100ml (3½fl oz): 10 cals; 1g fat (of which trace saturates); 1g carbohydrate

1 Put all the ingredients into a pan, cover and bring to the boil. Reduce the heat and simmer, skimming regularly, for 30 minutes.

2 Sieve, reserving the stock, then cool, cover and chill.

FISH STOCK

✋ HANDS-ON TIME: 10 MINUTES
🍲 COOKING TIME: 35 MINUTES
✗ MAKES 900ml (1½ pints)

900g (2lb) fish bones and trimmings, washed and dried
2 carrots, peeled and chopped
1 onion, peeled and chopped
2 celery sticks, trimmed and sliced
900ml (1½ pints) cold water
bouquet garni (bay leaf, thyme and parsley)

6 white peppercorns

½ tsp sea salt

Per 100ml (3½fl oz): 5 cals; trace fat; 1g carbohydrate

1 Put the fish trimmings into a large pan.

2 Add the vegetables together with the water, bouquet garni, peppercorns and salt. Bring slowly to the boil and skim the surface. Cover and simmer gently for about 30 minutes.

3 Sieve the stock through a fine sieve into a bowl and adjust the seasoning. Cool quickly, cover and keep in the fridge for up to two days. Use as required.

VARIATION: For an enriched court bouillon, add 150ml (5fl oz) dry white wine and 3 tbsp white wine vinegar at step 2.

GRAVY

A rich gravy is traditionally served with roast meat and poultry. If possible, make the gravy in the roasting tin while the joint (or bird) is resting. This will incorporate the meat juices that have escaped during roasting.

☞ HANDS-ON TIME: 2 MINUTES

☕ COOKING TIME: 2–3 MINUTES

✕ MAKES about 300ml (10 fl oz)

Per 100ml (3½fl oz): 20 cals; 2g fat (of which 1g saturates); 1g carbohydrate

1 Carefully pour (or skim) off the fat from a corner of the roasting tin, leaving the sediment behind. Put the tin on the hob over a medium heat and pour in 300–450ml (10–15fl oz) vegetable water, or chicken, vegetable or meat stock, as appropriate.

2 Stir thoroughly, scraping up the sediment, and boil steadily until the gravy is a rich brown colour.

COOK'S TIP: A little gravy browning can be added to intensify the flavour and colour.

VARIATIONS

RICH WINE GRAVY Deglaze the roasting tin with about 150ml (5fl oz) red or white wine, or 90ml (3fl oz) fortified wine such as sherry or

Madeira, and leave to bubble for a minute or two before adding the stock or water. For a sweeter flavour, add 2 tbsp redcurrant jelly the wine.

THICK GRAVY Sprinkle 1–2 tbsp plain flour into the roasting tin and cook, stirring, until browned, then gradually stir in the liquid and cook, stirring for 2–3 minutes until smooth and slightly thickened.

FRENCH DRESSING

☞ HANDS-ON TIME: 10 MINUTES

✕ MAKES 100ml (3½fl oz)

1 tsp Dijon mustard

pinch of sugar

1 tbsp white or red wine vinegar

6 tbsp extra-virgin olive oil

Per 1 tbsp serving: 110 cals; 11g fat; trace carbohydrate

1 Whisk the mustard, sugar, vinegar and seasoning together in a bowl, then gradually whisk in the olive oil until the dressing is amalgamated and thickened.

WHITE SAUCE

☞ HANDS-ON TIME: 2 MINUTES

☕ COOKING TIME: 5 MINUTES

✕ MAKES 300ml (10fl oz)

15g (½oz) butter

15g (½oz) plain flour

300ml (10fl oz) milk

freshly grated nutmeg

Per 15ml: 45 cals; 3g fat (of which 2g saturates); 4g carbohydrate

1 Melt the butter in a pan, stir in the flour and cook, stirring, for 1 minute until cooked but not coloured.
   (This is called a roux.)

2 Remove from the heat and gradually pour in the milk, whisking all the time. Season lightly with salt, pepper and nutmeg.

3 Put the pan back on the heat and cook, stirring constantly, until the sauce is thick and smooth.

Simmer gently for 2 minutes.

VARIATIONS

CHEESE (MORNAY) SAUCE Take the pan off the heat and stir 50g (2oz) finely grated mature Cheddar or Gruyère cheese and a large pinch of mustard powder or cayenne pepper into the finished sauce. Heat gently to melt the cheese. Use for cauliflower cheese or macaroni cheese (see pages 223).

PARSLEY SAUCE Stir in 2 tbsp freshly chopped parsley at step 3.

TO MAKE CHEESE SAUCE IN THE MICROWAVE Pour the milk into a measuring jug or microwaveable bowl. Add the butter and flour and whisk to combine. The butter won't mix in, but don't worry. Microwave on High (based on a 900W oven) for 2 minutes, then remove and whisk together. Cook for another 2 minutes and whisk again. The sauce should be thick and smooth. Season well, then add the cheese and mustard or pepper and stir until melted.

HOLLANDAISE SAUCE

Hollandaise is a wonderfully rich sauce. Serve with hot or cold vegetables, such as asparagus and globe artichokes, and poached fish and shellfish.

☞ HANDS-ON TIME: 20 MINUTES

☕ COOKING TIME: 23 MINUTES

✕ SERVES 6

4 tbsp white wine vinegar

6 black peppercorns

1 mace blade

1 onion slice

1 bay leaf

3 egg yolks

150g (5oz) unsalted butter, at room temperature, cut into pieces

2 tbsp single cream (optional)

lemon juice, to taste

Per serving: 230 cals; 24g fat (of which 15g saturates); trace carbohydrate

1 Put the vinegar into a small pan with the peppercorns, mace, onion slice and bay leaf. Bring to the boil and reduce to 1 tbsp liquid. Dip the base of the pan in cold water to stop further evaporation; set aside.

2 Put the egg yolks into a heatproof bowl with 15g (½oz) butter and a pinch of salt. Beat until well combined, then strain in the reduced vinegar.

3 Put the bowl over a pan of barely simmering water and whisk for 3–4 minutes until the mixture is pale and beginning to thicken.

4 Beat in the remaining butter, a piece at a time, until the mixture begins to emulsify. Ensure that each addition of butter is incorporated before adding the next. Do not allow the mixture to overheat or the eggs will scramble and split. Remove from the heat.

5 Whisk in the cream if using. Season the sauce with salt and pepper, and add a little lemon juice to taste. Serve at once.

COOK'S TIP: If the sauce shows signs of curdling, add an ice cube and whisk thoroughly; the hollandaise should re-combine.

BEARNAISE SAUCE

Serve this classic butter sauce with grilled beef and lamb steaks.

🖐 HANDS-ON TIME: 20 MINUTES
🍲 COOKING TIME: 2–3 MINUTES
✕ SERVES 4–6

4 tbsp white wine vinegar or tarragon vinegar
2 shallots, peeled and finely chopped
6 black peppercorns
a few tarragon sprigs, chopped
2 egg yolks
75g (3oz) butter, at room temperature, cut into pieces
salt and white pepper
2 tsp chopped flat-leafed parsley or chervil (optional)

Per serving: 170–110 cals; 18–12g fat (of which 11–7g saturates); 0–0g carbohydrate

1 Put the vinegar, shallots, peppercorns and tarragon into a very small pan. Bring to the boil and reduce to 1 tbsp. Dip the base of the pan in cold water to stop further evaporation; allow to cool, then strain.

2 Beat the egg yolks and reduced vinegar together in a heatproof bowl.

3 Put the bowl over a pan of barely simmering water and whisk for 3–4 minutes until the mixture is pale and beginning to thicken.

4 Beat in the butter a piece at a time, until the mixture begins to thicken and emulsify. Ensure each addition of butter is incorporated before adding the next. Do not allow the mixture to overheat or the eggs will scramble and split. Take off the heat.

5 Season with salt and pepper to taste. Stir in the chopped herbs if using.

CRANBERRY SAUCE

Serve this tangy relish with the traditional Christmas turkey or the Croûte above.

🖐 HANDS-ON TIME: 30 MINUTES
🍲 COOKING TIME: 1 HOUR, 5 MINUTES
✕ SERVES 8

2 tbsp olive oil
450g (1lb) red onions, thinly sliced
grated zest and juice of 1 large orange
1 tsp coriander seeds, lightly crushed
¼ tsp ground cloves
1 bay leaf
150g (5oz) dark muscovado sugar
150ml (¼ pint) red wine
450g (1lb) cranberries

Per serving: 140 cals, 3g fat (of which trace saturates), 26g carbohydrate

1 Heat the oil in a medium pan, add the onions and cook gently for 5 minutes. Add the orange zest and juice, coriander seeds, ground cloves, bay leaf, sugar and red wine. Simmer gently for 40 minutes.

2 Add the cranberries, bring back to the boil and simmer for 20 minutes. Cool and chill until required. Bring to room temperature before serving.

THE BEST CHOCOLATE SAUCE

🖐 HANDS-ON TIME: 2 MINUTES
🍲 COOKING TIME: 10 MINUTES
✕ SERVES 4

75g (3oz) good-quality plain dark chocolate, roughly chopped
142ml carton double cream

Per serving: 260 cals; 23g fat (of which 14g saturates); 13g carbohydrate

1 Put the chocolate into a small, heatproof bowl set over a pan of simmering water, making sure the bottom of the bowl doesn't touch the water. Pour the double cream over the top of the chocolate.

2 Leave the chocolate to melt at the lowest heat. It will take about 10 minutes. Don't stir, or it will thicken to a sticky mess. Once melted, gently stir the chocolate and cream together until smooth and serve with fresh fruit, ice cream or poached pears.

VARIATIONS

- Add a shot of espresso coffee to the cream and chocolate while they're melting together.
- Use a mint-flavoured chocolate instead of plain.
- Pour a little orange coffee-flavoured liqueur into the bowl while the chocolate and cream are melting together.

PASTRY

SHORTCRUST PASTRY

This is the most widely used pastry. The proportion of flour to fat is 2:1. The choice of fat is largely a matter of taste – butter gives a rich pastry, but using half white vegetable fat improves the texture.

🖐 HANDS-ON TIME: 10 MINUTES
✕ MAKES 225ml (8oz)

225g (8oz) plain flour, plus extra to dust
a pinch of salt
125g (4oz) butter, or half white vegetable fat and half butter, cut into pieces

Per 25g (1oz): 100 cals; 6g fat (of which 2g saturates); 11g carbohydrate;

1   Sift the flour and salt into a bowl, add the fat and mix lightly.

2   Using your fingertips, rub the fat into the flour until the mixture resembles fine breadcrumbs.

3   Sprinkle 3–4 tbsp cold water evenly over the surface and stir with a round-bladed knife until the mixture begins to stick together in large lumps. If the dough seems dry, add a little extra water. With one hand, collect the dough together to form a ball.

4   Knead gently on a lightly floured surface for a few seconds to form a smooth, firm dough; do not overwork. Wrap in clingfilm and leave to rest in the fridge for 30 minutes before rolling out.

VARIATIONS

HERB Add 2 tbsp freshly mixed herbs to the flour.

OLIVE Mix 25g (1oz) finely chopped black olives into the pastry before adding the water.

Watchpoints

■   Equipment and fingers should be cool. Run hot hands under the cold tap and dry them well before you start.

■   You can prepare the pastry in a food processor, but don't overwork it. Whizz the butter, flour and salt until the mixture resembles fine breadcrumbs, then add the water until just blended. Knead lightly on the worksurface.

■   Rub in the butter until evenly mixed but not sticky. If over-rubbed, the dough will be difficult to handle.

■   Always add at least the minimum amount of water suggested in the recipe. The dough may seem sticky at first but will dry out as it cooks. If insufficient liquid is added, the pastry will crumble and fall apart; too much liquid and the pastry will be tough.

■   Treat the pastry gently; if you

over-knead the dough, it will become tough and hard.

■   Always roll the pastry away from you. If you try to lean over the dough and roll it from side to side, it will stretch unevenly, causing it to shrink when cooked.

■   If you're in a hurry, the pastry can be chilled for 10 minutes in the freezer instead of leaving to rest in the fridge.

CHOUX PASTRY

Choux pastry is unlike any other as it is cooked twice. At the first attempt, it can be quite alarming to make – when the flour is added it will look very lumpy, but don't panic as it will beat to a smooth and shiny paste. The paste can be made the day before; cover and leave to chill.

✋ HANDS-ON TIME: 10 MINUTES
✕ MAKES A '2–EGG QUANTITY'

65g (2½oz) plain flour
pinch of salt
50g (2oz) butter
2 eggs, lightly beaten

Per 25g (1oz): 50 cals; 4g fat; 3g carbohydrate

1   Sift the flour and salt on to a generous sheet of greaseproof paper.

2   Pour 150ml (¼ pint) cold water into a medium pan, add the butter and melt over a low heat. Increase the heat and bring to a rolling boil.

3   Take off the heat, immediately tip in all of the flour and beat vigorously, using a wooden spoon. Continue beating until the mixture is smooth and leaves the sides of the pan to form a ball; do not over-beat. Leave to cool slightly, for 1–2 minutes.

4   Gradually add the eggs, beating well between each addition, adding just enough to give a smooth dropping consistency. The choux pastry should be smooth and shiny. Use as required.

Watchpoints

■   Don't let the water boil before the butter melts or it will evaporate.

It is this water turning to steam that helps to make the choux rise.

■   Slowly add the beaten eggs, making sure that the choux paste is thick, smooth and shiny after each addition.

■   If the choux paste starts to thin down and refuses to thicken despite constant beating, a small amount of beaten egg can be omitted.

■   It's best to bake one sheet of choux paste at a time; pastry on a lower shelf won't rise as well.

■   Don't be tempted to open the oven door while the choux pastry is baking; the dough will flatten.

■   When the pastry is made into buns, always split the cooked buns to allow the steam to escape, then return them to the oven for a few minutes so that they dry out properly.

SUET CRUST PASTRY

This pastry is used for sweet and savoury steamed puddings, and dumplings. It has a light, spongy texture provided it is handled gently, and cooked by steaming or simmering. Vegetarian suet can be used.

✋ HANDS-ON TIME: 10 MINUTES
✕ MAKES A '300G (11OZ) QUANTITY'

300g (11oz) self-raising flour
½ tsp salt
150g (5oz) shredded suet

Per 25g (1oz): 90 cals; 5g fat (of which 3g saturates); 10g carbohydrate

1   Sift the flour and salt into a bowl, add the shredded suet and stir to mix.

2   Using a round-bladed knife, mix in enough cold water to make a soft dough; you will need about 175ml (6fl oz). If the dough seems too dry, add a little extra liquid.

3   Knead very lightly until smooth. Use as required.

2

COOK NOW
EAT LATER

ITALIAN LAMB

✋ **HANDS-ON TIME:** 35 MINUTES　🍲 **COOKING TIME:** 3¾ HOURS　✗ **SERVES:** 6

INGREDIENTS

2 half-leg knuckles of lamb
2 tbsp olive oil
75g (3oz) butter
275g (10oz) onions, peeled and
　finely chopped
175g (6oz) carrots, peeled and
　finely chopped
175g (6oz) celery, trimmed and
　finely chopped
2 tbsp dried porcini pieces (see
　Cook's Tip) or 125g (4oz) finely
　chopped brown-cap mushrooms
9 pieces sun-dried tomato, finely
　chopped
150g (5oz) Italian-style spicy
　sausage or salami, thickly sliced
600ml (1 pint) red wine
400g (14oz) passata
600ml (1 pint) vegetable stock
125g (4oz) dried pasta shapes
15g (½oz) freshly grated Parmesan
　cheese
fresh flat-leafed parsley sprigs to
　garnish

PER SERVING

610 cals
34g fat (of which 16g saturates)
26g carbohydrate

METHOD

1　Preheat the oven to 240°C (220°C fan oven) mark 9. Put the lamb in a large roasting tin and drizzle over 1 tbsp oil. Roast for 35 minutes.

2　Meanwhile, melt the butter with the remaining oil in a large flameproof casserole. Stir in the vegetables and cook, stirring, for 10–15 minutes until golden and soft. Stir in the porcini pieces or mushrooms and cook for a further 2–3 minutes.

3　Add the sun-dried tomatoes, sausage, wine, passata and stock to the pan, then bring to the boil and simmer for 10 minutes.

4　Lift the lamb from the roasting tin, add to the tomato sauce and cover with a tight-fitting lid. Turn the heat down to 170°C (150°C fan oven) mark 3 and cook for a further 3 hours or until the lamb is falling off the bone.

5　Lift the lamb from the casserole on to a deep, heatproof serving dish. Cover loosely with foil and keep warm in a low oven.

6　Put the casserole on the hob, stir in the pasta and bring back to the boil. Simmer for 10 minutes or until the pasta is tender. Stir in the Parmesan just before serving.

7　Serve the lamb carved into large pieces and serve with the pasta sauce, garnished with parsley.

TO FREEZE

■　Complete to the end of step 4. Cool quickly, pack and freeze.
■　To use, thaw overnight at a cool room temperature.
　On the hob, bring the lamb and sauce to the boil and simmer gently for 30 minutes. Complete the recipe.

COOK'S TIP

Look out for bags of dried porcini pieces in supermarkets. These chopped dried mushrooms are ideal for adding a rich depth of flavour to stews or casseroles.

PEPPERED WINTER STEW

✋ **HANDS-ON TIME:** 30 MINUTES   🍲 **COOKING TIME:** 2 HOURS 20 MINUTES   ✕ **SERVES:** 6

METHOD

1 Preheat the oven to 180°C (160°C fan oven) mark 4. Season the flour with salt and pepper. Toss the meat in the seasoned flour.

2 Heat 3 tbsp oil in a large, deep, flameproof casserole and fry the meat in small batches until browned on all sides. Remove and put to one side.

3 Wipe out the casserole, heat the remaining oil, add the baby onions and fry for 4–5 minutes until golden. Drain and set aside. Add the chopped onion and garlic to the casserole and cook, stirring, for 5–7 minutes until soft and golden. Add the tomato purée and cook for a further 2 minutes. Add the vinegar and wine and bring to the boil. Let bubble for 10 minutes. Add the redcurrant jelly, thyme, bay leaves, pepper, cloves and meat to the casserole. Add enough stock to barely cover the meat then bring to the boil, cover and cook in the oven for 1–1½ hours until the meat is very tender.

4 Remove the meat from the casserole and put to one side. Sieve the liquid through a fine sieve, pushing the residue through. Put the liquid with the meat, root vegetables and browned baby onions back into the casserole, bring to the boil, then cover and cook in the oven for a further 45–50 minutes until the vegetables are tender.

5 Serve the stew from the casserole, garnished with thyme sprigs.

TO FREEZE

■ Prepare and cook to the end of step 4. Cool quickly, cover and freeze.

■ To use, thaw overnight at a cool room temperature. Add an extra 150ml (5fl oz) stock. Bring slowly to the boil. Cover and reheat the stew at 180°C (160°C fan oven) mark 4 for 30 minutes.

COOK'S TIPS

■ If using carrots, cut into smaller chunks.

■ To make peeling baby onions or shallots easier, blanch them for a minute or two in boiling water.

INGREDIENTS

25g (1oz) plain flour
900g (2lb) stewing venison, beef or lamb, cut into 4cm (1½in) cubes
5 tbsp oil
225g (8oz) baby onions or shallots, peeled with root end still attached
225g (8oz) onions, peeled and finely chopped
4 garlic cloves, crushed
2 tbsp tomato purée
125ml (4fl oz) red wine vinegar
75cl bottle red wine
2 tbsp redcurrant jelly
a small bunch of fresh thyme
4 bay leaves
1 tbsp coarsely ground black pepper
6 cloves
600–900ml (1–1½ pints) beef stock
900g (2lb) mixed root vegetables such as carrots, parsnips, turnips and celeriac, peeled and cut into about 4cm (1½in) chunks (see Cook's Tips)
fresh thyme sprigs to garnish

PER SERVING
440 cals
19g fat (of which 5g saturates)
24g carbohydrate

WINTER HOTPOT

✋ **HANDS-ON TIME:** 20 MINUTES, PLUS MARINATING   🍲 **COOKING TIME:** 2 HOURS 20 MINUTES   ✕ **SERVES:** 8

METHOD

1 Put the pork in a large bowl with the garlic, 2 tbsp oil, the vinegar, sugar, chilli, salt, pepper, 2 tsp oregano and all the thyme. Combine all the ingredients, cover and leave in the fridge for at least 8 hours to marinate.

2 Drain the pork, putting the marinade to one side.

3 Preheat the oven to 180°C (160°C fan oven) mark 4. Heat 3 tbsp oil in a large flameproof casserole and fry the pork in batches until well browned and sealed on all sides. Put to one side. Add the remaining oil with the onions and cook for 10 minutes over a high heat, stirring occasionally, until they are soft and caramelized. Add the tomato purée and cook for 1 minute. Put the meat back into the casserole with the drained bean juice, tomatoes, wine, bay leaves and the reserved marinade. Bring to the boil, stirring, then cover and cook in the oven for 2 hours or until the pork is very tender.

4 About 20 minutes before the end of the cooking time, stir in the beans.

5 Increase the oven temperature to 200°C (180°C fan oven) mark 6 and move the pork to a lower shelf. Heat the butter in a roasting tin, add the breadcrumbs, the remaining oregano and seasoning. Brown on the top shelf for 10 minutes. Sprinkle the hotpot with the breadcrumbs and grated cheese. Garnish with thyme sprigs and serve.

TO FREEZE

■ Complete to the end of step 4. Cool quickly, cover and freeze.

■ To use, thaw overnight at a cool room temperature. Add 150ml (5fl oz) stock and bring to the boil. Cover and reheat at 180°C (160°C fan oven) mark 4 for 25 minutes; complete the recipe.

COOK'S TIP

Curly kale would make a good accompaniment to this dish. Remove the frilly leaf from the coarse stalk and drop into a large pan of boiling salted water. Return to the boil and cook for 2–3 minutes, then drain, season with pepper and serve.

INGREDIENTS

1.4kg (3lb) boned shoulder of pork, cut into 2.5cm (1in) cubes
6 garlic cloves, crushed
7 tbsp olive oil
2 tbsp red wine vinegar
4 tbsp soft brown sugar
2 tsp minced chilli or a few drops of chilli sauce
3 tsp dried oregano
2 tsp dried thyme
450g (1lb) onions, peeled, halved and sliced
2 tbsp tomato purée
2 × 400g cans haricot or flageolet beans, drained and juice put to one side
2 × 400g cans chopped tomatoes
300ml (10fl oz) red wine
4 bay leaves
25g (1oz) butter
125g (4oz) white breadcrumbs from French bread or ciabatta
125g (4oz) grated Gruyère cheese
fresh thyme sprigs to garnish

PER SERVING
580 cals
28g fat (of which 10g saturates)
31g carbohydrate

CHUNKY ONE-POT BOLOGNESE

✋ HANDS-ON TIME: 15 MINUTES　**🍲 COOKING TIME:** ABOUT 1 HOUR　**✗ SERVES:** 6

INGREDIENTS

3 tbsp olive oil

2 large red onions, peeled and
　finely diced

a few fresh rosemary sprigs

1 large aubergine, finely diced

8 plump, coarse sausages

350ml (12fl oz) full-bodied red wine

700g (1½lb) passata

4 tbsp sun-dried tomato paste

300ml (10fl oz) hot vegetable stock

175g (6oz) small dried pasta, such
　as orecchiette

PER SERVING

506 cals

31g fat (of which 11g saturates)

40g carbohydrate

METHOD

1　Heat 2 tbsp olive oil in a large, shallow, non-stick pan. Add the onions and rosemary and cook over a gentle heat for 10 minutes or until soft and golden.

2　Add the aubergine and remaining oil and cook over a medium heat for 8–10 minutes until soft and golden.

3　Meanwhile, pull the skin off the sausages and divide each into four rough chunks. Tip the aubergine mixture on to a plate and add the sausage chunks to the hot pan. You won't need any extra oil.

4　Stir the sausage pieces over a high heat for 6–8 minutes until golden and beginning to turn crisp at the edges. Pour in the wine and let bubble for 6–8 minutes until only a little liquid remains. Return the aubergine mixture to the pan, along with the passata, tomato paste and stock.

5　Stir the pasta into the liquid, cover, then simmer for 20 minutes or until the pasta is cooked. Taste and season if needed.

TO FREEZE

■　Complete up to the end of step 4. Add the pasta and cook for 10 minutes – it will continue to cook right through when you reheat the bolognese. Cool, put in a freezerproof container and freeze for up to three months.

■　To use, thaw overnight at cool room temperature, put in a pan and add 150ml (5fl oz) water. Bring to the boil, then simmer gently for 10 minutes or until the sauce is hot and the pasta is cooked.

COOK'S TIPS

■　You need coarse-textured butcher's sausages for this. The better the sausages, the better the sauce.

■　At the end of step 4 it may look as if you have too much sauce, but it will be absorbed by the pasta on reheating.

CHEESE AND PASTA BEEF BAKE

👋 **HANDS-ON TIME:** 25 MINUTES, PLUS CHILLING 🍲 **COOKING TIME:** 55 MINUTES 🍴 **SERVES:** 6

METHOD

1 Grease a 3.4 litre (6 pint) ovenproof dish with butter.
2 Combine the salami, beef, garlic, parsley, 75g (3oz) Parmesan cheese, the breadcrumbs and plenty of seasoning with the beaten egg and water in a large bowl. Mix the ingredients together with your hands or use a mixer with the flat beater attached. Shape into walnut-size balls. Chill for 30 minutes.
3 Preheat the oven to 200°C (180°C fan oven) mark 6. Heat the oil in a non-stick frying pan and fry the meatballs in batches until golden brown and cooked through (about 5 minutes).
4 Cook the pasta in a large pan of boiling salted water. Drain well, then mix with the passata, herbs, half the mozzarella, 50g (2oz) Parmesan cheese and the meatballs. Season generously with salt and pepper, then spoon into the prepared dish. Sprinkle with the remaining mozzarella and Parmesan.
5 Cook in the oven for 30 minutes or until golden brown.

TO PREPARE AHEAD

■ One day ahead, complete to the end of step 4. Cover and chill.
■ To use, complete the recipe and allow an extra 10 minutes cooking time.

INGREDIENTS

butter to grease
75g (3oz) peppered salami, finely chopped
450g (1lb) minced beef
3 garlic cloves, crushed
2 tbsp freshly chopped parsley
225g (8oz) freshly grated Parmesan cheese
50g (2oz) fresh white breadcrumbs
1 medium egg, beaten
150ml (5fl oz) water
3 tbsp olive oil
250g (9oz) dried pasta
1kg (2¼lb) passata
2 tbsp freshly chopped basil, parsley, thyme or chives, or 2 tsp dried mixed Italian herbs
400g (14oz) mozzarella cheese, diced

PER SERVING

770 cals
42g fat (of which 21g saturates)
41g carbohydrate

BRAISED BEEF

👋 **HANDS-ON TIME:** 20 MINUTES 🍲 **COOKING TIME:** ABOUT 3½ HOURS ✖ **SERVES:** 4

METHOD

1 Preheat the oven to 170°C (150°C fan oven) mark 3. Fry the pancetta or bacon in a shallow flameproof casserole for 2–3 minutes until golden. Add the leeks and cook for a further 2 minutes or until the leeks are just beginning to colour. Remove with a slotted spoon and put to one side.

2 Heat the oil in the casserole and fry the beef in batches for 2–3 minutes until a rich golden colour on all sides. Remove from the casserole and set aside. Add the onion and fry over a gentle heat for 5 minutes or until golden. Stir in the carrots and parsnips and fry for 1–2 minutes.

3 Put the beef back into the casserole and stir in the flour to soak up the juices. Gradually add the red wine and water, then stir in the redcurrant jelly. Season with pepper and bring to the boil. Cover with a tight-fitting lid and cook in the oven for 2 hours.

4 Stir in the fried leeks, pancetta and mushrooms, re-cover and cook for a further 1 hour or until everything is tender. Serve scattered with chopped flat-leafed parsley.

TO FREEZE

■ Put in a freezerproof container, cool and freeze for up to three months.

■ To use, thaw overnight at a cool room temperature. Preheat the oven to 180°C (160°C fan oven) mark 4. Bring to the boil on the hob, cover tightly and reheat in the oven for about 30 minutes until piping hot.

COOK'S TIP

Leeks can trap a lot of fine soil, so need to be washed thoroughly: trim the ends of the leaves, then cut a cross about 7.5cm (3in) into the top and hold under cold running water.

INGREDIENTS

175g (6oz) smoked pancetta or smoked streaky bacon, cut into cubes

2 medium leeks, thickly sliced

1 tbsp olive oil

450g (1lb) braising steak, cut into 5cm (2in) pieces

1 large onion, peeled and finely chopped

2 carrots and 2 parsnips, peeled and thickly sliced

1 tbsp plain flour

300ml (10fl oz) red wine

300ml (10fl oz) water

1–2 tbsp redcurrant jelly

125g (4oz) chestnut mushrooms, halved

freshly chopped flat-leafed parsley to garnish

PER SERVING

490 cals

27g fat (of which 10g saturates)

23g carbohydrate

BEEF WITH FRUITY STUFFING

HANDS-ON TIME: 35 MINUTES, PLUS MARINATING   **COOKING TIME:** 1 HOUR   **SERVES:** 6

INGREDIENTS

- 1.4kg (3lb) piece topside or top rump of beef
- 1 tbsp balsamic vinegar or red wine vinegar blended with a pinch of sugar
- 2 tbsp white wine vinegar
- 3 tbsp olive oil
- 3 tbsp freshly chopped coriander or thyme, or 2 tsp dried mixed Italian herbs
- 1 red pepper, quartered and deseeded
- 1 yellow pepper, quartered and deseeded
- 75g (3oz) fresh spinach, cooked, excess water squeezed out, and roughly chopped, or 150g (5oz) frozen leaf spinach, thawed, drained and roughly chopped
- 75g (3oz) pitted black olives, roughly chopped
- 50g (2oz) smoked ham, roughly chopped
- 75g (3oz) raisins or sultanas
- 100ml (3½fl oz) water

PER SERVING

270 cals

9g fat (of which 3g saturates)

10g carbohydrate

METHOD

1. Make a deep incision along the length of the beef to create a large pocket, season liberally with pepper and put in a shallow dish. Mix the balsamic vinegar, white wine vinegar, oil and herbs together. Pour over the beef and into the pocket. Leave to marinate for about 4 hours or overnight.

2. Preheat the oven to 190°C (170°C fan oven) mark 5 and preheat the grill. Cook the peppers under the hot grill until the skins are blackened. Leave to cool then remove the skins. Put to one side.

3. Mix the spinach, olives, ham and raisins together, then season with salt and pepper.

4. Line the pocket of the beef with the peppers, keeping two pieces of pepper to one side for the gravy. Spoon the spinach mixture into the pocket and spread evenly. Reshape the meat and tie at intervals with string.

5. Put in a shallow roasting tin (just large enough to hold the joint) with the marinade, and cook in the oven for 1 hour for rare (see Cook's Tip), basting occasionally. Remove from the oven and cover with foil while preparing a gravy.

6. Skim off the excess fat. Bring the pan juices to the boil and add the water. Let bubble for 2–3 minutes. If the flavour is too concentrated, add more water. Finely chop the remaining pepper pieces and add to the gravy.

7. Serve the beef sliced with the gravy.

TO PREPARE AHEAD

- Up to one day ahead, prepare to the end of step 4, cover loosely and chill.
- To use, complete the recipe.

COOK'S TIP

Topside tends to be tough when cooked well done, so serve it either rare or medium rare. Allow an extra 10–15 minutes for medium rare.

CHICKEN IN RED WINE

👋 **HANDS-ON TIME:** 15 MINUTES 🍲 **COOKING TIME:** 1 HOUR 10 MINUTES ✕ **SERVES:** 4

METHOD

1 Wrap a slice of prosciutto around each chicken thigh. Heat the oil in a large, non-stick frying pan and fry the chicken pieces for 8–10 minutes until golden all over. Transfer to a plate and set aside.

2 Add the garlic and shallots and fry over a gentle heat for 5 minutes or until the shallots are beginning to soften and turn golden. Stir in the mushrooms and flour and cook over a gentle heat for 1–2 minutes.

3 Put the chicken back in the pan and add the wine, stock, Worcestershire sauce and bay leaf. Season lightly with salt and pepper, bring to the boil for 5 minutes, then cover and simmer over a low heat for 45 minutes or until the chicken is tender. Serve with crusty bread.

TO FREEZE

■ Cool quickly, put in a freezerproof container and freeze for up to three months.

■ To use, thaw overnight at a cool room temperature, then put back into a pan. Bring slowly to the boil, then simmer gently for 10–15 minutes until piping hot.

COOK'S TIP

If you can't buy prosciutto, thinly cut smoked streaky bacon will work just as well.

INGREDIENTS

8 slices prosciutto ham
8 large boned and skinned chicken thighs
1 tbsp olive oil
1 fat garlic clove, crushed
about 12 shallots or button onions, peeled and halved
225g (8oz) shiitake mushrooms
1 tbsp plain flour
300ml (10fl oz) red wine
300ml (10fl oz) hot chicken stock
1 tbsp Worcestershire sauce
1 bay leaf

PER SERVING

350 cals
13g fat (of which 4g saturates)
15g carbohydrate

MUSHROOM AND ROASTED POTATO BAKE

🖐 **HANDS-ON TIME:** 15 MINUTES   🍲 **COOKING TIME:** 1¼ HOURS   ✕ **SERVES:** 6   V

METHOD

1   Preheat the oven to 200°C (180°C fan oven) mark 6. Toss the potatoes with 4 tbsp oil in a large roasting tin and cook in the oven for 40 minutes or until tender and golden.

2   Heat the remaining oil in a large, heavy-based pan. Add the onion and cook for 10 minutes or until soft, then add the chopped mixed mushrooms and garlic and cook over a high heat for 5 minutes. Stir in the tomato pastes, porcini mushrooms, if using, and the thyme and wine. Bring to the boil and simmer for 2 minutes.

3   Add the stock and cream, bring back to the boil and bubble for 20 minutes or until well reduced and syrupy. Pour into a 2.4 litre (4 pint) ovenproof dish. Stir in the potatoes, spinach, Gruyère and half the Parmesan cheese. Season well with salt and pepper.

4   Combine the yogurt with the eggs and season. Spoon over the vegetable mixture and sprinkle with the remaining Parmesan cheese.

5   Cook in the oven for 30–35 minutes until golden and bubbling. Garnish with parsley and thyme sprigs, if you like, before serving.

TO FREEZE

■   Cool and freeze at the end of step 4.

■   To use, thaw overnight at cool room temperature, then cook as above for 40–45 minutes until golden and bubbling.

COOK'S TIP

In recipes, mix cultivated mushrooms with wild to reduce the cost of the dish.

INGREDIENTS

900g (2lb) small potatoes, quartered
6 tbsp olive oil
225g (8oz) onions, peeled and roughly chopped
450g (1lb) mixed mushrooms, such as shiitake and brown-cap, roughly chopped
2 garlic cloves, crushed
2 tbsp tomato purée
4 tbsp sun-dried tomato paste
25g (1oz) dried porcini mushrooms (optional)
2 tsp freshly chopped thyme
300ml (10fl oz) white wine
300ml (10fl oz) vegetable stock
284ml carton double cream
400g (14oz) large fresh spinach leaves, roughly chopped
175g (6oz) Gruyère cheese, grated
125g (4oz) freshly grated Parmesan cheese
300ml (10fl oz) Greek yogurt
2 eggs, beaten
fresh flat-leafed parsley and thyme sprigs to garnish (optional)

PER SERVING

720 cals
54g fat (of which 29g saturates)
30g carbohydrate

COURGETTE AND THYME TART

INGREDIENTS

125g (4oz) chilled butter, cut into
    cubes
125g (4oz) plain flour, plus extra
    to dust
a pinch of salt
4 tbsp cold water
2 tbsp olive oil
a bunch of spring onions, trimmed
    and sliced
350g (12oz) courgettes, trimmed
    and roughly chopped
1 tbsp small fresh thyme sprigs
300g (11oz) medium-fat soft goat's
    cheese
3 eggs, beaten
200ml (7fl oz) double cream
125g (4oz) feta cheese, crumbled
    into large pieces
salad leaves to serve

PER SERVING

630 cals
53g fat (of which 31g saturates)
20g carbohydrate

METHOD

1   To make the pastry, put the butter in a food processor with the
    flour and salt and whiz for 2–3 seconds. Add the water and whiz
    for 3–4 seconds until the mixture just comes together in a ball.
    Turn out on to a floured worksurface and knead lightly until the
    ball of dough has a smooth surface but the butter is still in small
    pieces. Wrap and leave to chill for at least 2 hours.

2   To make the filling, heat the olive oil in a large frying pan. Add the
    spring onions and cook for 1–2 minutes. Add the courgettes and
    cook for a further 2–3 minutes. Season with salt and pepper and
    add the thyme. Turn into a wide bowl to cool.

3   Combine the goat's cheese, 2 eggs, cream, feta cheese and the
    cooled courgettes in a large bowl. Put to one side in a cool place.

4   Preheat the oven to 200°C (180°C fan oven) mark 6. Roll out the
    pastry thinly on a lightly floured worksurface and use to line a
    23cm (9in) loose-based flan tin. Leave to chill for 20 minutes.

5   Line the pastry case with greaseproof paper and fill with baking
    beans. Bake in the oven for 15 minutes, then remove the paper and
    baking beans and bake for a further 10–15 minutes until the pastry
    is a deep russet brown colour. Leave to cool for 5 minutes, then
    brush the inside of the pastry case with the remaining beaten egg
    and put it back into the oven for 4–5 minutes until the egg has
    formed a seal. Pour in the courgette and cheese mixture and bake
    for 30–35 minutes until the filling is just set.

6   Leave the tart to cool for 5 minutes then carefully take it out of
    the flan tin and put on a wire rack. Serve warm or cold with
    salad leaves.

TO FREEZE

■   Complete to the end of step 6, cool quickly on a wire rack, wrap
    and freeze.

■   To use, put the frozen tart on a preheated baking sheet and bake at
    200°C (180°C fan oven) mark 6 for 50 minutes. (You might need to
    cover the tart with a tent of foil to prevent over-browning.) If the
    tart has been defrosted beforehand, reheat for 30 minutes.

SPANISH FISH STEW

HANDS-ON TIME: 20 MINUTES   **COOKING TIME:** 1 HOUR 10 MINUTES   **SERVES:** 4

METHOD

1 Preheat the oven to 170°C (150°C fan oven) mark 3. Put the potatoes, chorizo, roasted peppers, garlic, onions, wine and passata into a large, non-stick, flameproof casserole with 2 tbsp of the oil from the peppers. Season with salt and pepper.

2 Bring to the boil over a medium heat, cover with a tight-fitting lid, and cook in the oven for 45 minutes.

3 Add the olives and fish and put back into the oven for 15 minutes until the fish is opaque and completely cooked through.

TO FREEZE

- Complete up to the end of step 2. Put in a large freezerproof container, cool, then stir in the fish and olives. Freeze for up to three months.

- To use, thaw overnight at a cool room temperature, then put back into the casserole. Bring to the boil with 150ml (5fl oz) water, and simmer gently for 10–15 minutes until the fish is cooked through and the sauce is piping hot.

COOK'S TIP

Because of the colour of their skins, red onions have a wonderfully sweet, mild flavour.

INGREDIENTS

350g (12oz) small salad potatoes, unpeeled and halved
175g (6oz) chorizo sausage, skinned and roughly chopped
350g jar roasted peppers in olive oil, drained and chopped, oil put to one side
1 garlic clove, crushed
2 small red onions, peeled and cut into thick wedges
175ml (6fl oz) dry white wine
300g jar passata
25g (1oz) pitted black olives
450g (1lb) chunky white fish such as cod or haddock, cut into large cubes

PER SERVING

420 cals
19g fat (of which 6g saturates)
29g carbohydrate

PANETTONE BREAD AND BUTTER PUDDING

✋ **HANDS-ON TIME:** 30 MINUTES, PLUS SOAKING   🍲 **COOKING TIME:** 1¼ HOURS   ✗ **SERVES:** 8

INGREDIENTS
125g (4oz) raisins
100ml (3½fl oz) brandy
2 × 500g cartons fresh custard,
about 900ml (1½ pints) in total
600ml carton milk
panettone, weighing about 700g
(1½lb)
75g (3oz) softened butter, plus
extra to grease
200g (7oz) plain chocolate, roughly
chopped
icing sugar to dust

PER SERVING
730 cals
30g fat (of which 14g saturates)
97g carbohydrate

METHOD
1 Put the raisins in a bowl, add the brandy and leave to soak overnight. Stir the custard and milk together.
2 Slice the panettone into circles, about 5mm (¼in) thick, and spread with the butter. Cut each circle into quarters. Grease a 3.4 litre (6 pint) ovenproof dish and pour a thin layer of custard over the base of the dish.
3 Layer the panettone, raisins, chocolate and custard in the dish, finishing with a layer of custard. Set aside and leave to soak for 1 hour.
4 Preheat the oven to 180°C (160°C fan oven) mark 4. Put the dish in a roasting tin and pour hot water around the dish to come halfway up the sides. Bake in the oven for 1–1¼ hours until the custard is set and the top has turned a deep brown. If necessary, cover with foil after 40 minutes to prevent the top from burning.
5 Dust the pudding lightly with icing sugar and serve (not suitable for children due to the alcohol content).

TO FREEZE
■ Freeze at the end of step 3.
■ To use, thaw the pudding overnight in the fridge, then complete the recipe.

COOK'S TIP
Panettone is a dome-shaped yeasted cake with sultanas, orange and citrus peel. You'll find it in major supermarkets and delicatessens.

DOUBLE CHOCOLATE TERRINE WITH CARAMEL SAUCE

✋ **HANDS-ON TIME:** 1 HOUR, PLUS CHILLING   🍲 **COOKING TIME:** 55 MINUTES   ✗ **SERVES:** 6

INGREDIENTS

**4 eggs, separated, plus
    4 yolks**
250g (9oz) caster sugar
**85g (3½oz) cocoa powder, plus
    extra to dust**
65g (2½oz) unsalted butter
65g (2½oz) plain chocolate
284ml carton double cream
25g (1oz) icing sugar

PER SERVING
670 cals
46g fat (of which 26g saturates)
58g carbohydrate

METHOD

1   Preheat the oven to 150°C (130°C fan oven) mark 2. Line a 23 × 30cm (9 × 12in) Swiss roll tin with non-stick baking parchment.

2   Mix the four egg yolks with 25g (1oz) caster sugar and 25g (1oz) cocoa. In a separate bowl, whisk the four egg whites until stiff, then gradually whisk in 75g (3oz) caster sugar until stiff and glossy. Beat a quarter of the meringue into the egg yolk mix, then gently fold the mixture back into the remaining meringue. Spread over the base of the tin. Bake in the oven for 45–55 minutes until just firm to the touch in the centre. Leave to cool, then cover with a damp cloth.

3   Heat the butter, chocolate and remaining cocoa powder in a bowl set over a pan of gently simmering water. Stir until the butter and chocolate have melted. Leave to cool.

4   Whisk the cream with the icing sugar until it begins to thicken. Beat the four extra egg yolks with the remaining 150g (5oz) caster sugar until thick and light in colour, then beat into the cooled chocolate mixture. Slowly whisk in the double cream.

5   Line a 1.3 litre (2¼ pint) loaf tin with non-stick baking parchment. Cut the cake into three rectangles that will fit in the tin. Place a third of the mousse in the tin and put a piece of cake on top. Repeat until all the mousse and cake are used, finishing with cake. Cover with foil and leave to chill overnight.

6   Turn out the terrine and slice thickly. Lightly dust with cocoa powder. Serve with chilled single cream and Caramel Sauce.

CARAMEL SAUCE

✋ **HANDS-ON TIME:** 5 MINUTES   🍲 **COOKING TIME:** 15 MINUTES, PLUS COOLING   ✗ **SERVES:** 6

INGREDIENTS

50g (2oz) caster sugar
142ml carton double cream

PER SERVING
140 cals
11g fat (of which 7g saturates)
9g carbohydrate

METHOD

1   Melt the sugar slowly in a small, heavy-based pan until liquid and golden, then cook over a gentle heat until a dark caramel colour.

2   Add the cream immediately in a slow, steady stream. Take care – the hot caramel will cause the cream to boil up in the pan. Stir over a gentle heat until the caramel has melted, then leave to cool. Serve with Double Chocolate Terrine.

BAKED ALASKA

METHOD

1. Put the sponge case on a board and use a 5cm (2in) cutter to make four rounds. Put the rounds on a non-stick baking sheet, spoon over the cassis, then spread evenly with the jam.

2. Spoon four scoops of ice cream from the tub and put one on top of each jam-covered sponge. Pop them into the freezer for at least an hour.

3. Meanwhile, make the meringue. Put the egg whites into a large bowl and whisk with an electric hand whisk until stiff. Mix in the cream of tartar along with a pinch of salt. Using a large metal spoon, fold in the sugar a teaspoonful at a time, then whisk at high speed until very stiff and shiny.

4. Spoon the meringue into a piping bag fitted with a star nozzle, then pipe to cover the sponge and ice cream completely. Fill in any gaps. Freeze overnight or for up to one month, covered loosely with clingfilm.

5. Preheat the oven to 230°C (210°C fan oven) mark 8. Scatter the almonds over the meringue, then bake for 3–5 minutes until just golden brown. Serve immediately with extra cassis drizzled around, or, if the puddings have been in the freezer for longer than one night, leave to sit for 15 minutes before serving.

COOK'S TIP

Freeze the leftover egg yolks to use in other recipes. If you will be using them in savoury dishes, add a pinch of salt; for sweet, a pinch of sugar. This stops them becoming gelatinous during the freezing process. Don't forget to label the container.

INGREDIENTS

1 sponge flan case, 20cm (8in) in diameter
3 tbsp cassis, plus extra to drizzle
4 tbsp raspberry jam, beaten
½ × 500ml tub luxury ice cream
3 egg whites
a small pinch of cream of tartar
a pinch of salt
150g (5oz) golden caster sugar
25g (1oz) flaked almonds

PER SERVING

440 cals
9g fat (of which 3g saturates)
83g carbohydrate

CHOCOLATE AND ORANGE CHEESECAKE

HANDS-ON TIME: 35 MINUTES   **COOKING TIME:** 1 HOUR 10 MINUTES   **SERVES:** 6–8

INGREDIENTS
3 eggs
125g (4oz) caster sugar
3 × 200g tubs full-fat soft cheese
6 tbsp crème fraîche or thick Greek
   yogurt
125ml (4oz) plain chocolate
zest of 2 large oranges

To decorate
orange segments
chocolate curls
strips of deep-fried orange peel
   (optional, see Cook's Tips)
icing sugar

PER SERVING
770–580 cals
64–48g fat (of which 39–29g saturates)
43–32g carbohydrate

METHOD

1   Preheat the oven to 180°C (160°C fan oven) mark 4. Line the base of a 23cm (9in) spring-release cake tin with non-stick baking parchment.

2   Separate the eggs. Beat the egg yolks with 50g (2oz) sugar until pale in colour and thick. Add the full-fat soft cheese and crème fraîche or Greek yogurt and beat until smooth.

3   Melt the chocolate in a large bowl set over a pan of simmering water (see Cook's Tips). Add a third of the cheese mixture to the chocolate, mix until smooth and put to one side.

4   Add the orange zest to the remaining cheese mixture.

5   Whisk the egg whites in a separate bowl until stiff, then gradually whisk in the remaining sugar until the mixture is stiff and shiny.

6   Fold a third of the egg whites into the chocolate mixture, spoon into the prepared cake tin and smooth the top. Fold the remaining egg whites into the orange mixture, spoon on top of the chocolate mixture and smooth the surface.

7   Bake in the oven for 55–60 minutes until the centre is just firm to the touch. Turn off the oven and leave the cheesecake to cool in the oven.

8   Take the cheesecake out of the tin. Decorate with orange segments, chocolate curls and strips of deep-fried orange peel, if you like. Dust with icing sugar.

TO FREEZE
■   Complete to the end of step 6. Wrap and freeze.
■   To use, bake from frozen for 1 hour–1 hour 10 minutes, then complete the recipe.

COOK'S TIPS
■   If you are in a hurry, chocolate can be melted in the microwave on the Defrost setting. (It will take about 2½ minutes in a 650W oven.)
■   For the deep-fried orange peel, pare the zest thinly and deep-fry in a small amount of hot oil until crisp; drain on kitchen paper. Leave to cool then use as required.

FRUIT COMPOTE

✋ **HANDS-ON TIME:** 45 MINUTES, PLUS COOLING AND CHILLING 🍲 **COOKING TIME:** 8 MINUTES ✗ **SERVES:** 6

METHOD

1 Put the honey, wine, fruit juice and spices in a medium pan and warm gently until the honey has dissolved. Bring to the boil and simmer gently for about 3 minutes.

2 Add the dried fruit, bring back to the boil and simmer for 3 minutes. Pour into a heatproof bowl and stir in the grapes and redcurrants. Remove and discard the cinnamon stick and leave the fruit to cool.

3 Stir the clementines, mango and pineapple into the mixed fruit with the drained apricot halves. Put in the fridge and chill for 30 minutes before serving (not suitable for children due to the alcohol content).

TO FREEZE

■ Spoon the compote into a sealable container and freeze. (The fruit will soften.)

■ To use, thaw overnight in the fridge.

COOK'S TIP

To save time, you can buy ready-chopped pineapple and mango from the fruit salad bar of many supermarkets.

INGREDIENTS

2 tbsp runny honey
300ml (10fl oz) dessert wine
300ml (10fl oz) fresh fruit juice
    such as orange, apple and mango
    or pineapple
½ tsp freshly grated nutmeg
1 cinnamon stick and/or 3 thick
    slices fresh root ginger, peeled
225g (8oz) mixed dried fruits
125g (4oz) small black seedless
    grapes
125g (4oz) redcurrants
3 clementines, peeled and thickly
    sliced
1 small fresh mango, peeled and
    thickly sliced
1 small ripe pineapple, peeled,
    cored and thinly sliced, and each
    slice cut into quarters
400g can apricot halves in natural
    juice, drained

PER SERVING

260 cals
trace fat
57g carbohydrate

SPICED WINTER FRUIT

HANDS-ON TIME: 20 MINUTES **COOKING TIME:** ABOUT 20 MINUTES **SERVES:** 6

METHOD

1 First, make the syrup. Pour the port and orange juice into a small pan, then add the sugar and water. Bring to the boil, stirring all the time. Add the cinnamon stick, cardamom pods and ginger, then bubble gently for 15 minutes.

2 Put all the fruit into a serving bowl. Remove the cinnamon stick and cardamom pods from the syrup, then pour the syrup over the fruit. Serve warm or cold (not suitable for children due to the alcohol content).

TO FREEZE

- Tip the fruit and syrup into a freezerproof container, leave to cool, then cover with a tight-fitting lid and freeze for up to three months.
- To use, thaw overnight in the fridge and serve cold.

COOK'S TIP

It might sound odd freezing a fruit salad, but it saves all the last-minute chopping and slicing.

INGREDIENTS

150ml (5fl oz) port
150ml (5fl oz) freshly squeezed orange juice
75g (3oz) light muscovado sugar
300ml (10fl oz) cold water
1 cinnamon stick
6 whole cardamom pods, lightly crushed
5cm (2in) piece fresh root ginger, peeled and thinly sliced
50g (2oz) large muscatel raisins or dried blueberries
1 small pineapple, peeled, cored and thinly sliced
1 mango, peeled and thickly sliced
3 tangerines, peeled and halved horizontally
3 fresh figs, halved

PER SERVING

180 cals

0g fat

42g carbohydrate

PECAN, MAPLE AND WHISKY PIE

HANDS-ON TIME: 40 MINUTES, PLUS CHILLING **COOKING TIME:** 1 HOUR 20 MINUTES **SERVES:** 6–8

INGREDIENTS
225g (8oz) plain flour, plus extra
    to dust
225g (8oz) butter
3 tbsp iced water
200g (7oz) pecan nuts
3 eggs, beaten
75g (3oz) dark muscovado or
    molasses sugar
1 tsp cornflour
50ml (2fl oz) maple syrup, plus
    extra to drizzle
250ml (8fl oz) golden syrup
4 tbsp whisky
1 tsp vanilla extract
ice cream or whipped cream to
    serve

PER SERVING
900–670 cals
58–43g fat (of which 23–17g saturates)
83–63g carbohydrate

METHOD
1   Preheat the grill. To make the pastry, put the flour and 150g (5oz)
    butter in a food processor and pulse until the mixture resembles
    fine crumbs. Add the iced water, pulse until the mixture comes
    together in a ball, then wrap in clingfilm and chill for 30 minutes.
    Put the nuts on a baking sheet and toast lightly under the hot grill.
    Leave to cool then chop roughly.
2   Roll out the pastry on a lightly floured worksurface and use to line
    a 23cm (9in) loose-based tart tin. Prick the base well, line with
    greaseproof paper and baking beans and chill for 30 minutes.
3   Preheat the oven to 200°C (180°C fan oven) mark 6 and bake the
    pastry case for 15 minutes, then remove the paper and beans and
    bake for a further 15 minutes or until golden. Brush the base and
    sides of the pastry case with a little of the beaten egg and put back
    in the oven for 3–4 minutes. Set aside.
4   Reduce the oven temperature to 180°C (160°C fan oven) mark 4.
    Beat the remaining butter with the sugar until light, then slowly
    add the remaining beaten eggs and cornflour. Stir in the syrups,
    whisky and vanilla extract. Don't worry if the mixture appears
    curdled. Stir in the toasted pecans and pour into the cooked
    pastry case.
5   Bake the pie for 45 minutes or until the filling is just set. Leave
    to cool slightly, then drizzle with maple syrup and serve with ice
    cream or whipped cream (not suitable for children due to the
    alcohol content).

TO FREEZE
- Complete to step 4. Cool, pack and freeze.
- To use, thaw overnight at a cool room temperature and serve, or
  warm through at 200°C (180°C fan oven) mark 6 for 20 minutes.

RASPBERRY AND ALMOND TRIFLE

HANDS-ON TIME: 1 HOUR 10 MINUTES, PLUS FREEZING ⬛ **COOKING TIME:** 20 MINUTES ✕ **SERVES:** 6

METHOD

1 Warm 5 tbsp golden syrup and 8 tbsp Drambuie together in a small pan. Stir in the raspberries and take the pan off the heat. Put the sponge cake in a deep, 3 litre (5 pint) freezerproof serving bowl, spoon the raspberry mixture on top. then leave to cool.

2 Oil a baking sheet. Put the almonds in a small pan with the caster sugar and heat gently, stirring occasionally, until the sugar dissolves and turns a golden caramel colour. Spoon the almonds on to the oiled baking sheet and leave to cool. When cold, whiz to a rough powder in a food processor or blender.

3 Whip the double cream until it begins to thicken, then continue more slowly while gradually adding the remaining Drambuie.

4 Heat the remaining golden syrup in a small pan. Using an electric whisk, whisk the egg yolks for 2 minutes, then gradually add the hot syrup. Keep whisking until the mixture is slightly thickened. Fold into the whipped cream with half the powdered nuts.

5 Roughly spoon the raspberry sorbet on top of the raspberries, top with the nut cream and freeze overnight.

6 When ready to serve, spoon the double cream on top of the frozen trifle. Decorate with raspberries, holly leaves (if the trifle's for Christmas), the remaining powdered nuts and a dusting of icing sugar. Leave the trifle to chill in the fridge for at least 3 hours before serving (not suitable for children due to the alcohol content).

COOK'S TIP

If you don't have a whisky liqueur use another such as Grand Marnier or Cointreau.

INGREDIENTS

200g (7oz) golden syrup
175ml (6fl oz) Drambuie
225g (8oz) fresh or frozen raspberries
125g (4oz) light sponge cake such as Madeira, chopped
25g (1oz) flaked almonds
50g (2oz) caster sugar
284ml carton double cream
8 egg yolks
500ml tub raspberry sorbet

To decorate

284ml carton extra-thick double cream
125g (4oz) fresh raspberries and a few holly leaves
icing sugar to dust

PER SERVING

690 cals
44g fat (of which 24g saturates)
58g carbohydrate

CHERRY AND TANGERINE STICKY PUDDINGS

✋ **HANDS-ON TIME:** 20 MINUTES, PLUS SOAKING ♨ **COOKING TIME:** 25 MINUTES ✗ **SERVES:** 8

INGREDIENTS

about 25g (1oz) white vegetable fat, melted
200g (7oz) dried cherries
150ml (5fl oz) boiling water
2 tbsp orange-flavoured liqueur
¾ tsp bicarbonate of soda
75g (3oz) unsalted butter, softened
150g (5oz) golden caster sugar
2 eggs, beaten
175g (6oz) self-raising flour

For the sauce

175g (6oz) light muscovado sugar
125g (4oz) unsalted butter
6 tbsp double cream
25g (1oz) pecan nuts, chopped
juice of 1 tangerine

PER SERVING

580 cals
33g fat (of which 19g saturates)
67g carbohydrate

METHOD

1   Preheat the oven to 180°C (160°C fan oven) mark 4. Using the melted fat, lightly oil eight 175ml (6fl oz) metal pudding basins or ramekins, then put a circle of non-stick baking parchment into the base of each.

2   Put 175g (6oz) dried cherries into a bowl and pour the boiling water over them. Stir in the liqueur and bicarbonate of soda, then leave to soak for 1 hour.

3   Whisk the butter and sugar in a large bowl until pale and fluffy, then beat in the eggs a little at a time. Fold in the cherry mixture.

4   Add the flour and fold in with a large metal spoon. Divide the mixture equally among the basins, then bake on a baking sheet for about 25 minutes or until well risen and firm.

5   Meanwhile, make the sauce. Put the sugar, butter, cream, pecans and remaining cherries in a pan. Heat gently until the sugar has dissolved, then stir in the tangerine juice.

6   Leave the puddings to cool for 5 minutes, then turn out. Serve topped with the sauce.

TO FREEZE

■   Leave the puddings to cool completely, then wrap in clingfilm. Pour the sauce into a freezerproof container and leave to cool. Freeze both for up to one month.

■   To use, thaw the puddings and sauce overnight in the fridge. Warm the sauce. Meanwhile, put the puddings on a microwaveable plate. Spoon 1 tbsp sauce over each. Warm in the microwave on High for 2 minutes. Alternatively, preheat the oven to 150°C (130°C fan oven) mark 2. Put the puddings on an edged baking sheet, spoon 1 tbsp sauce over each and reheat for about 10 minutes. Serve with the remaining sauce.

TOASTED HAZELNUT MERINGUE CAKE

✋ **HANDS-ON TIME:** 10 MINUTES   🍰 **COOKING TIME:** ABOUT 30 MINUTES, PLUS COOLING   ✕ **SERVES:** 8

INGREDIENTS
175g (6oz) skinned hazelnuts, toasted
3 large egg whites
175g (6oz) golden caster sugar
250g tub mascarpone cheese
284ml carton double cream
3 tbsp Baileys Irish Cream liqueur, plus extra to serve
125g (4oz) frozen raspberries
340g jar redcurrant jelly

PER SERVING
610 cals
40g fat (of which 21g saturates)
58g carbohydrate

METHOD

1 Preheat the oven to 190°C (170°C fan oven) mark 5. Lightly oil two 18cm (7in) sandwich tins and line the bases with non-stick baking parchment. Put the hazelnuts into a food processor and whiz until finely chopped (see Cook's Tips).

2 Put the egg whites into a spotlessly clean, grease-free bowl and whisk until stiff peaks form. Whisk in the sugar, a spoonful at a time. Fold in half the nuts with a metal spoon.

3 Divide the mixture between the tins and spread evenly. Bake in the middle of the oven for about 30 minutes, then leave to cool in the tins for 30 minutes.

4 Meanwhile, make the filling. Put the mascarpone cheese into a bowl and beat in the cream and liqueur until smooth.

5 Put the raspberries and redcurrant jelly into a small pan and heat gently until the jelly has melted. Sieve to remove any pips, then leave the purée to cool.

6 When the meringues are cool, use a palette knife to loosen the edges, then carefully turn out on to a wire rack. Peel off the baking parchment and discard. Put a large sheet of baking parchment on a board and sit one meringue on top, flat side down.

7 Spread a third of the mascarpone mixture over the meringue, then drizzle with the raspberry purée. Top with the other meringue, then cover the whole cake with the rest of the mascarpone mixture. Sprinkle with the remaining hazelnuts.

8 Carefully put the cake on a serving plate and drizzle with more liqueur, if you like (not suitable for children due to the alcohol content).

TO FREEZE
■ Make the cake up to the end of step 7. Using the paper, lift the cake into the freezer, then freeze until solid. Once solid, freeze in a sturdy container for up to one month.
■ To use, thaw overnight in the fridge, then complete the recipe.

COOK'S TIPS
■ Freezing the meringue makes it slightly softer but no less delicious.
■ Chop the nuts in the food processor in short bursts of 2–3 seconds at a time. If they are over-processed they will become oily and spoil the meringue.

CRANBERRY, APPLE AND CALVADOS TART

METHOD

1 Roll out the pastry on a lightly floured worksurface and use to line a 23cm (9in) round and 4cm (1½in) deep, loose-based fluted flan tin. Prick the base all over with a fork.

2 Carefully cover the base and sides with foil, pressing it firmly into the edges of the pastry, then wrap over the top edge to cover the pastry completely. Chill for 30 minutes.

3 Preheat the oven to 190°C (170°C fan oven) mark 5. Bake the pastry case for 20 minutes or until the pastry has set. Remove the foil.

4 Meanwhile, put 225g (8oz) dried cranberries into a bowl and stir in the grated apple, Calvados, orange zest and all but 1 tbsp of the orange juice. In another bowl, mix together the melted butter, ground almonds, eggs and sugar. Stir in the cranberry mixture, then spoon into the pastry case. Sprinkle with toasted almonds, then bake for 30 minutes or until golden. Leave to cool for 20 minutes. Sprinkle with the remaining cranberries.

5 Heat the jam and remaining orange juice in a small pan until it bubbles. Brush over the tart. Turn out of the tin and serve (not suitable for children due to the alcohol content).

TO FREEZE

■ Complete the recipe and leave the tart in the tin until cooled. Wrap in foil and freeze for up to one month.

■ To use, thaw overnight in the fridge. Serve cold or heat in the oven for 15 minutes at 180°C (160°C fan) mark 4, covering the tart loosely with foil.

COOK'S TIP

The secret of a good glaze is to keep the jam bubbling as you brush it on, so take the tart to the hob to do this.

INGREDIENTS

375g pack ready-rolled shortcrust pastry
a little plain flour to dust
250g (9oz) dried cranberries
1 eating apple, peeled and coarsely grated
3 tbsp Calvados
zest and juice of 1 orange
125g (4oz) unsalted butter, melted
225g (8oz) ground almonds
2 eggs, beaten
75g (3oz) golden caster sugar
25g (1oz) flaked almonds, lightly toasted
100g (3½oz) apricot jam

PER SERVING
500 cals
36g fat (of which 13g saturates)
36g carbohydrate

3

WEEKDAY MEALS

If you're cooking a sauce for a meal, it makes sense to cook double the quantity and freeze half. Once you've made up a big batch you can ring the changes for speedy midweek meals. Two very versatile sauces are Tomato and Bolognese (see below), so always try to keep a quantity of each in the freezer. The Tomato Sauce can be the basis for lots of pasta recipes, while the bolognese sauce will stand you in good stead for dishes such as cottage pie, chilli con carne and lasagne.

TOMATO SAUCE

This sauce is easy and keeps well in an airtight container for up to four days in the fridge. Serve with pasta, grilled fish or chicken.

- ✋ **HANDS-ON TIME:** 5 MINUTES
- 🍲 **COOKING TIME:** ABOUT 20 MINUTES
- ✕ **SERVES:** 4

2 tbsp olive oil
1 medium onion, peeled and finely chopped
2 garlic cloves, crushed
900g (2lb) very ripe tomatoes, preferably on the vine, roughly chopped
3 tbsp sun-dried tomato paste
a pinch of sugar, if needed

PER SERVING: 120 cals; 7g fat (of which 1g saturates); 13g carbohydrate

1 Heat the oil in a large frying pan. Add the onion and garlic and fry over a low heat for 10 minutes until the onion is soft. Don't stint on the cooking time as, properly softened, golden onions will melt into the finished sauce and give it depth of flavour.

2 Add the tomatoes and tomato paste then simmer, uncovered, over a low heat until the sauce is thick and pulpy. This will take about 10 minutes. Taste the sauce and season. If it tastes a little too acidic, add a pinch of sugar. Serve with pasta, grilled fish or chicken.

VARIATIONS

CHILLI TOMATO SAUCE Fry half a finely chopped red chilli with the onion, then complete the recipe.

BASIL AND TOMATO SAUCE After cooking the sauce, stir in a handful of freshly chopped basil.

BACON AND TOMATO SAUCE Chop 2 rashers of rindless streaky bacon and add to the pan with the onion. Cook for 10–15 minutes until the bacon is browned, then add the tomatoes and complete the recipe.

TOMATO SAUCE WITH RED PEPPER AND OLIVES Add 1 deseeded and sliced red pepper to the pan when frying the onion. When the sauce has finished simmering, add 6 pitted, chopped olives and cook for 1–2 minutes to heat through.

TUNA AND TOMATO SAUCE Reheat 1 quantity of tomato sauce. Drain an 80g can tuna in oil or brine and add to the pan, then cook for 2–3 minutes to warm through. Toss with pasta. Serves 4

SIMPLE BOLOGNESE SAUCE

This sauce tastes even better the day after it's been made.

- ✋ **HANDS-ON TIME:** 15 MINUTES
- 🍲 **COOKING TIME:** ABOUT 1 HOUR
- ✕ **SERVES:** 4

1 tbsp olive oil
1 large onion, peeled and finely chopped
1 carrot, peeled and finely chopped
1 celery stick, trimmed and finely chopped
1 garlic clove, crushed
125g (4oz) button mushrooms, chopped
450g (1lb) minced meat
300ml (10fl oz) stock
300ml (10fl oz) dry red or white wine
400g can chopped tomatoes

1 tbsp tomato purée
2 tsp dried oregano
2 tbsp freshly chopped parsley

To serve
freshly cooked pasta
freshly grated Parmesan cheese

PER SERVING: 250 cals; 9g fat (of which 3g saturates);
10g carbohydrate;

1   Heat the oil in a frying pan. Add the onion, carrot, celery
    and garlic, and fry gently for 5 minutes or until softened.
    Add the mushrooms and fry for a further minute.
2   Stir in the minced meat and cook, stirring, over a high
    heat until browned. Stir in the stock, wine, tomatoes,
    tomato purée, oregano and seasoning. Bring to the
    boil, cover and simmer for 1 hour or until the meat is
    tender and the sauce is well reduced.
3   Adjust the seasoning and stir in the parsley before
    serving with freshly cooked pasta and freshly grated
    Parmesan cheese.

VARIATIONS

COTTAGE PIE Preheat the oven to 200ºC (180ºC fan oven)
mark 6. Add 1 tbsp plain flour once the meat has
browned. Omit the tomatoes and add 450ml (15fl oz) beef
stock. Add 1 medium carrot, peeled and diced, with the
mushrooms. Spoon the sauce into a 1.7 litre (3 pint)
ovenproof dish and top with 1kg (2lb 3½oz) mashed potato.
Cook for 20–25 minutes.
LASAGNE Preheat the oven to 200ºC (180ºC fan oven)
mark 6. Make a quantity of bolognese sauce. When it is
nearly finished make a double quantity of cheese sauce
(page 25). Spoon half the bolognese sauce into a shallow
1.7 litre (3 pint) ovenproof dish. Top with 2 sheets of
lasagne (the 'no precooking required' type) and half the
cheese sauce. Repeat with the rest of the bolognese,
lasagne and cheese sauce. Sprinkle with 1 tbsp grated
cheese. Cook for 35 minutes.
CHILLI CON CARNE Follow the bolognese recipe, but
after cooking the onions for 15 minutes, add 1 deseeded,
chopped red pepper and cook for 5 minutes. Add 2 tsp
mild chilli powder with the mince. Drain a 400g can of red
kidney beans and add to the pan for the final 5 minutes of
cooking time. Serve with rice, jacket potatoes or in a flour
tortilla. Grate over some Cheddar cheese, if you like.

- **VARIATIONS:** Replace half the quantity of mince with
  200g (7oz) red lentils, and add them after browning
  the mince. There's no need to soak them, so just stir
  them in, then complete the recipe.

PLANNING MIDWEEK MEALS

If you plan a week's menus in advance, it will
take the stress out of deciding what to cook
each day and can turn leftovers into meals in
their own right. For example, the remains of
the roast chicken on Sunday can be made into
Leftover Roast Chicken Soup (page 65)

For a family hooked on takeaways, the
week's menu might look like the one below,
but these home-cooked versions are a healthy
version:

MONDAY
Ham and Mushroom Pasta (page 81)

TUESDAY
Tuna Melt Pizza (page 95)

WEDNESDAY
Chilli-Fried Chicken with Coconut Noodles
(page 93)

THURSDAY
Grilled Burger (page 101)

FRIDAY
Quick Fish and Chips (page 95)

Choose fresh fruit, yogurt or ice cream for
quick midweek desserts, or check out the
freeze- ahead puddings in Chapter 2, Cook Now
Eat Later.

HEALTHY BREAKFASTS

QUICK MEALS TO START THE DAY

TOAST Two slices of wholemeal stoneground bread, toasted and spread with yeast extract or 1 tbsp low-sugar jam. Serve with half a grapefruit.

SMOOTHIE Whiz together 150g pot low-fat natural yogurt, 1 banana, 2 tbsp oats, 1 tbsp honey and 4 ice cubes in a blender until smooth.

CEREAL Serve 50g (2oz) unsweetened, no-added-salt muesli with 100ml (3½fl oz) skimmed milk and 1 grated apple per person. Or make porridge with 40g (1½oz) oats per person and water or skimmed milk.

CONTINENTAL 1 small wholemeal stoneground roll, toasted and topped with 2 ripe chopped tomatoes and 1 tsp olive oil.

LIGHT 200g (7oz) chopped fresh fruit with 150g pot low-fat natural yogurt, 1 tsp honey and 5 chopped almonds.

MORE TIME? TRY THESE...

POSH SCRAMBLED EGGS
Snip a couple of slices of smoked salmon into scrambled eggs with some chives. Stir to combine, then spoon onto buttered granary toast.

EGGS BENEDICT
Top a toasted muffin with a layer of wilted spinach, a slice of good-quality cooked ham and a poached egg. Spoon over hollandaise sauce and flash under the grill before serving.

THE BEST BACON BUTTY
Grill smoked streaky bacon until crisp. Toast slices of thick, good quality bread. Sandwich togther with sliced plum tomatoes, avocado, bacon and a good dollop each of mayonnaise and tomato ketchup.

MUSHROOM OMELETTE
Top a plain omelette with a handful each of fried button mushrooms and grated cheese. Fold in half and serve straightaway.

SPECIAL PANCAKE
Top warmed pancakes with rashers of crispy bacon and drizzle over maple syrup. If you prefer your pancake sweet, leave out the bacon and serve with sliced exotic fruit such as banana, mango and pineapple and a dollop of natural yogurt.

LUNCH

MIXED MUSHROOM SOUP

✋ **HANDS-ON TIME:** 15 MINUTES, PLUS SOAKING ▦ **COOKING TIME:** 35 MINUTES ✕ **SERVES:** 4 V

INGREDIENTS

15g (½oz) dried porcini mushrooms
75ml (2½fl oz) boiling water
1 tbsp sunflower oil, plus 50ml
   (2fl oz) to shallow-fry
1 small onion, peeled and chopped
450g (1lb) chestnut mushrooms,
   chopped
600ml (1 pint) hot vegetable stock
salt and pepper
2 slices white bread, crusts
   removed, cut into cubes
2 garlic cloves, finely sliced
freshly chopped flat-leafed parsley
   to garnish

PER SERVING

210 cals
15g fat (of which 2g saturates)
14g carbohydrate

METHOD

1 Put the porcini into a bowl, pour over the boiling water and leave to soak for 10 minutes. Sieve the mushrooms, put the liquid to one side, then roughly chop the porcini, keeping 1 tbsp to use as garnish.

2 Heat 1 tbsp oil in a pan. Add the onion and porcini and cook over a medium heat for 5 minutes. Add the chestnut mushrooms, increase the heat and brown lightly for 5 minutes.

3 Add the porcini liquid and stock, then bring to the boil. Season well with salt and pepper and simmer for 20 minutes.

4 To make croûtons, heat 50ml (2fl oz) oil in a frying pan. Add the bread and garlic and stir-fry for 2 minutes until golden. Drain on kitchen paper.

5 Take the soup off the heat and leave to cool slightly. Whiz in a blender until smooth, then transfer to a clean pan. Gently reheat, then divide among four warmed bowls. Serve topped with the croutons, reserved porcini and a sprinkling of parsley.

SPICY BEAN AND COURGETTE SOUP

✋ **HANDS-ON TIME:** 10 MINUTES 🍲 **COOKING TIME:** 30 MINUTES ✗ **SERVES:** 4 V

METHOD

1 Heat the oil in a pan. Add the onion and garlic and sauté for
   2 minutes. Add the spices and cook, stirring, for 1 minute. Mix in
   the courgettes and potatoes and cook for 1–2 minutes.
2 Add the remaining ingredients, cover and simmer for 25 minutes,
   stirring occasionally, or until the potatoes are tender. Adjust the
   seasoning before serving with crusty bread.

COOK'S TIP

Courgettes are baby marrows. Look for small, firm vegetables.
They lose their flavour as they grow larger.

INGREDIENTS

2 tbsp olive oil
**175g (6oz) onions, peeled and finely
   chopped**
2 garlic cloves, crushed
2 tsp ground coriander
1 tbsp paprika
1 tsp mild curry powder
**450g (1lb) courgettes, trimmed,
   halved and sliced**
225g (8oz) potatoes, peeled and diced
400g can red kidney beans, drained
425g can flageolet beans, drained
1.5 litres (2½ pints) vegetable stock

PER SERVING

250 cals
8g fat (of which 1g saturates)
34g carbohydrate

LEFTOVER ROAST CHICKEN SOUP

✋ **HANDS-ON TIME:** 15 MINUTES 🍲 **COOKING TIME:** 45 MINUTES ✗ **SERVES:** 4

METHOD

1 Heat the oil in a large pan. Add the onion, carrot, celery and thyme
   and fry gently for 20–30 minutes until soft but not brown. Add the
   bay leaf, stripped roast chicken carcass and the boiling water to
   the pan. Bring to the boil, then simmer for 5 minutes.
2 Remove the bay leaf and carcass and add the chopped roast
   chicken and cooked potato. Simmer for 5 minutes.
3 Whiz the soup in a food processor, pour back into the pan and
   bring to the boil. Stir in the double cream.

INGREDIENTS

3 tbsp olive oil
1 onion, peeled and chopped
1 carrot, peeled and chopped
2 celery sticks, chopped
2 fresh thyme sprigs, chopped
1 bay leaf
a stripped roast chicken carcass
900ml (1½ pints) boiling water
150–200g (5–7oz) chopped roast chicken
200g (7oz) mashed or roast potato
1 tbsp double cream

PER SERVING

230 cals
14g fat (of which 3g saturates)
15g carbohydrate

TOMATO SALAD SOUP WITH BRUSCHETTA

HANDS-ON TIME: 15 MINUTES, PLUS MARINATING & CHILLING **COOKING TIME:** 5 MINUTES **SERVES:** 4

METHOD

1 Put the tomatoes in a large, shallow dish and scatter over the spring onions, lemon zest and chopped basil.

2 Blend together the olive oil, vinegar, one garlic clove, the sugar, vodka, Worcestershire sauce and Tabasco. Season to taste with salt and pepper and pour over the tomatoes. Cover and leave to marinate for 2 hours at room temperature.

3 Whiz the tomato salad and tomato juice in a blender until very smooth. Transfer to a bowl and leave to chill in the fridge for 1 hour.

4 Just before serving, preheat the grill. Put the bread slices on the grill rack and toast lightly on both sides. Rub each one with the remaining crushed garlic and drizzle with extra-virgin olive oil. Spoon the soup into serving bowls and serve with the bruschetta. Garnish with fresh basil leaves and serve at once (not suitable for children due to the alcohol content).

INGREDIENTS

700g (1½lb) ripe plum tomatoes, thinly sliced
6 spring onions, trimmed and finely chopped
zest of ½ lemon
2 tbsp freshly chopped basil
125ml (4fl oz) extra-virgin olive oil, plus extra to drizzle
2 tbsp balsamic vinegar
2–3 garlic cloves
a pinch of sugar
60ml (2fl oz) chilled vodka
1 tbsp Worcestershire sauce
a few drops of Tabasco
150ml (5fl oz) tomato juice
8 thin slices French bread
fresh basil leaves to garnish

PER SERVING
490 cals
33g fat (of which 5g saturates)
36g carbohydrate

SMOKED MACKEREL AND PASTA SALAD

✋ **HANDS-ON TIME:** 10 MINUTES   🍲 **COOKING TIME:** 20 MINUTES   ✗ **SERVES:** 4

INGREDIENTS

225g (8oz) dried pasta shapes, such as shells or spirals

3 medium courgettes, about 275g (10oz) total weight, trimmed and sliced

grated zest and juice of 2 oranges

3 tbsp olive oil

350g (12oz) smoked mackerel fillets, flaked

freshly snipped chives to garnish

PER SERVING

620 cals

38g fat (of which 7g saturates)

48g carbohydrate

METHOD

1 Cook the pasta in a large pan of boiling salted water until *al dente*, then drain. Cook the courgettes in another pan of boiling salted water until just tender, about 2–3 minutes, then drain.

2 Whisk together the oil, orange zest and juice. Season well with salt and pepper and stir in the cooked pasta. Leave to cool.

3 Combine all the ingredients, with the flaked mackerel, in a bowl. Season with salt and pepper and garnish with snipped chives. Cover and chill until required.

COOK'S TIP

You could also use canned salmon, tuna or sardines, or smoked trout – just keep the quantities the same.

CHORIZO SALAD

✋ **HANDS-ON TIME:** 15 MINUTES   🍲 **COOKING TIME:** ABOUT 15 MINUTES   ✗ **SERVES:** 4

INGREDIENTS

225g (8oz) chorizo sausage, diced

175ml (6fl oz) olive oil

125g (4oz) French baguette, diced

2 tsp freshly chopped thyme

1 garlic clove, crushed

2 tbsp Dijon mustard

2 tbsp sherry vinegar

1 medium egg yolk

salad leaves

125g (4oz) fennel, finely sliced

125g (4oz) cucumber, finely sliced

200g (7oz) goat's cheese, crumbled

PER SERVING

800 cals

68g fat (of which 21g saturates)

20g carbohydrate

METHOD

1 Fry the diced chorizo over a high heat until golden, stirring occasionally, then put to one side.

2 Heat 50ml (2fl oz) oil in a pan. Add the bread and cook until it is golden. Add the thyme and garlic and set aside.

3 For the dressing, whisk together the mustard, vinegar, one egg yolk and the remaining oil. Season with salt and pepper.

4 Put the salad leaves, fennel, cucumber, goat's cheese, chorizo and bread in a bowl, add the dressing and toss well until combined. Serve immediately.

COOK'S TIP

For the salad leaves, use chicory, batavia, rocket or spinach.

HOT SPICED CHICKPEA SALAD

✋ **HANDS-ON TIME:** 5 MINUTES 🍲 **COOKING TIME:** 10 MINUTES ✗ **SERVES:** 4 V

METHOD

1. Heat the oil in a medium pan. Add the onion and sauté until golden brown.
2. Add the turmeric and cumin seeds and cook, stirring, for 1–2 minutes. Add the remaining ingredients and sauté for 1–2 minutes, stirring frequently.
3. Adjust the seasoning, garnish with fresh coriander and serve with wholemeal bread.

COOK'S TIP

To stop yourself crying when chopping an onion, place it, unpeeled, in the freezer for 10 minutes before using.

INGREDIENTS

1 tbsp oil
125g (4oz) onion, peeled and roughly chopped
2 tsp ground turmeric
1 tbsp cumin seeds
450g (1lb) tomatoes, roughly chopped
2 x 400g cans cooked chickpeas, drained
1 tbsp lemon juice
4 tbsp fresh coriander
fresh coriander leaves to garnish
wholemeal bread to serve

PER SERVING

210 cals
7g fat (of which 1g saturates)
27g carbohydrate

NEW POTATO AND PRAWN SALAD

✋ **HANDS-ON TIME:** 25 MINUTES, PLUS MARINATING 🍲 **COOKING TIME:** 20 MINUTES ✗ **SERVES:** 6

METHOD

1. Cook the potatoes in a pan of boiling salted water until tender, then drain. While still warm, halve or quarter the potatoes, depending on size.
2. Whisk together the oil, vinegar and seasoning in a large bowl. Stir in the warm potatoes and leave to marinate for 20–30 minutes, stirring occasionally.
3. Stir the peppers, tomatoes and prawns into the cold potatoes, Season with salt and pepper, then cover and leave to chill for at least 2 hours.
4. Leave at room temperature for at least 30 minutes before serving and stir well to mix.

INGREDIENTS

700g (1½lb) new potatoes, scrubbed
100ml (3½fl oz) olive oil
2 tbsp red wine vinegar
1 red pepper, diced
225g (8oz) ripe red tomatoes, halved, deseeded and roughly chopped
350–450g (12oz–1lb) large cooked peeled prawns

PER SERVING

300 cals
16g fat (of which 2g saturates)
21g carbohydrate

QUICK CHICKEN AND GRUYERE SALAD

✋ **HANDS-ON TIME:** 15 MINUTES, PLUS CHILLING   🍲 **COOKING TIME:** 0 MINUTES   ✗ **SERVES:** 8

INGREDIENTS
900–1kg (2–2¼lb) cooked, boned
   chicken, skinned and cut into
   bite-size pieces
4 celery sticks, thinly sliced
125g (4oz) Gruyère or Emmenthal
   cheese, coarsely grated
2 firm red apples, halved, cored and
   roughly chopped
125g (4oz) seedless black grapes,
   halved
200ml (7fl oz) oil
2 tbsp white wine vinegar
4 tbsp soured cream
4 tbsp mayonnaise
4 tbsp freshly chopped parsley
75g (3oz) toasted pecan nuts or
   walnuts
mixed green salad to serve

PER SERVING
580 cals
47g fat (of which 10g saturates)
7g carbohydrate

METHOD
1 Put the chicken, celery, cheese, apple and grapes into a large
   bowl. Add all the other ingredients and toss well.
2 Adjust the seasoning, cover and leave to chill for at least
   10–15 minutes. Serve with a mixed green salad.

COOK'S TIPS
- Any strongly flavoured cheese can be used for this recipe. You
  could try crumbled Danish blue or blue Stilton.
- The whole salad can be completed the day before and kept covered
  in the fridge until required. Stir well before serving.

CHARGRILLED VEGETABLES WITH FRUITY COUSCOUS

✋ **HANDS-ON TIME:** 20 MINUTES, PLUS SOAKING 🍲 **COOKING TIME:** 50 MINUTES ✗ **SERVES:** 4–6 ✓

INGREDIENTS

2 tsp hot chilli purée
4 tbsp mayonnaise
2 tbsp balsamic vinegar
1 tsp sugar
1 garlic clove, halved and bruised
300ml (10fl oz) olive oil
300ml (10fl oz) hot vegetable stock
150g (5oz) couscous
75g (3oz) ready-to-eat dried
  apricots, roughly chopped
50g (2oz) shelled pistachio nuts,
  toasted
50g (2oz) pinenuts
50g (2oz) raisins
4 tbsp freshly chopped flat-leafed
  parsley
1 tbsp freshly chopped tarragon
1 tbsp freshly chopped chives
275g (10oz) aubergine, sliced into
  1cm (½in) rounds
275g (10oz) courgettes, sliced into
  1cm (½in) rounds
275g (10oz) fennel, quartered
275g (10oz) onions, peeled and
  quartered
450g (1lb) red and yellow peppers,
  halved and deseeded
paprika to sprinkle

PER SERVING
1140–760 cals
93–62g fat (of which 12–8g saturates)
62–41g carbohydrate

METHOD

1 Preheat the oven to 240°C (220°C fan oven) mark 9. Stir the chilli purée into the mayonnaise, cover and put to one side. To make the balsamic vinaigrette, whisk together the vinegar, sugar, garlic and seasoning, then whisk in 8 tbsp oil.

2 Pour the hot stock over the couscous and leave to soak for 5 minutes. Stir in the apricots, nuts, raisins, herbs, seasoning and half the vinaigrette and set aside.

3 Brush the aubergine, courgettes, fennel, onions and peppers with the remaining oil and roast in the oven until well coloured and softened. The onion and fennel take about 50 minutes; the others 30 minutes.

4 Peel the peppers and cut into strips. Mix all the vegetables together in a bowl.

5 Stir the remaining vinaigrette, discarding the garlic, into the vegetables and serve with the couscous and chilli mayonnaise sprinkled with paprika.

TO PREPARE AHEAD

■ The day before, complete the recipe to the end of step 4. Cover and leave to chill separately.

■ To use, bring the couscous and vegetables back to room temperature; complete the recipe.

QUICK CAMEMBERT AND TOMATO TARTS

🤚 **HANDS-ON TIME:** 5 MINUTES   🍲 **COOKING TIME:** 15–18 MINUTES   ✖ **SERVES:** 4   V

METHOD

1 Preheat the oven to 220°C (200°C fan oven) mark 7. Cut the puff pastry into four pieces and put on a baking sheet. Cook in the oven for 8–10 minutes until risen.

2 Press down the centres of the tarts slightly with the back of a fish slice, then spread with the black olive tapenade. Top with the halved cherry tomatoes and sliced Camembert. Put back into the oven for a further 7–8 minutes, then serve with a crisp green salad.

INGREDIENTS

375g pack ready-rolled puff pastry
2 tbsp black olive tapenade
200g (7oz) cherry tomatoes, halved
75g (3oz) Camembert cheese, sliced

PER SERVING

480 cals
34g fat (of which 13g saturates)
36g carbohydrate

TUNA ON TOASTED OLIVE BREAD

🤚 **HANDS-ON TIME:** 10 MINUTES   🍲 **COOKING TIME:** 5 MINUTES   ✖ **SERVES:** 4

METHOD

1 Put the tuna into a bowl with the spring onions, yellow pepper and olives.

2 Whisk 2 tbsp of reserved tuna oil with the extra-virgin olive oil, vinegar and 1 tsp soured cream in a separate bowl. Toss into the tuna mix.

3 Toast the slices of olive bread and divide among four plates. Spoon over the tuna mixture, then scatter over a handful of rocket, followed by a dollop of the remaining soured cream.

COOK'S TIP

If you want to cut down on the fat, omit the 2 tbsp extra-virgin olive oil and replace the soured cream with fat-free Greek yogurt. Each serving will contain 320 calories, 11g fat (of which 2g saturates) and 32g carbohydrate.

INGREDIENTS

2 x 185g cans tuna in oil, drained and oil put to one side
8 spring onions, trimmed and chopped
1 yellow pepper, deseeded and sliced
20 Kalamata olives, pitted and halved
2 tbsp extra-virgin olive oil
1 tbsp white wine vinegar
142g carton soured cream
8 slices olive bread
a handful of rocket

PER SERVING

470 cals
25g fat (of which 7g saturates)
38g carbohydrate

BLUE CHEESE AND SWEET ONION TART

🖐 **HANDS-ON TIME:** ABOUT 20 MINUTES ⬛ **COOKING TIME:** ABOUT 1¾ HOURS ✕ **SERVES:** 4–8 ✓

INGREDIENTS
150g (5oz) plain flour, plus extra to dust
150g (5oz) butter
125g (4oz) freshly grated Parmesan cheese
a pinch of cayenne pepper
4 eggs
175g (6oz) onion, peeled and finely chopped
2 tsp caster sugar
225g (8oz) fresh spinach or 125g (4oz) frozen leaf spinach
a grating of nutmeg
450ml (15fl oz) double cream
175g (6oz) soft blue cheese such as Dolcelatte, Roquefort, Bleu d'Auvergne or Lanark Blue, crumbled into large pieces
fresh baby spinach leaves to garnish

PER SERVING
1320–660 cals
114–57g fat (of which 70–35g saturates)
39–29g carbohydrate

METHOD

1 Whiz the flour with 125g (4oz) butter in a food processor until fine crumbs form. Add the Parmesan cheese, cayenne pepper and 1 egg yolk. Put the egg white to one side. Whiz until the mixture begins to form a crumbly dough, then turn out on a floured worksurface and knead lightly. Wrap the dough in clingfilm and leave to chill for 20 minutes.

2 Heat the remaining butter in a small frying pan. Add the onions and sugar and cook very slowly for at least 20 minutes or until the onions are very soft and a golden colour.

3 Cook the spinach in a pan, with just the water that still clings to the leaves, for 2–3 minutes until the leaves have just wilted. Drain and squeeze out any excess moisture. Chop the leaves roughly. (Squeeze the moisture from the frozen spinach, if using.) Season the spinach well with salt, pepper and nutmeg. Whisk together the cream and remaining whole eggs. Season with salt and pepper.

4 Roll out the pastry on a floured worksurface and use to line a 23cm (9in) flan tin then leave to chill for 30 minutes.

5 Preheat the oven to 200°C (180°C fan oven) mark 6. Line the base and sides of the flan tin, with foil to cover completely. Make a steam hole in the centre of the foil and put some baking beans around the edge to keep the sides of the pastry up. Bake for 20–25 minutes until the pastry looks dry. Remove the foil and beans and bake for a further 5 minutes. Brush the pastry with the reserved egg white. Don't worry if there are cracks in the pastry as the egg white will seal up any holes that appear. Put the flan tin back in the oven and bake for a further 3–5 minutes.

6 Turn the heat down to 170°C (150°C) mark 3. Spoon the onion mixture into the flan. Scatter with the cheese and spinach and finally pour on the egg mixture. Cook for about 50 minutes or until the filling is lightly set. Leave the tart to cool in the tin for 15 minutes before serving garnished with fresh baby spinach leaves.

TO PREPARE AHEAD
Complete to the end of step 4 the day before required. Cover and chill everything separately. To use, complete the recipe.

CHICKEN RAREBIT

HANDS-ON TIME: 5 MINUTES   **COOKING TIME:** 25 MINUTES   **SERVES:** 4

METHOD

1 Preheat the oven to 200°C (180° fan oven) mark 6. Roast the chicken in a single layer in a heatproof serving dish for 20 minutes, or until cooked through.

2 Meanwhile, melt the butter in a pan over a low heat, then add the flour and stir for 1 minute. Gradually stir in the milk to make a smooth sauce.

3 Add the cheese, breadcrumbs, mustard and garlic and cook for 1 minute. Leave to cool briefly, then beat in the egg yolk. Preheat the grill.

4 Discard the skin from the cooked chicken and beat any pan juices into the cheese mixture. Spread the paste over each chicken breast, then grill for 2–3 minutes until golden. Serve with boiled new potatoes.

INGREDIENTS

4 large chicken breasts, with skin
15g (½oz) butter
1 tbsp plain flour
75ml (3fl oz) milk
175g (6oz) Gruyère cheese, grated
25g (1oz) fresh white breadcrumbs
1 tsp English mustard
2 fat garlic cloves, crushed
1 egg yolk

PER SERVING

430 cals
26g fat (of which 14g saturates)
7g carbohydrate

GARDEN FRITTATA

✋ **HANDS-ON TIME:** 10 MINUTES　　🍲 **COOKING TIME:** 10–15 MINUTES　　✗ **SERVES:** 6

METHOD

1　Preheat the grill. Cook the potatoes and broad beans separately in boiling salted water until just tender, then drain. Whisk together the cheese, eggs, thyme and seasoning.

2　Heat the oil in a large, shallow, flameproof pan. Add the onion, courgettes, potatoes and beans and cook, stirring for 2–3 minutes, then add the prawns and salmon. Pour over the egg mixture.

3　As the eggs cook, push the mixture into the centre of the pan to allow the raw egg to flow down to the edge. When the mixture is lightly set, put the pan under the hot grill for 2–3 minutes until golden. Sprinkle with thyme to serve.

COOK'S TIPS

- You could substitute fresh sorrel for the thyme.
- The broad beans can be skinned for extra colour.

INGREDIENTS

125g (4oz) small new potatoes
125g (4oz) shelled broad beans
50g (2oz) soft cheese, preferably fresh goat's cheese
4 eggs
2 tbsp freshly chopped thyme
2 tbsp olive oil
125g (4oz) onions, peeled and roughly chopped
225g (8oz) courgettes, trimmed and sliced
125g (4oz) cooked peeled prawns
125g (4oz) lightly cooked salmon
freshly chopped thyme to serve

PER SERVING

220 cals
13g fat (of which 4g saturates)
7g carbohydrate

CHEESE AND CHIVE OMELETTE

✋ **HANDS-ON TIME:** 5 MINUTES　　🍲 **COOKING TIME:** ABOUT 10 MINUTES　　✗ **SERVES:** 4

METHOD

1　Preheat the grill. Grill the bacon until golden and crisp (leave the grill on). Meanwhile, melt the butter in a large, non-stick ovenproof frying pan, then add the garlic and fry for 1–2 minutes until golden. Add the tomato pieces and half the chives. Stir over the heat for a further minute.

2　Spread the mixture over the base of the pan and add the beaten eggs. Tilt the pan to coat the base with the mixture, then leave the omelette to cook for 2–3 minutes.

3　Crumble the goat's cheese over the top of the omelette and put the pan under the hot grill for about 1 minute or until the egg is lightly cooked and the cheese is melting. Crumble the bacon and remaining chives over the top. Serve immediately.

INGREDIENTS

175g (6oz) smoked rindless streaky bacon
a large knob of butter
2 garlic cloves, crushed
about 12 sunblush tomato pieces, halved
20g pack chives, finely chopped
8 eggs, beaten with 3 tbsp water and seasoning
150g (5oz) soft goat's cheese

PER SERVING:

440 cals
33g fat (of which 14g saturates)
1g carbohydrate

GOLDEN MUSHROOM AND TARRAGON OMELETTE

✋ **HANDS-ON TIME:** 5 MINUTES   🍲 **COOKING TIME:** 10 MINUTES   ✗ **SERVES:** 2   V

INGREDIENTS

3 eggs

1 tbsp freshly chopped tarragon or a large pinch of dried (look out for frozen chopped tarragon, use about 1 tsp in this recipe)

1 tsp Dijon mustard

2 tbsp olive oil

225g (8oz) button or cup mushrooms, halved or quartered

a small bunch of spring onions, trimmed and roughly chopped with coarse green leaves discarded

25g (1oz) reduced-fat Cheddar-type cheese

endive and apple salad to serve

PER SERVING

310 cals

26g fat (of which 6g saturates)

2g carbohydrate

METHOD

1   Preheat the grill. Whisk together the eggs, herbs, mustard and seasoning.

2   Heat the oil in a medium non-stick frying pan. Add the mushrooms and onions and fry over a high heat until all excess moisture has evaporated.

3   Pour the egg mixture into the pan and cook over a medium heat until almost set.

4   Grate over the cheese and lightly brown under the hot grill, being careful to protect the pan handle.

5   Serve cut into wedges with an endive and apple salad.

COOK'S TIP

Grilling the cooked omelette gives it an attractive golden finish.

STORECUPBOARD OMELETTE

✋ **HANDS-ON TIME:** 5 MINUTES　🍲 **COOKING TIME:** 15–18 MINUTES　✖ **SERVES:** 4　∨

METHOD

1　Heat the oil or butter in a 25cm (10in) non-stick, ovenproof frying pan. Add the onion and fry for 6–8 minutes until golden. Add the potatoes and petit pois and cook, stirring, for 2–3 minutes. Preheat the grill.

2　Spread the mixture over the base of the pan and pour in the eggs. Tilt the pan to coat the base with egg. Leave the omelette to cook undisturbed for 2–3 minutes, then top with the cheese.

3　Put the pan under the hot grill for 1–2 minutes until the egg is just set (no longer, or it will turn rubbery) and the cheese starts to turn golden. Season with salt and pepper and serve immediately with a green salad.

VARIATIONS

■　Use 100g (3½oz) sundried tomatoes instead of the new potatoes.

■　Throw in a handful of halved pitted black olives as you pour the egg into the pan.

INGREDIENTS

a drizzle of olive oil or knob of butter
1 large onion, peeled and finely chopped
225g (8oz) cooked new potatoes, sliced
125g (4oz) frozen petit pois, thawed
6 eggs, beaten
150g pack soft goat's cheese, sliced
green salad to serve

PER SERVING

300 cals
18g fat (of which 8g saturates)
17g carbohydrate

HERB TORTILLA

✋ **HANDS-ON TIME:** 15 MINUTES　🍲 **COOKING TIME:** 25 MINUTES　✖ **SERVES:** 4　∨

METHOD

1　Preheat the grill. Heat 2 tbsp oil in a large, non-stick sauté pan. Add the onion and cook for 5–6 minutes until beginning to soften.

2　Add the potatoes to the pan and cook over a medium heat, stirring frequently, for about 10–15 minutes until the potatoes are golden and almost tender.

3　Whisk together the eggs and herbs, then season with salt and pepper. Stir in the potatoes and onions and put the mixture to one side.

4　Heat a fine film of oil in a clean frying pan. Add the potato and onion mixture and press down gently. Cook for about 4–5 minutes until the egg is nearly set.

5　Put the pan under the grill until browned, then garnish with tarragon and serve warm or cold.

INGREDIENTS

olive oil
175g (6oz) onions, peeled and sliced
450g (1lb) old potatoes, peeled and thinly sliced
4 eggs
1 tsp freshly chopped tarragon or ½ tsp dried
4 tbsp freshly chopped parsley
fresh tarragon to garnish (optional)

PER SERVING

260 cals
15g fat (of which 3g saturates)
23g carbohydrate

TOMATO AND ARTICHOKE PASTA

HANDS-ON TIME: 10 MINUTES   **COOKING TIME:** 10-12 MINUTES   ✕ **SERVES:** 4   V

INGREDIENTS
300g (11oz) penne
6 pieces sunblush tomatoes in oil
1 red onion, sliced
About 10 pieces roasted artichoke
   hearts in oil
50g (2oz) pitted black olives
50g (2oz) pecorino cheese
100g (3½oz) rocket

PER SERVING
360 cals

7g fat (of which 3g saturates)

61g carbohydrate per serving

METHOD
1   Cook the pasta in a pan of boiling water according to the packet instructions; keep it *al dente*. Drain well.

2   Meanwhile, drain the sunblush tomatoes, reserving the oil, and roughly chop. Heat 1 tbsp oil from the tomatoes in a large frying pan, add the onion and fry for 5-6 minutes until softened and turning golden. Drain the artichokes and roughly chop with the olives. Add to the pan with the tomatoes and heat for 3-4 minutes until hot.

3   Grate in half the pecorino cheese and stir through. Remove from the heat and stir in the rocket and pasta. Divide the pasta among four bowls and grate the remaining pecorino over the top to serve.

ROCKET PESTO PASTA

METHOD

1 Cook the pasta in a large pan of boiling water according to the packet instructions; keep it al dente.
2 Meanwhile, blend all the remaining ingredients in a food processor to form a smooth pesto. Drain the pasta, tip back into the pan and add the pesto. If the sauce seems too thick loosen with ½ tbsp of hot water. Toss well and serve.

INGREDIENTS

425g (15oz) dried pasta
75g (3oz) goat's cheese or low-fat soft cheese
25g (1oz) grated Gruyere or Emmental cheese
100ml (4fl oz) olive oil
25g (1oz) shelled unsalted pistachio nuts
1 fresh garlic clove
75g (3oz) rocket leaves

PER SERVING

440 cals, 21g fat (of which 4g saturates),
53g carbohydrate per serving

HAM AND MUSHROOM PASTA

METHOD

1 Cook the pasta in a large pan of boiling salted water until al dente.
2 Meanwhile, heat the oil in a pan. Add the shallots and fry gently for 3 minutes until starting to soften. Add the mushrooms and fry for 5–6 minutes.
3 Drain the pasta, put back into the pan and add the shallots and mushrooms. Stir in the crème fraîche, smoked ham and parsley. Toss everything together, season to taste with salt and pepper, and heat through to serve.

INGREDIENTS

350g (12oz) penne pasta
1 tbsp olive oil
2 shallots, peeled and sliced
200g (7oz) small button mushrooms
3 tbsp crème fraîche
125g (4oz) smoked ham, roughly chopped
2 tbsp freshly chopped flat-leafed parsley

PER SERVING

380 cals
12g fat (of which 5g saturates)
49g carbohydrate

RIBBON PASTA WITH COURGETTES AND CAPERS

HANDS-ON TIME: ABOUT 5 MINUTES **COOKING TIME:** 8–10 MINUTES **SERVES:** 4

METHOD

1 Cook the pappardelle in a large pan of boiling water until *al dente*. About 1 minute before the end of the cooking time, add the courgettes, then simmer until the pasta is just cooked.

2 Meanwhile, put the anchovies into a small pan and add the chilli, capers, garlic, olives and olive oil. Stir over a low heat for 2–3 minutes.

3 Drain the pasta and put back in the pan. Pour the hot anchovy mixture on top, mix well and toss with the parsley. Season with salt and pepper and serve immediately.

COOK'S TIP

If cooking for vegetarians, omit the anchovies and serve with freshly grated Parmesan cheese.

INGREDIENTS

450g (1lb) dried pappardelle pasta

2 large courgettes, trimmed and coarsely grated

50g can anchovies, drained and roughly chopped

1 red chilli, deseeded and finely chopped

2 tbsp salted capers, rinsed

1 garlic clove, crushed

4 tbsp pitted black Kalamata olives, roughly chopped

4 tbsp extra-virgin olive oil

2 tbsp freshly chopped flat-leafed parsley

PER SERVING

560 cals

19g fat (of which 2g saturates)

84g carbohydrate

SAUSAGE AND PEPPER PASTA

✋ HANDS-ON TIME: 5 MINUTES   🍲 **COOKING TIME:** ABOUT 10 MINUTES   ✗ **SERVES:** 4

INGREDIENTS

300g (11oz) dried pasta, such as
    fusilli
6 good-quality sausages, skinned
    and roughly chopped
1 large onion, peeled and finely
    chopped
290g jar peperonata antipasto
20g pack fresh basil, roughly
    chopped
1–2 tbsp lemon juice

PER SERVING

720 cals
39g fat (of which 15g saturates)
75g carbohydrate

METHOD

1 Cook the pasta in a pan of boiling water until *al dente*.
2 Put the sausages into a large, non-stick pan with the onion and
   fry for 10 minutes until golden and cooked. Stir in the peperonata
   antipasto, basil and 1 tbsp lemon juice.
3 Drain the pasta, leaving about 2 tbsp cooking water, and put it
   back into the pan. Add the sausage sauce and the remaining
   lemon juice, then toss together and serve at once.

TO FREEZE

■ The sauce for this recipe freezes well, so make double the quantity
   and, once it's cool, freeze half in a freezerproof container.
■ To use, thaw the sauce overnight in the fridge, then heat through
   gently while the pasta is cooking.

CANNELLONI WITH ROASTED GARLIC

HANDS-ON TIME: 40 MINUTES   **COOKING TIME:** ABOUT 1 HOUR   **SERVES:** 6

METHOD

1 Preheat the oven to 180°C (160°C fan oven) mark 4. Put the garlic cloves in a small roasting tin with 1 tbsp oil. Toss to coat the garlic in the oil and cook for 25 minutes or until soft. Leave to cool.

2 Meanwhile, drain the porcini mushrooms, putting the liquor to one side, then rinse to remove any grit. Chop the mushrooms finely.

3 Heat the remaining oil in a pan. Add the shallots and cook over a medium heat for 5 minutes until soft. Increase the heat and stir in the meat. Cook, stirring frequently, until browned. Add the wine, mushrooms with their liquor, and thyme. Cook over a medium heat for 15–20 minutes until the liquid has almost evaporated. The mixture should be quite moist.

4 Peel the garlic cloves and mash them to a rough paste with a fork. Stir into the meat mixture, then season with salt and pepper and set aside.

5 Cook the lasagne in a large pan of boiling salted water until *al dente*. Drain, rinse with cold water and drain again.

6 Lay each lasagne sheet flat. Spoon the meat mixture along one long edge and roll up to enclose the filling. Cut the tube in half.

7 Mix the cream and sun-dried tomato paste together in a small bowl, then season with pepper. Preheat the oven to 200°C (180°C fan oven) mark 6 and grease a shallow baking dish.

8 Arrange a layer of filled tubes in the base of the baking dish. Spoon over half the tomato cream and sprinkle with half the cheese. Arrange the remaining tubes on top and cover with the remaining tomato cream and cheese.

9 Cover the dish with foil and cook in the oven for 10 minutes. Uncover and cook for a further 5–10 minutes until lightly browned. Serve immediately.

COOK'S TIP

To save time, you can buy ready-to-use cannelloni tubes instead of using lasagne.

INGREDIENTS

20 garlic cloves, unpeeled
2 tbsp extra-virgin olive oil
15g (½oz) dried porcini
    mushrooms, soaked for
    20 minutes
150ml (5fl oz) boiling water
5 shallots or button onions, peeled
    and finely chopped
700g (1½lb) lean minced meat
175ml (6fl oz) red wine
2 tbsp freshly chopped thyme
about 12 lasagne sheets
    (see Cook's Tip)
142ml carton single cream
2 tbsp sun-dried tomato paste
butter to grease
75g (3oz) Gruyère cheese, finely
    grated

PER SERVING

430 cals
20g fat (of which 9g saturates)
29g carbohydrate

SAFFRON RISOTTO WITH LEMON CHICKEN

✋ **HANDS-ON TIME:** 20 MINUTES　　🍲 **COOKING TIME:** 30 MINUTES　　✗ **SERVES:** 4

INGREDIENTS

zest and juice of 1 lemon
a small handful of fresh parsley
25g (1oz) blanched almonds
1 tbsp dried thyme
1 garlic clove
75ml (3fl oz) olive oil
4 chicken breast fillets with skin
50g (2oz) butter
225g (8oz) onions, peeled and finely
　chopped
a small pinch of saffron
225g (8oz) risotto (arborio) rice
125ml (4fl oz) white wine
450ml (15fl oz) hot chicken stock
50g (2oz) freshly grated Parmesan
　cheese
fresh thyme sprigs to garnish

PER SERVING

840 cals
52g fat (of which 18g saturates)
50g carbohydrate

METHOD

1　Preheat the oven to 200°C (180°C fan oven) mark 6. Whiz the lemon zest, parsley, almonds, thyme and garlic in a food processor for a few seconds, then slowly add the oil and whiz until combined. Season with salt and pepper.

2　Spread the mixture under the skin of the chicken.

3　Put the chicken in a roasting tin, brush with 25g (1oz) melted butter and pour over the lemon juice. Cook in the oven for 25 minutes, basting occasionally.

4　Heat the remaining butter in a pan. Add the onion and fry until soft. Stir in the saffron and rice.

5　Add the wine and hot stock a little at a time, allowing the rice to absorb the liquid after each addition. This will take about 25 minutes.

6　Take the pan off the heat and stir in the Parmesan. Serve with the chicken, pouring over any juices from the roasting tin. Garnish with thyme.

TO PREPARE AHEAD

Prepare to the end of step 2. Cover and chill until required. To use; complete the recipe.

DOS AND DON'TS FOR THE PERFECT RISOTTO

- Always use risotto (arborio) rice: the grains are thicker and shorter than long-grain rice and have a high starch content. They absorb more liquid slowly, producing a creamy-textured risotto.
- Stock should be hot when it's added: this swells the grains, yet keeps them firm. Keep stock simmering gently in a pan and add it ladle by ladle to the risotto, allowing it to be absorbed by the rice after each addition.
- The correct heat is vital. If the risotto gets too hot, the liquid evaporates too quickly and the rice won't cook evenly. If the heat is too low, the risotto will go gluey. Over a medium heat, the rice should cook in about 25 minutes.
- Don't leave your risotto! Stir constantly to loosen the rice from the bottom of the pan.
- The quantity of liquid given is an approximate amount – adjust it so that, when cooked, the rice is tender but firm to the bite. It should be creamily bound together, neither runny nor dry.

GARLIC RISOTTO WITH FRESH MUSSELS

✋ **HANDS-ON TIME:** ABOUT 5 MINUTES   🍲 **COOKING TIME:** 30 MINUTES   ✕ **SERVES:** 4

INGREDIENTS
50g (2oz) butter
175g (6oz) onions, peeled and finely chopped
4 garlic cloves, crushed
225g (8oz) risotto (arborio) rice
450ml (15fl oz) white wine
450ml (15fl oz) hot fish or vegetable stock
3 tbsp pesto sauce
50g (2oz) freshly grated Parmesan cheese
4 tbsp freshly chopped parsley
1.4kg (3lb) mussels in their shells or 350g (12oz) cooked shelled mussels or prawns

PER SERVING
620 cals
28g fat (of which 11g saturates)
48g carbohydrate

METHOD

1 Heat 25g (1oz) butter in a large pan. Add the onion and fry for about 5 minutes or until soft but not coloured. Add two crushed garlic cloves and the rice and stir well.

2 Increase the heat to medium and add 300ml (10fl oz) wine and the hot fish stock a little at a time, allowing the rice to absorb the liquid after each addition. This should take about 25 minutes.

3 Stir in the pesto, Parmesan cheese and 2 tbsp chopped parsley. Keep warm.

4 Put the mussels in a large pan with the remaining 25g (1oz) butter, garlic and 150ml (5fl oz) wine. Cover with a tight-fitting lid and cook for 3–5 minutes, shaking the pan frequently. Discard any mussels that do not open.

5 Spoon the risotto on to four serving plates. Pile the mussels on top, allowing the cooking juices to seep into the risotto and scatter over with the remaining chopped parsley.

COOK'S TIP
Fresh mussels are available from most major supermarkets. Look out for ready-prepared marinated mussels or moules marinières – quick and easy to use.

GRILLED CHICKEN BREASTS WITH A CHEESE AND HERB CRUST

✋ HANDS-ON TIME: 15 MINUTES   **🍲 COOKING TIME:** 15 MINUTES   **✖ SERVES:** 4

METHOD

1 Preheat the grill. Whiz the bread in a food processor until fine crumbs form. Transfer to a bowl, stir in the grated cheese and season well with salt and pepper.

2 Coat each chicken breast with 1 tbsp garlic mayonnaise or hollandaise, then dip in the crumbs until coated. Put on a baking sheet and drizzle each chicken breast with 1 tsp oil.

3 Cook the chicken under the hot grill, as far away from the heat as possible, for 5–6 minutes on each side.

4 Slice the chicken, garnish with parsley and serve with a fresh tomato salad and garlic mayonnaise or hollandaise.

COOK'S TIP

The crisp cheesy crumbs used for the crust keep the chicken tender and moist as it cooks.

INGREDIENTS

125g (4oz) olive oil bread, such as ciabatta, roughly chopped

75g (3oz) Gruyère cheese, grated

4 chicken breast fillets, skinless, weighing about 450g (1lb)

4 tbsp garlic mayonnaise or hollandaise sauce, plus extra to serve

4 tsp olive oil

fresh flat-leafed parsley to garnish

PER SERVING

600 cals
53g fat (of which 11g saturates)
trace carbohydrate

CHICKEN AND VEGETABLE HOTPOT

✋ HANDS-ON TIME: 5 MINUTES   **🍲 COOKING TIME:** 25–30 MINUTES   **✖ SERVES:** 4

METHOD

1 Heat a non-stick frying pan or flameproof casserole until hot, then fry the chicken breasts, skin-side down, for 5–6 minutes. Turn them over, add the parsnips and carrots and cook for a further 7–8 minutes.

2 Pour over the gravy, then cover and cook gently for 10 minutes.

3 Season with pepper and stir in the cabbage, then cover and cook for a further 4–5 minutes until the chicken is cooked through, the cabbage has wilted and the vegetables are tender.

INGREDIENTS

4 chicken breasts

2 parsnips, peeled and chopped

2 carrots, peeled and chopped

300ml (10fl oz) ready-made, good-quality gravy

a handful of chopped cabbage

PER SERVING

390 cals
27g fat (of which 9g saturates)
13g carbohydrate

SIMPLE CHICKEN

👋 **HANDS-ON TIME:** 5 MINUTES 🍲 **COOKING TIME:** ABOUT 25 MINUTES ✕ **SERVES:** 4

INGREDIENTS
6 fresh tarragon sprigs
4 chicken breasts, skin on
50g (2oz) butter, diced
4 garlic cloves, sliced
a little olive oil
pepper
1 large glass of dry white wine

PER SERVING
350 cals
27g fat (of which 12g saturates)
0g carbohydrate

METHOD
1 Preheat the oven to 220°C (200°C fan oven) mark 7. Push a sprig of tarragon under the skin of each chicken breast. Place skin-side up, into a small roasting tin just large enough to hold the chicken comfortably.
2 Dot half the butter over the top, scatter over the garlic, drizzle with a little oil and season with pepper. Roast for 20–25 minutes until cooked through. The juices should run clear when the chicken is pierced with a sharp knife. Halfway through cooking baste with the juices.
3 Remove the chicken from the tin and keep warm. Put the tin over a high heat and whisk in the wine, scraping up the sticky bits from the bottom.
4 While still bubbling, whisk the remaining butter into the sauce. Stir in the remaining tarragon. Divide the chicken among four plates and serve with the warm juices and lightly crushed new potatoes and broad beans.

ONE-PAN CHICKEN WITH TOMATOES

👋 **HANDS-ON TIME:** 5 MINUTES 🍲 **COOKING TIME:** 25 MINUTES ✕ **SERVES:** 4

INGREDIENTS
4 chicken thighs
1 red onion, peeled and sliced
400g can chopped tomatoes with
    herbs
400g can mixed beans, drained and
    rinsed
2 tsp good-quality balsamic vinegar

PER SERVING
140 cals
31g fat (of which 9g saturates)
12g carbohydrate

METHOD
1 Heat a non-stick pan and fry the chicken thighs, skin-side down, until golden. Turn over and fry for a further 5 minutes.
2 Add the onion and fry for 5 minutes, then add the chopped tomatoes, mixed beans and balsamic vinegar. Cover and simmer for 10–12 minutes until piping hot. Serve immediately.

CREAMY CURRIED CHICKEN

✋ **HANDS-ON TIME:** 15 MINUTES   🍲 **COOKING TIME:** 25 MINUTES   ✗ **SERVES:** 4

METHOD

1 Heat the butter in a pan. Add the chicken and fry for 15–20 minutes until cooked, then set aside. Add the onion and celery to the pan and fry for 5 minutes until soft.

2 Stir in the curry paste, chutney and lemon juice and cook, stirring, for 2 minutes.

3 Take the pan off the heat, add the yogurt, mayonnaise and milk and stir well.

4 Put the chicken back into the pan and bring to simmering point. Cook until piping hot. Divide among four serving plates, garnish with parsley and serve with pilau rice.

INGREDIENTS

25g (1oz) butter
700g (1½lb) skinless chicken breast fillets, cut into bite-size pieces
1 small onion, peeled and chopped
4 celery sticks, trimmed and chopped
2 tbsp each mild curry paste and mango chutney
2 tbsp lemon juice
2 tbsp each Greek-style natural yogurt and mayonnaise
3 tbsp milk
fresh flat-leafed parsley to garnish

PER SERVING

380 cals
21g fat (of which 7g saturates)
9g carbohydrate

INSTANT FLAVOUR IDEAS FOR CHICKEN

■ Snip bacon into a frying pan, cook until crisp and golden, then stir into warm, boiled new potatoes with shredded roast chicken and mustard mayonnaise. Serve with green salad.

■ Roast a chicken with lots of tarragon, peppers, whole garlic cloves and olive oil. Serve with couscous, into which you've stirred the roasting juices.

■ Pan-fry chicken breasts that have been marinating in olive oil with rosemary, thyme and crushed garlic. Serve with a fresh tomato sauce made by whizzing together ripe tomatoes, olive oil, basil and seasoning.

■ Pan-fry chicken breasts in butter and set aside. Add flaked almonds and pitted fresh cherries to the pan, toss over a high heat for 1–2 minutes and serve with the chicken.

CHILLI-FRIED CHICKEN WITH COCONUT NOODLES

HANDS-ON TIME: 15–20 MINUTES **COOKING TIME:** 15 MINUTES **SERVES:** 6

METHOD

1 Mix the flour, chilli powder, ground ginger, salt and sugar in a bowl. Dip the chicken into the spiced flour and coat well.
2 Cook the noodles according to the pack instructions, then drain.
3 Heat the oil in a frying pan. Add the chicken and fry for 5 minutes or until cooked. Set aside, cover and keep warm. Add the spring onions to the pan and fry for 1 minute. Put to one side and keep warm.
4 Add the curry paste to the pan with 75g (3oz) peanuts and fry for 1 minute. Add the noodles and fry for 1 minute. Stir in the coconut milk and toss the noodles over a high heat for 30 seconds.
5 Put the chicken and spring onions on the coconut noodles. Scatter with the remaining peanuts and serve.

COOK'S TIP

Coconut milk gives a thick creaminess to stir-fries, soups and curries.

INGREDIENTS

2 tbsp plain flour
1 tsp mild chilli powder
1 tsp ground ginger
½ tsp salt
1 tsp caster sugar
6 skinless chicken breast fillets, about 150g (5oz) each, cut diagonally into three
250g (9oz) thread egg noodles
3 tbsp groundnut oil
a large bunch of spring onions, trimmed and sliced
1½ tsp Thai red curry paste or tandoori paste
150g (5oz) salted roasted peanuts, finely chopped
6 tbsp coconut milk

PER SERVING
580 cals
29g fat (of which 8g saturates)
37g carbohydrate

QUICK FISH BAKE

HANDS-ON TIME: 10 MINUTES   **COOKING TIME:** 45 MINUTES   **SERVES:** 4

INGREDIENTS

3 tbsp vegetable oil

350g (12oz) onion, peeled and roughly chopped

1 large green pepper, halved, deseeded and roughly chopped

1 garlic clove, peeled and crushed

1 tbsp plain flour

397g can chopped tomatoes with herbs

1 tbsp tomato purée

½ tsp dried marjoram

about 575g (1¼lb) thick-cut cod fillet, skinned and cut into 6 or 8 pieces

freshly cooked pasta tossed in pesto or crusty bread to serve

PER SERING:

260 cals

11g fat (of which 1g saturates)

14g carbohydrate

METHOD

1   Preheat the oven to 180°C (160°F) mark 4. Heat the oil in a medium flameproof casserole. Add the onion and sauté for 3–4 minutes until it starts to brown. Stir in the green pepper and garlic and sauté for a further 2–3 minutes.

3   Mix in the flour, cook for 1 minute, then stir in the tomatoes, tomato purée, marjoram and plenty of seasoning. Bring to the boil, stirring.

4   Add the fish to the casserole and baste with the sauce mixture.

5   Cover tightly and cook in the oven for about 30 minutes or until the fish is just beginning to flake apart. Serve with pasta tossed in pesto or with crusty bread.

TUNA MELT PIZZA

HANDS-ON TIME: 5 MINUTES   **COOKING TIME:** 10–12 MINUTES   **SERVES:** 4

INGREDIENTS

2 tbsp sun-dried tomato pesto

2 large pizza bases

185g can tuna, drained

½ x 50g can anchovies, drained and chopped

50g (2oz) grated mature Cheddar cheese

rocket to serve

PER SERVING

550 cals

26g fat (of which 10g saturates)

44g carbohydrate

METHOD

1   Preheat the oven to 220°C (200°C fan oven) mark 7. Spread the sun-dried tomato pesto over the pizza bases. Top each with tuna, anchovies and grated cheese.

2   Put the pizzas on to a baking sheet and cook in the oven for 10–12 minutes until cheese has melted. Sprinkle with rocket to serve.

QUICK FISH AND CHIPS

✋ **HANDS-ON TIME:** 15 MINUTES   🍲 **COOKING TIME:** 12 MINUTES   ✗ **SERVES:** 2

METHOD

1 Pour the oil into a deep-fat fryer and heat it to 190ºC or until a 2.5cm (1in) cube of bread browns in 60 seconds.
2 Put the flour, baking powder, salt, egg and water into a processor and blend to combine. (Or put the ingredients in a bowl and beat everything together until smooth.) Remove the blade and drop one fillet into the batter to coat it.
3 Put half the chips in the deep-fat fryer, then add the battered fish. Fry for 6 minutes until just cooked, then remove and drain well on kitchen paper. Keep warm if not serving immediately.
4 Drop the remaining fillet into the batter to coat, then repeat step 3 with the remaining chips. Serve both portions with salt, vinegar and garlic mayonnaise.

INGREDIENTS

4 litres (7 pints) sunflower oil
125g (4oz) self-raising flour
½ tsp baking powder
¼ tsp salt
1 egg
150ml (5fl oz) sparkling mineral water
2 x 125g (4oz) haddock or hake fillets
450g (1lb) Desirée potatoes, cut into 1cm (½in) chips

PER SERVING

460 cals
20g fat (of which 4g saturates)
43g carbohydrate

FISHCAKES WITH HERBS

✋ **HANDS-ON TIME:** 15 MINUTES   🍲 **COOKING TIME:** 10 MINUTES   ✗ **SERVES:** 4

METHOD

1 Whiz the fish, lemon juice, Worcestershire sauce and horseradish in a food processor until puréed. Transfer to a bowl and stir in the milk, herbs and potatoes until blended. Season with salt and pepper.
2 Shape the mixture into 4 fishcakes, brush with beaten egg and coat with the breadcrumbs.
3 Heat the oil in a pan. Add the fishcakes and shallow-fry for 4–5 minutes on each side until golden brown and cooked through. Serve with tomato salad, peas and ketchup.

INGREDIENTS

275g (10oz) haddock fillet, skinned
1 tbsp lemon juice
1 tbsp Worcestershire sauce
1 tbsp creamed horseradish
100ml (3½fl oz) milk
1 tbsp freshly snipped chives
1 tbsp freshly chopped parsley
350g (12oz) cooked potatoes, mashed
1 egg
50g (2oz) wholemeal breadcrumbs
sunflower oil to shallow-fry

PER SERVING

250 cals
2g fat (of which 0g saturates)
22g carbohydrate

SMOKED HADDOCK AND POTATO PIE

✋ **HANDS-ON TIME:** 15 MINUTES   🫕 **COOKING TIME:** 1¼ HOURS–1 HOUR 25 MINUTES   ✗ **SERVES:** 4

INGREDIENTS
142ml carton double cream
150ml (5fl oz) fish stock
3 medium baking potatoes, thinly
    sliced
300g (11oz) skinless smoked
    haddock fillets, roughly chopped
20g packet fresh chives, chopped
1 large onion, peeled and finely
    chopped
lemon slice to garnish

PER SERVING
380 cals
18g fat (of which 11g saturates)
34g carbohydrate

METHOD
1   Preheat the oven to 200°C (180°C fan oven) mark 6. Pour the cream into a large bowl. Add the fish stock and stir well to combine.
2   Add the potatoes, haddock, chives and onion and season with salt and pepper. Toss everything together to coat. Spoon the mixture into a shallow 2.4 litre (4 pint) ovenproof dish.
3   Cover the dish with foil, put it on a baking tray and cook for 45 minutes. Remove the foil and cook for 30–40 minutes until bubbling and the top is golden.
4   To check that the potatoes are cooked, insert a skewer or small knife – it should push in easily. If you like, you can put it under a hot grill to make the top layer crisp. Leave to cool slightly, then serve with a green salad or green beans, garnished with a slice of lemon.

COOK'S TIPS
■   For the lightest texture, make sure you use floury baking potatoes, as salad potatoes are too waxy.
■   To cook the beans, put 200g (7oz) fine green beans into a bowl, pour in enough boiling water to cover them, and put a lid on top. Leave for 10 minutes, then drain.

SPICY SAUSAGES

👋 **HANDS-ON TIME:** 5 MINUTES   🍲 **COOKING TIME:** 30 MINUTES   ✕ **SERVES:** 4

INGREDIENTS
4 tbsp hot chilli sauce
4 tbsp runny honey
450g (1lb) coarse pork sausages
   (about 8)

PER SERVING
460 cals
36g fat (of which 14g saturates)
22g carbohydrate

METHOD
1. Preheat the oven to 200°C (180°C fan oven) mark 6. Mix together the hot chilli sauce and honey.
2. Put the sausages in a small roasting tin and cook in the oven for about 10 minutes. Add the sauce and stir to coat the sausages on all sides. Cook for a further 20 minutes or until golden brown and cooked through. Serve with potatoes mashed with olive oil and chives, or stir-fried vegetables.

PORK AND MOZZARELLA PARCELS

👋 **HANDS-ON TIME:** 5 MINUTES   🍲 **COOKING TIME:** 10–15 MINUTES   ✕ **SERVES:** 4

INGREDIENTS
150g (5oz) mozzarella cheese,
   thinly sliced
4 pork escalopes or shoulder
   steaks
4 thin slices prosciutto ham or
   pancetta
4 fresh sage leaves
2 tbsp olive oil
1 large garlic clove, crushed
150ml (5fl oz) pure unsweetened
   apple juice
25g (1oz) chilled butter
a squeeze of lemon juice or 1 tsp
   sherry vinegar

PER SERVING
420 cals
29g fat (of which 13g saturates)
4g carbohydrate

METHOD
1. Put one or two mozzarella slices on each piece of pork. Wrap a slice of ham or pancetta around each one and top with a sage leaf. Carefully secure everything to the pork with a thin wooden skewer, then season with plenty of pepper.
2. Heat the oil in a shallow frying pan over a high heat. Add the garlic and fry for 1 minute until golden. Add the pork parcels, cheese-side up, and cook for 7–10 minutes, then turn over and cook the other side for 2–3 minutes until golden and the cheese is beginning to melt. Remove the parcels and set aside.
3. Pour the apple juice into the hot pan: it will sizzle immediately. Scrape the bottom to loosen the crusty bits and leave to bubble until reduced by half.
4. Add the butter bit by bit and swirl it around until it melts into the pan juices. Finish with a squeeze of lemon juice or a splash of sherry vinegar. Put the pork parcels back into the pan and warm through in the juices for 1–2 minutes. Serve immediately with a tomato salad and crusty bread.

PORK WITH APPLE MASH

👋 **HANDS-ON TIME:** 5 MINUTES 🍲 **COOKING TIME:** ABOUT 15 MINUTES ✗ **SERVES:** 4

METHOD

1 Cook the potatoes in a pan of salted water for 10–12 minutes until tender. Meanwhile, rub the spice mix into the pork chops.
2 Heat the butter in a pan. Add the chops and fry for 5 minutes on each side. Remove from the pan and put on warm plates. Add a splash of hot water to the pan and swirl the juices around to make a thin gravy. Drain the potatoes.
3 Melt a knob of butter in another pan. Add the apple and fry for 1–2 minutes until starting to soften. Tip the drained potatoes into the pan, season with salt and pepper and mash roughly. Serve with the chops and gravy.

INGREDIENTS

4 large potatoes, chopped
4 tsp ready-made spice mix
4 pork chops
25g (1oz) butter
knob of butter
1 red apple, chopped

PER SERVING
480 cals
7g fat (of which 2g saturates)
6g carbohydrate

PAN-FRIED LAMB STEAKS

👋 **HANDS-ON TIME:** 5 MINUTES 🍲 **COOKING TIME:** 10 MINUTES ✗ **SERVES:** 4

METHOD

1 Soften the garlic butter and stir in the lemon and orange juices, honey and coriander.
2 Fry the lamb for 3–4 minutes on each side. When cooked, put on warm serving plates.
3 Add the butter to the pan and swirl around until melted, whisking for 1 minute only.
4 Sprinkle with parsley. Serve with rosti and French beans.

INGREDIENTS

100g (3½oz) garlic butter
1 tbsp lemon juice
2 tbsp orange juice
1 tbsp runny honey
2 tbsp ground coriander
4 boneless lamb leg steaks
1 tbsp freshly chopped parsley

PER SERVING
390 cals
31g fat (of which 19g saturates)
1g carbohydrate

SPICED LAMB CHOPS WITH MANGO SALSA

👋 **HANDS-ON TIME:** 15 MINUTES, PLUS MARINATING   🍲 **COOKING TIME:** 15 MINUTES   ✕ **SERVES:** 4

INGREDIENTS

1 tbsp oil
175g (6oz) onions peeled and finely
   chopped
2 tsp cumin seeds, plus 1 tbsp each
   mustard and coriander seeds
½ tsp cayenne pepper
300ml (10fl oz) Greek yogurt
4 lamb chops, about 175g (6oz) each
1 ripe mango, peeled and roughly
   chopped
1 tbsp freshly chopped parsley
1 tbsp freshly chopped mint
1 tbsp lemon juice
lemon wedges to serve

PER SERVING
390 cals
23g fat (of which 10g saturates)
16g carbohydrate

METHOD

1   Heat the oil in a small frying pan. Add the onion and cook, stirring, for 7 minutes or until soft. Add the seeds and cook for 1 minute. Leave to cool. Put the onion mixture in a shallow, non-metallic dish with the cayenne pepper, salt and pepper and 150ml (5fl oz) yogurt. Add the chops, coat in the mixture, then cover and leave to marinate in the fridge for several hours or overnight.

2   Preheat the grill. Combine the mango, remaining yogurt, parsley, mint, lemon juice and seasoning in a bowl.

3   Secure each chop with a wooden cocktail stick and cook under the hot grill for 3–5 minutes on each side. Serve with any pan juices, the mango salsa and lemon wedges.

GRILLED BURGER WITH SALSA

HANDS-ON TIME: 10 MINUTES **COOKING TIME:** 30 MINUTES **SERVES:** 4

METHOD

1 Preheat the oven to 200°C (180°C fan oven) mark 6. Brush the pineapple slices and burgers with a little oil and season well with salt and pepper.
2 Put the onion rings on a baking sheet and cook in the oven for 10–15 minutes until crisp. Keep warm.
3 Heat a grill pan or barbecue and cook the burgers for 4–5 minutes on each side. Alternatively, put the burgers on a baking sheet under a hot grill and cook for 4–5 minutes on each side. Add the pineapple for the last minute of cooking time. Drizzle the baps with the remaining oil, then toast.
4 Arrange the baps on serving plates and spread each with mustard. Top with lettuce, Smoky Salsa (see below), a burger, a pineapple slice and onion rings. Serve with the remaining Smoky Salsa.

INGREDIENTS

4 thin slices fresh pineapple, skin removed if you like
4 venison burgers, about 450g (1lb) total weight
1 tbsp olive oil
175g (6oz) frozen onion rings in batter or breaded
2 large granary baps, halved

PER SERVING

390 cals
12g fat (of which 2g saturates)
38g carbohydrate

SMOKY SALSA

HANDS-ON TIME: 5 MINUTES **COOKING TIME:** 10 MINUTES **SERVES:** 4

METHOD

1 Put the onion, barbecue sauce, maple syrup, vinegar, sugar, water, lemon juice and zest in a pan. Bring to the boil and leave to bubble for 10–15 minutes until syrupy.
2 Take the pan off the heat, and add the spring onions and pineapple. Serve warm or cold.

COOK'S TIP

The salsa can be kept, covered, in the fridge overnight.

INGREDIENTS

75g (3oz) onions or shallots, peeled and finely chopped
150ml (5fl oz) shop-bought barbecue sauce
100ml (4fl oz) maple syrup
1 tbsp cider vinegar
1 tbsp soft brown sugar
100ml (3½fl oz) water
1 tsp lemon juice
a little lemon zest
6 spring onions, trimmed and finely chopped
175g (6oz) fresh pineapple, peeled and finely chopped

PER SERVING

160 cals
trace fat (of which trace saturates)
41g carbohydrate

COUSCOUS-STUFFED MUSHROOMS

HANDS-ON TIME: 3 MINUTES **COOKING TIME:** ABOUT 12 MINUTES **SERVES:** 4 V

METHOD

1 Preheat the oven to 220°C (200°C fan oven) mark 7. Put the couscous in a bowl with the boiling water, parsley, antipasti, and 1 tbsp of the reserved oil. Stir well.

2 Put the mushrooms on to a non-stick baking tray and spoon a little of the couscous mixture into the centre of each. Cook in the oven while you make the sauce.

3 Whisk together the butter, flour and milk in a small pan over a high heat until the mixture comes to the boil. Reduce the heat as soon as it starts to thicken and whisk constantly until smooth. Take the pan off the heat and stir in the cheese.

4 Spoon the sauce over the mushrooms and sprinkle with the remaining cheese. Put back into the oven for a further 7–10 minutes until golden. Serve with a green salad.

INGREDIENTS

125g (4oz) couscous
200ml (7fl oz) boiling water
20g pack fresh flat-leafed parsley,
  roughly chopped
280g jar mixed antipasti in oil,
  drained and oil put to one side
8 large flat Portabellini mushrooms
25g (1oz) butter
25g (1oz) plain flour
300ml (10fl oz) skimmed milk
75g (3oz) mature Cheddar cheese,
  grated, plus extra to sprinkle
green salad to serve

PER SERVING
390 cals
17g fat (of which 10g saturates)
35g carbohydrate

QUICK-AS-A-FLASH STEAK

HANDS-ON TIME: 2 MINUTES **COOKING TIME:** ABOUT 10 MINUTES **SERVES:** 4

METHOD

1 Rub the steaks all over with a little olive oil and pepper. Heat a large frying pan or cast iron griddle until very hot. Add the steaks to the pan and leave to cook undisturbed for at least 2 minutes. Depending on their thickness, cook the steaks for 2–3 minutes in total for rare; 3–4 minutes for medium rare and 4–5 minutes for well done.

2 Turn over the steaks briefly, season with salt and pepper, then lift on to warm plates. Take the pan off the heat, leave to cool for 1–2 minutes, then spoon in the crème fraîche and mustard. Swirl around with the pan juices to make an instant sauce. Season to taste, then spoon over the steaks and serve with boiled new potatoes and a green salad.

INGREDIENTS

4 rump sirloin steaks, about 200g
  (7oz) each
a little olive oil
2 tbsp crème fraîche
2 tsp Dijon mustard

PER SERVING
290 cals
14g fat (of which 5g saturates)
trace carbohydrate

CURRIED TOFU BURGERS

✋ **HANDS-ON TIME:** 20 MINUTES 🍲 **COOKING TIME:** 6–8 MINUTES ✗ **SERVES:** 4 V

INGREDIENTS

1 tbsp oil, plus extra to fry
1 large carrot, peeled and finely
    grated
1 large onion, peeled and finely
    grated
2 tsp coriander seeds, finely
    crushed (optional)
1 garlic clove, crushed
1 tsp curry paste
1 tsp tomato purée
225g pack tofu
25g (1oz) fresh wholemeal
    breadcrumbs
25g (1oz) finely chopped mixed nuts
plain flour to dust
fresh thyme sprigs to garnish

PER SERVING

190 cals
11g fat (of which 1g saturates)
29g carbohydrate

METHOD

1   Heat the oil in a large frying pan. Add the carrot and onion and fry
    for 3–4 minutes until the vegetables are softened, stirring all the
    time. Add the coriander seeds, if using, the garlic, curry paste and
    tomato purée. Increase the heat and cook for 2 minutes, stirring
    all the time.

2   Mash the tofu with a potato masher, then stir in the vegetables,
    breadcrumbs and nuts. Season with salt and pepper and beat
    thoroughly until the mixture starts to stick together. With floured
    hands, shape the mixture into eight burgers.

3   Heat some oil in a frying pan and fry the burgers for 3–4 minutes
    on each side until golden brown. Alternatively, brush lightly with
    oil and cook under a hot grill for about 3 minutes on each side or
    until golden brown. Drain on kitchen paper and serve hot,
    garnished with fresh thyme sprigs.

COOK'S TIP

Some steamed rice and summer vegetables would go well with
these burgers.

BLACK-EYED BEAN CHILLI

HANDS-ON TIME: 5 MINUTES **COOKING TIME:** 25 MINUTES **SERVES:** 4 V

METHOD

1 Heat the oil in a large frying pan. Add the onion and celery and fry for 10 minutes until softened.
2 Add the beans to the pan with the tomatoes and 2–3 splashes of Tabasco. Bring to the boil, then simmer for 10 minutes. Stir in the coriander. Spoon on to warm tortillas and serve with a spoonful of soured cream.

INGREDIENTS

1 tbsp olive oil
1 onion, peeled and chopped
3 celery sticks, trimmed and finely sliced
425g can black-eyed beans, drained
2 x 400g cans chopped tomatoes
2–3 splashes of Tabasco
3 tbsp freshly chopped coriander
pack of ready-made tortillas

PER SERVING

150 cals
4g fat (of which 1g saturates)
23g carbohydrate

HOT SPICED CHICKPEAS

HANDS-ON TIME: 5 MINUTES **COOKING TIME:** 10–15 MINUTES **SERVES:** 4 V

METHOD

1 Heat the oil in a pan. Add the onion and cook for 5–10 minutes until golden brown, stirring constantly.
2 Add the turmeric and cumin seeds and cook, stirring, for 1–2 minutes. Add the tomatoes and chickpeas to the pan together with the lemon juice, coriander and seasoning. Cook for 1–2 minutes, stirring frequently.
3 Garnish with coriander leaves and serve with baked potatoes, rice or wholemeal bread.

INGREDIENTS

1 tbsp oil
1 onion, peeled and chopped
2 tsp ground turmeric
1 tbsp cumin seeds
450g (1lb) tomatoes, roughly chopped
2 x 425g cans chickpeas, drained
1 tbsp lemon juice
4 tbsp freshly chopped coriander
fresh coriander leaves to garnish

PER SERVING

220 cals
8g fat (of which 1g saturates)
29g carbohydrate

4

COOKING
FOR ONE

EGGY BREAD SANDWICHES

🖐 **HANDS-ON TIME:** 5 MINUTES   🍲 **COOKING TIME:** 5–7 MINUTES   ✖ **SERVES:** 1

INGREDIENTS
2 slices bread
a little Dijon mustard (optional)
a small piece of Cheddar cheese, grated
1 tomato, sliced
1 slice ham
1 egg
a little vegetable oil

PER SERVING
486 cals
29g fat (of which 7g saturates)
36g carbohydrate

METHOD
1 Spread the slices of bread with a little mustard, if you like, then make a sandwich with the cheese, tomato and ham. Press down on the sandwich.
2 Beat the egg lightly in a shallow dish, then season with salt and pepper. Dip the sandwich into the egg, then turn over to coat on both sides.
3 Heat a little oil in a frying pan until hot. Fry the sandwich, pouring over any remaining egg, for 2–3 minutes on each side until golden.

QUICK-AS-A-FLASH TUNA PASTA

🖐 **HANDS-ON TIME:** 5 MINUTES   🍲 **COOKING TIME:** 10–15 MINUTES   ✖ **SERVES:** 1

INGREDIENTS
1 tbsp sunflower oil
1 onion, peeled and sliced
1 tsp granulated sugar
75g (3oz) pasta
a small handful of broccoli
185g can tuna in oil, drained

PER SERVING
560 cals
16g fat (of which 2g saturates)
76g carbohydrate

METHOD
1 Heat the oil in a pan. Add the onion and sugar and fry over a medium heat for 8–10 minutes until the onion is golden and starting to turn very soft.
2 Meanwhile, cook the pasta in a large pan of boiling water until *al dente*. Add the broccoli to the pasta for the last 5 minutes of cooking time. Drain, then tip back into the pan.
3 Add the tuna and onions, and toss everything together before serving immediately.

THROW-IT-ALL-TOGETHER NAAN PIZZA

🖐 **HANDS-ON TIME:** 5 MINUTES 🍲 **COOKING TIME:** 7–8 MINUTES ✗ **SERVES:** 1

METHOD

1 Preheat the grill. Spread the cream cheese over the naan bread, then spoon over the mango chutney. Top with the ham and scatter on the pepper strips and scatter on top.

2 Drizzle with a little olive oil and cook under the hot grill for 7–8 minutes until the pepper is tender.

INGREDIENTS

50g (2oz) cream cheese
1 naan bread
2 tbsp mango chutney
2 slices ham
½ yellow pepper, cut into strips
a little olive oil

PER SERVING

482 cals
23g fat (of which 10g saturates)
88g carbohydrate

RICE AND PEPPER STIR-FRY

🖐 **HANDS-ON TIME:** 5 MINUTES 🍲 **COOKING TIME:** 15 MINUTES ✗ **SERVES:** 1

METHOD

1 Put the rice in a pan and pour in the hot stock. Cover, bring to the boil and simmer for 10 minutes until the rice is tender and the liquid has been absorbed.

2 Heat the oil in a frying pan over a medium heat. Add the onion and fry for 5 minutes, then add the bacon and pepper. Fry for 5 minutes until the bacon is crisp. Stir in the cooked rice and the peas. Cook, stirring occasionally, for 2–3 minutes until the rice is hot and the peas are tender. Add a dash of Worcestershire sauce and serve.

INGREDIENTS

75g (3oz) rice
200ml (7fl oz) hot vegetable stock
½ onion, peeled and chopped
2 rashers streaky bacon
1 small red pepper, halved, deseeded and cut into chunks
2 tsp vegetable oil
a handful of frozen peas
a dash of Worcestershire sauce

PER SERVING

670 cals
29g fat (of which 9g saturates)
80g carbohydrate

PORK STIR-FRY WITH CHILLI AND MANGO

HANDS-ON TIME: 5 MINUTES   **COOKING TIME:** 10 MINUTES   **SERVES:** 1

INGREDIENTS
75g (3oz) medium egg noodles
1 tsp groundnut oil
½ red chilli, deseeded and finely chopped
125g (4oz) pork stir-fry strips
1 head pak choi, roughly chopped
1 tbsp soy sauce
½ ripe mango, sliced

PER SERVING
390 cals
11g fat (of which 4g saturates)
44g carbohydrate

METHOD
1 Cook the egg noodles according to the pack instructions.
2 Meanwhile, put the oil into a wok or large frying pan and heat until very hot. Add the chilli and pork and stir-fry for 3–4 minutes. Add the pak choi and soy sauce and cook for a further 2–3 minutes. Add the mango and toss to combine.
3 Drain the noodles and add to the pan, then warm through and serve.

COOK'S TIP
The smaller the chilli, the hotter it is.

WARM LENTIL SALAD

✋ **HANDS-ON TIME:** 5 MINUTES   🍲 **COOKING TIME:** 12 MINUTES   ✗ **SERVES:** 1   V

INGREDIENTS
1 egg
1 tsp olive oil
1 small leek, trimmed and chopped
2 spring onions, trimmed and
    chopped
½ red pepper, chopped
½ × 400g can lentils, drained
250ml (8fl oz) vegetable stock
a small handful of rocket

PER SERVING
330 cals
12g fat (of which 3g saturates)
32g carbohydrate

METHOD
1   Gently lower the egg into a pan of boiling water and simmer for
    7 minutes.
2   Meanwhile, heat the oil in a separate pan. Add the leek, spring
    onions and red pepper and fry for 6–8 minutes until softened.
    Stir in the lentils and stock. Bring to the boil and simmer for
    1–2 minutes.
3   Peel the egg, then cut in half. Put the lentils on a plate and top
    with a small handful of rocket and the egg.

CAESAR SALAD

✋ **HANDS-ON TIME:** 5 MINUTES   🍲 **COOKING TIME:** 5 MINUTES   ✗ **SERVES:** 1

INGREDIENTS
15g (½oz) piece of Parmesan
    cheese
50g (2oz) low-fat natural yogurt
1 tsp lemon juice
1 garlic clove, crushed
4 anchovies in salt, 2 finely chopped
    and 2 halved
1 thick slice bread, cut into cubes
1 Little Gem lettuce

PER SERVING
275 cals
8g fat (of which 2g saturates)
26g carbohydrate

METHOD
1   Preheat the grill. To make the dressing, grate half the Parmesan
    cheese into a large bowl. Add the yogurt, lemon juice, garlic and
    finely chopped anchovies. Whisk, then season with pepper.
2   Cook the bread cubes under the hot grill until golden. Add to the
    bowl with the halved anchovies and the lettuce leaves. Slice the
    remaining Parmesan cheese and add it to the bowl, then toss all
    the ingredients together.

TUNA PASTA SALAD

HANDS-ON TIME: 3 MINUTES   **COOKING TIME:** 10–15 MINUTES   **SERVES:** 1

METHOD

1 Cook the pasta in a large pan of boiling water according to packet instructions.
2 Meanwhile, put the tomatoes in a pan with the peas and oil. Heat gently for 5 minutes, then stir in the spinach leaves, capers and balsamic vinegar.
3 Drain the pasta and tip back into the pan, then add the vegetables, tuna and basil.

INGREDIENTS

50g (2oz) pasta shapes
2 ripe tomatoes, roughly chopped
50g (2oz) frozen peas
1 tsp extra-virgin olive oil
a handful of baby spinach leaves
1 tbsp capers
1 tsp balsamic vinegar
80g can tuna in water, drained
a small handful of fresh basil
   leaves, toughly torn

PER SERVING

320 cals
3g fat (of which trace saturates)
48g carbohydrate

COOKING FOR ONE

ASIAN-STYLE BROTH

HANDS-ON TIME: 5 MINUTES   **COOKING TIME:** ABOUT 10 MINUTES   **SERVES:** 1

METHOD

1   Heat the oil in a pan. Add the chilli, ginger, spring onions and red pepper and fry gently for 2–3 minutes until starting to soften. Add the hot stock and bring to the boil. Add the rice noodles and cabbage. Cover and cook for 3–4 minutes until the noodles have softened.
2   Stir in the king prawns and cook for 1 minute or until piping hot. Serve immediately with a squeeze of lime, if you like.

INGREDIENTS

1 tsp groundnut oil
½ red chilli, deseeded and chopped
1 tsp grated fresh root ginger
4 spring onions, trimmed and chopped
½ red pepper, sliced
600ml (1 pint) weak vegetable or fish stock, heated
40g (1½oz) rice noodles
a handful of shredded cabbage
75g (3oz) cooked, peeled king prawns
a squeeze of lime (optional)

PER SERVING

300 cals
6g fat (of which 1g saturates)
39g carbohydrate

WHOLESOME BEAN SOUP

HANDS-ON TIME: 5 MINUTES   **COOKING TIME:** 1 HOUR 10 MINUTES   **SERVES:** 1

METHOD

1   Heat the oil in a large pan. Add the leek, carrot and bacon to the pan and fry for 10 minutes until starting to soften. Add the soup mix and hot stock. Cover and bring to a rapid boil for 10 minutes, then leave the soup to simmer for 45 minutes or until all the ingredients are tender.
2   Add the cabbage, cook for 1–2 minutes, then serve.

INGREDIENTS

2 tsp olive oil
1 leek, chopped
1 carrot, peeled and cut into chunks
2 rashers streaky bacon, chopped
50g (2oz) dried soup mix
600ml (1 pint) hot vegetable stock
a handful of shredded Savoy cabbage

PER SERVING

430 cals
13g fat (of which 3g saturates)
32g carbohydrate

VEGGIE CURRY

🤚 **HANDS-ON TIME:** 5 MINUTES   🍲 **COOKING TIME:** 12 MINUTES   ✗ **SERVES:** 1   V

INGREDIENTS

1 tbsp medium curry paste
227g can chopped tomatoes
150ml (5fl oz) hot vegetable stock
200g (7oz) vegetables, such as
   broccoli, courgettes and
   sugarsnap peas, roughly chopped
½ × 410g can chickpeas, drained
   and rinsed

PER SERVING

350 cals
4g fat (of which trace saturates)
66g carbohydrate

METHOD

1 Heat the curry paste in a large, heavy-based pan for 1 minute, stirring the paste to warm the spices. Add the tomatoes and hot stock. Bring to the boil, then reduce the heat to a simmer and add the vegetables. Simmer for 5–6 minutes until the vegetables are tender.

2 Stir in the chickpeas and heat for 1–2 minutes until hot. Serve the vegetable curry with a griddled wholemeal pitta and yogurt.

JACKET POTATO WITH COLESLAW

🤚 **HANDS-ON TIME:** 5 MINUTES   🍲 **COOKING TIME:** 50 MINUTES–1 HOUR   ✗ **SERVES:** 1   V

INGREDIENTS

1 medium baking potato, scrubbed
1 small carrot, peeled and grated
a small chunk of white cabbage,
   thinly sliced
½ red apple, thinly sliced
1 celery stick, sliced
a handful of salted peanuts
2 tbsp mayonnaise
a knob of butter

PER SERVING

472 cals
29g fat (of which 6g saturates)
50g carbohydrate

METHOD

1 Preheat the oven to 200°C (180°C fan oven) mark 6. Cook the potato for 50 minutes–1 hour until cooked through.

2 To make the coleslaw, put the carrot, cabbage, apple and celery into a bowl. Add the peanuts, mayonnaise and a good grinding of pepper and toss together.

3 When the potato is cooked, cut a cross in the top, add a knob of butter, season with salt and pepper and spoon the coleslaw on top.

LEEK AND POTATO COLD-NIGHT PIE

🖐 **HANDS-ON TIME:** 5 MINUTES   🍲 **COOKING TIME:** 25–35 MINUTES   ✕ **SERVES:** 1   V

INGREDIENTS

2 medium potatoes, chopped
1 large leek, chopped
butter
25g (1oz) grated Cheddar cheese

PER SERVING

456 cals
23g fat (of which 14g saturates)
55g carbohydrate

METHOD

1 Put the potatoes in a pan of lightly salted water, cover and bring to the boil. Simmer for 10–15 minutes until tender.

2 Heat a little butter in a frying pan. Add the leek and fry for 10–15 minutes until soft and golden. Preheat the grill.

3 Drain the potatoes and tip back into the pan. Season with salt and pepper, then mash with a small knob of butter. Put the leek into a small, ovenproof dish and cover with the mash. Top the pie with the cheese, then cook under the hot grill for 10 minutes or until hot and golden.

SPICY ONE-PAN CHICKEN

🖐 **HANDS-ON TIME:** 5 MINUTES   🍲 **COOKING TIME:** 1 HOUR   ✕ **SERVES:** 1

INGREDIENTS

½ red or white onion, peeled and
   sliced
½ yellow pepper, sliced
1 small parsnip, peeled and
   chopped
1 potato, cut into chunks
227g can chopped tomatoes
150ml (5fl oz) hot vegetable stock
1 tbsp medium curry paste
1 chicken leg
a little vegetable oil

PER SERVING

410 cals
10g fat (of which 2g saturates)
51g carbohydrate

METHOD

1 Preheat the oven to 200°C (180°C fan oven) mark 6. Put all the vegetables into a roasting tin or ovenproof dish, together with the tomatoes. Stir the curry paste into the hot stock and pour over the vegetables. Season with pepper and cook in the oven for 30 minutes.

2 Put the chicken leg on top of the vegetables and drizzle with a little oil, then season with salt and pepper. Put the casserole back in the oven for 30 minutes, until the vegetables are tender and the chicken is cooked through – the juices should run clear when the chicken leg is pierced with a sharp knife.

LEMON COD WITH TARTARE SAUCE

HANDS-ON TIME: 5 MINUTES   **COOKING TIME:** 8–10 MINUTES   **SERVES:** 1

METHOD

1 Heat the oil in a non-stick frying pan. Squeeze the lemon juice over the cod fillet, then fry, skin-side down, for 6–8 minutes.
2 Meanwhile, put the yogurt in a bowl and stir in the dill, gherkins and capers. Turn the fish over and fry for a further 2 minutes or until cooked through. Serve with the sauce, steamed broccoli and boiled new potatoes.

INGREDIENTS

½ tsp olive oil
juice of ¼ lemon
150g (5oz) piece of cod fillet
2 tbsp low-fat natural yogurt
1 tbsp freshly chopped dill
1 tbsp freshly chopped gherkins
1 tbsp freshly chopped whole
  capers

PER SERVING
290 cals
5g fat (of which 1g saturates)
25g carbohydrate

WEEKEND COOKING

POACHED EGGS WITH SMOKED HADDOCK AND MUFFINS

✋ **HANDS-ON TIME:** 10 MINUTES   🍲 **COOKING TIME:** 10 MINUTES   ✗ **SERVES:** 6

INGREDIENTS
50g (2oz) butter
225g (8oz) spinach, washed
1 tbsp water
225g (8oz) smoked haddock fillets,
    thinly sliced
1 tbsp vinegar
6 eggs
3 English muffins
4 tbsp ready-made Béarnaise sauce

PER SERVING
320 cals
21g fat (of which 10g saturates)
15g carbohydrate

METHOD

1   Heat 25g (1oz) of the butter in a pan and, when hot, add the spinach and cook over a high heat until just wilted. Season with salt and pepper and set aside.

2   Add the remaining butter and the water to the pan. When hot, add the haddock and cook for 1 minute on each side. Put to one side.

3   Bring a large, shallow, non-stick pan of water to a gentle simmer and add the vinegar. Carefully break the eggs into the water and cook for 2–3 minutes until the whites are just set. Remove and drain on kitchen paper.

4   Preheat the grill. Split the muffins and toast lightly under the hot grill until golden. Divide the spinach between each half-muffin and top with the smoked haddock. Put one egg on top of each muffin and coat with 2 tsp Béarnaise sauce.

5   Cook under the grill for 2–3 minutes until the Béarnaise is golden and bubbling.

STICKY GLAZED HAM WITH SPICED ORANGES

🖐 **HANDS-ON TIME:** 15 MINUTES, PLUS SOAKING   🍲 **COOKING TIME:** 1½ HOURS, PLUS COOLING

✕ **SERVES:** 6

METHOD

1 Soak the gammon in cold water overnight.
2 Drain the gammon and put in a large pan with the chopped vegetables. Add enough water to cover. Bring slowly to the boil then cover and simmer very gently for 1 hour. Leave to cool in the water for about 1 hour then drain and remove the rind.
3 Preheat the oven to 200°C (180°C fan oven) mark 6. Put the gammon in a small roasting tin. Combine the mustard with the sugar and marmalade and spread over the ham fat. Pour in the cider and cook in the oven for 20–30 minutes until the fat is crisp and golden, basting occasionally. Leave to cool.
4 Serve in thin slices.

INGREDIENTS

1.1kg (2½lb) gammon joint
125g (4oz) carrot, peeled and roughly chopped
125g (4oz) onions, peeled and roughly chopped
125g (4oz) celery, roughly chopped
1 tbsp Dijon mustard
1 tbsp light muscovado sugar
3 tbsp marmalade
300ml (10fl oz) cider

PER SERVING:
480 cals
32g fat (of which 13g saturates)
8g carbohydrate

BLUEBERRIES IN BAY SYRUP

🖐 **HANDS-ON TIME:** 10 MINUTES   🍲 **COOKING TIME:** 20 MINUTES   ✕ **SERVES:** 6   V

METHOD

1 Mix together the fromage frais and crème fraîche. Beat until smooth, then cover and leave to chill until required.
2 Put the bay leaves, vinegar, sugar and water in a large pan. Slowly bring to the boil, add the blueberries and simmer for 1–2 minutes. Remove the blueberries and put in a bowl. Boil the syrup hard to reduce by half. Remove from the heat and stir in lemon juice to taste.
3 Pour over the blueberries. Serve warm or chilled, with the cream.

INGREDIENTS

500ml tub fromage frais
500ml tub crème fraîche
2 bay leaves
1 tbsp raspberry vinegar
75g (3oz) caster sugar
300ml (10fl oz) water
575g (1¼lb) fresh or frozen blueberries
juice of 1 lemon

PER SERVING
490 cals
39g fat (of which 26g saturates)
270g carbohydrate

BRAISED BEEF WITH MUSTARD AND CAPERS

✋ **HANDS-ON TIME:** 15 MINUTES   🍲 **COOKING TIME:** 2 HOURS 20 MINUTES, PLUS COOLING   ✗ **SERVES:** 4

INGREDIENTS

50g (2oz) can anchovy fillets in oil, drained, chopped and oil put to one side
olive oil
700g (1½lb) braising steak, cut into small strips
4 tbsp cold water
2 large Spanish onions, peeled and thinly sliced
2 tbsp capers
1 tsp English mustard
6 fresh thyme sprigs
20g pack fresh flat-leafed parsley, roughly chopped

PER SERVING
330 cals
16g fat (of which 4g saturates)
8g carbohydrate

METHOD

1 Preheat the oven to 170°C (150°C fan oven) mark 3. Measure the anchovy oil into a deep flameproof casserole, then make up to 3 tbsp with the olive oil. Heat the oil and fry the meat, a few pieces at a time, until well browned. When all the meat has been browned, pour the water into the empty casserole and stir to loosen any bits on the bottom.

2 Put the meat back in the pan and add the onions, anchovies, capers, mustard, half the thyme and all but 1 tbsp of the parsley. Stir until thoroughly mixed.

3 Tear off a sheet of greaseproof paper big enough to cover the pan. Crumple it up and wet it under the cold tap. Squeeze out most of the water, open it out and press down over the surface of the meat.

4 Cover with a tight-fitting lid, and cook in the oven for 2 hours or until the beef is meltingly tender. Check the casserole after 1 hour to make sure it's still moist. If it looks dry, add a little water.

5 Adjust for seasoning, then stir in the remaining parsley and thyme. Serve with a green salad and crusty bread or mashed potato.

COOK'S TIP

To make a deliciously easy mash, put four baking potatoes in the oven when you put in the casserole. Leave to bake for 2 hours. Cut each potato in half, and use a fork to scrape out the flesh into a bowl. Add 50g (2oz) butter and season well with salt and pepper – the potato will be soft enough to mash with the fork.

STEAK AND KIDNEY PUDDING

HANDS-ON TIME: 20 MINUTES **COOKING TIME:** 3½ HOURS–4 HOURS, PLUS COOLING **SERVES:** 6

INGREDIENTS

butter to grease
about 3 tbsp oil
700g (1½lb) stewing steak, cut into
    large bite-size pieces
225g (8oz) ox kidney, cut into large
    bite-size pieces
225g (8oz) onions, peeled and
    chopped
3 tbsp plain flour
600ml (1 pint) beef stock
1 tbsp wholegrain mustard
4 tbsp freshly chopped parsley
275g (10oz) self-raising flour, plus
    extra to dust
150g (5oz) shredded suet
grated zest of 1 lemon
about 175–200ml (6–7fl oz) water
fresh flat-leafed parsley to garnish

PER SERVING
610 cals
33g fat (of which 16g saturates)
46g carbohydrate

METHOD

1 Preheat the oven to 170°C (150°C fan oven) mark 3 and grease a 1.7 litre (3 pint) pudding basin with butter. Heat the oil in a flameproof casserole and fry the steak and kidney in batches until browned, adding more oil if needed. Remove and drain on kitchen paper.

2 Add the onion to the casserole and lightly brown. Take the casserole off the heat, and stir in the plain flour, stock, mustard and seasoning. Bring to the boil, then put the steak and kidney back into the casserole.

3 Cover the casserole and cook in the oven for 2 hours or until the meat is tender. Adjust the seasoning, stir in the parsley and leave to cool.

4 To make the pastry, mix together the self-raising flour, suet, grated lemon zest and seasoning. Bind to a soft dough with the water and knead lightly until just smooth.

5 Roll out the dough to a 33cm (13in) round. Cut out a quarter and put to one side. Line the prepared pudding basin with the large piece of dough, damping and overlapping join to seal.

6 Spoon in the meat and juices. Roll out the reserved dough and use to top the pudding, damping the pastry edges to seal. Trim to neaten.

7 Cover the basin with greaseproof paper and foil, and tie securely with string. Stand the basin on a heatproof saucer in a pan and pour boiling water around the basin to come halfway up the side. Cover tightly and boil for 1½–2 hours, topping up if you need to. Garnish with parsley and serve.

TO FREEZE
■ Pack and freeze at the end of step 4.
■ To use, thaw overnight at a cool room temperature and complete the recipe from step 5.

COOK'S TIP
For extra-rich flavour, add a 105g can of smoked mussels at step 7. The mussels will break up during cooking, leaving a smoky gravy.

ONE-POT LAMB

HANDS-ON TIME: 15 MINUTES   **COOKING TIME:** 1 HOUR 10 MINUTES, PLUS RESTING   **SERVES:** 4

METHOD

1 Preheat the oven to 230°C (210°C fan oven) mark 8. Rub the meat all over with 1 tbsp oil, then season with salt and pepper. Cover and put to one side.
2 Put the parsnips, onions and carrots in a large roasting tin, drizzle with a little of the oil and toss together. Shake the tin to spread out the vegetables. Roast for 30 minutes, stirring halfway through.
3 Put the lamb on a small rack over the vegetables and turn the heat down to 200°C (180°C fan oven) mark 6. Cook the meat for a further 40 minutes or until the vegetables are tender and the lamb is golden on the outside but still a little pink in the middle.
4 Put the lamb on a large, warm plate, cover with foil and leave to rest for 10 minutes. Mix together the remaining oil and the balsamic vinegar, and drizzle over the vegetables. Slice the lamb and serve.

VARIATIONS

■ Stir a handful of freshly chopped parsley into the cooked vegetables before serving.
■ Spread 1–2 tbsp black olive tapenade (paste) over the lamb about 15 minutes before the end of the cooking time.
■ Add 6 garlic cloves to the vegetables.

INGREDIENTS

½ leg of lamb, about 1kg (2¼lb), cut from the thicker end of the leg, so it doesn't overcook
3 tbsp olive oil, plus extra to drizzle
4 large parsnips, peeled and sliced into rounds as thick as a £1 coin
3 small red or white onions, peeled and cut into thin wedges
4 large carrots, peeled and sliced
1 tbsp balsamic vinegar

PER SERVING
470 cals
21g fat (of which 6g saturates)
30g carbohydrate

LAMB STEAKS WITH BEANS AND POLENTA CHIPS

INGREDIENTS

900ml (1½ pints) chicken stock
175g (6oz) quick-cook polenta
75g (3oz) Parmesan cheese, grated
50g (2oz) Emmenthal cheese,
    grated
50g (2oz) butter
freshly ground nutmeg
50g (2oz) plain flour, seasoned
oil, to fry
4 lamb leg steaks, about 175g (6oz)
    each
2 garlic cloves, crushed
175g (6oz) flat mushrooms, roughly
    chopped
290g jar red and yellow peppers,
    drained and roughly chopped
290g jar mixed beans, drained
1 tbsp balsamic vinegar
1 tsp sugar
1 tbsp sage leaves
1 tbsp chopped fresh parsley

PER SERVING

830 cals
43g fat (of which 21g saturates)
53g carbohydrate

METHOD

1 Bring the stock to the boil in a large pan. Add the polenta, stirring, and simmer for 5 minutes. Beat the cheeses into the polenta with 25g (1oz) butter and season well with salt, pepper and nutmeg. Leave to cool in a shallow tin.

2 Cut the polenta into 5cm (2in) sticks and coat in seasoned flour. Heat the oil in a frying pan and fry the polenta in batches for 2–3 minutes until golden. Drain on kitchen paper and season with salt. Keep warm in a low oven.

3 Wipe out the frying pan and heat the remaining butter. Add the lamb and fry for 2–3 minutes on each side, then remove and keep warm. Add the garlic and the mushrooms to the pan . Cook for 2 minutes, then add the peppers, beans, vinegar, sugar, salt and pepper. Cook for 1 minute, then add the sage and parsley.

4 Serve the lamb with the bean mixture and polenta chips.

TO PREPARE AHEAD

Complete to end of step 2 up to one day ahead. Put the polenta chips in the fridge. To use, heat the polenta chips for 10 minutes at 200°C (180°C fan oven) mark 6.

COOK'S TIP

Quick-cook polenta is a precooked, fine type of polenta.

PORK KEBABS WITH MUSTARD MARINADE

HANDS-ON TIME: 20 MINUTES, PLUS MARINATING   **COOKING TIME:** 15 MINUTES   **SERVES:** 4

METHOD

1 To make the marinade, put the chopped sage leaves in a bowl, together with the mustards, apple juice and vinegar. Season with salt and pepper.

2 Put the pork in the marinade, cover and leave in a cool place for at least 1 hour.

3 Preheat the grill. Put the marinade to one side, then thread the pork and apple alternately on to skewers, interspersing them with one or two fresh sage leaves. Put the skewers under the hot grill for 10–15 minutes until cooked, basting occasionally with the marinade. Serve on a bed of rocket or watercress, garnished with coarse sea salt.

INGREDIENTS

1 tbsp fresh sage leaves, finely chopped, plus a few extra leaves
2 tbsp Dijon mustard
2 tbsp wholegrain mustard
50ml (2fl oz) apple juice
2 tbsp cider vinegar
350g (12oz) pork tenderloin, cut into small cubes
2 crisp red apples, cut into quarters, cored and thickly sliced
coarse sea salt to garnish
rocket or watercress salad to serve

PER SERVING

150 cals
6g fat (of which 2g saturates)
6g carbohydrate

DEVILLED ROAST CHICKEN

👋 **HANDS-ON TIME:** 10 MINUTES   🍲 **COOKING TIME:** 1¼ HOURS   ✗ **SERVES:** 4–6

METHOD

1 Preheat the oven to 200°C (180°C fan oven) mark 6. Heat the oil in a large roasting tin. Add the onion, peppers and garlic and fry, stirring, for about 4–5 minutes until golden. Add the Worcestershire sauce, cider vinegar, marjoram, thyme, muscovado sugar and lager. Bring to the boil and simmer, uncovered, for 5 minutes.

2 Cook the corn on the cob in a pan of boiling salted water for 5–7 minutes then strain, putting the cooking liquid to one side, and slice thickly. Add the corn and chickpeas to the roasting tin.

3 Mix together the butter, paprika and seasoning. Spread all over the chicken. Put in a roasting tin, lying on one breast, and spoon over the corn and chickpea mixture.

4 Cook in the oven for about 1¼ hours. After 20 minutes cooking time, turn the chicken on to the other breast for 20 minutes, then on to its back for the remainder of the cooking time. Cover the breast with foil if it shows signs of over-browning.

5 When cooked, put the chicken on a warm serving plate and cover with foil to keep warm. Pour off the excess fat and add 300ml (10fl oz) reserved corn cooking liquid to the roasting tin. Bring the juices to the boil on the hob and bubble gently for 4–5 minutes. Adjust the seasoning and serve with the carved chicken.

VARIATION

Make with chicken breasts or suprêmes: complete steps 1 and 2. Spread six chicken pieces with flavoured butter and put in a roasting tin on top of the sauce, corn and chickpea mixture. Cook at 200°C (180°C fan oven) mark 6 for 20–25 minutes until golden and tender. Complete the sauce as in step 5, bubbling the juices until well reduced and syrupy.

INGREDIENTS

2 tbsp olive oil
125g (4oz) onions, peeled and roughly chopped
2 red peppers, deseeded and roughly chopped
2 garlic cloves, crushed
1 tbsp Worcestershire sauce
1 tbsp cider vinegar
1 tsp dried marjoram
1 tsp dried thyme
2 tbsp dark muscovado sugar
300ml (10fl oz) lager
700g (1½lb) corn on the cob
400g can chickpeas, drained and rinsed
50g (2oz) butter, softened
2 tsp ground paprika
1.4kg (3lb) oven-ready chicken

PER SERVING

580–390 cals
33–22g fat (of which 14–19g saturates)
31–21g carbohydrate

CHICKEN SOUP WITH GARLIC AND PARMESAN CROUTONS

✋ **HANDS-ON TIME:** 30 MINUTES   🍲 **COOKING TIME:** ABOUT 1¼ HOURS   ✗ **SERVES:** 6

INGREDIENTS

1 small chicken, about 1kg (2¼lb),
   cut into pieces
300ml (10fl oz) dry white wine
a few peppercorns
1–2 red chillies
2 bay leaves
2 fresh rosemary sprigs
1 celery stick, trimmed and roughly
   chopped
4 carrots, peeled, 3 roughly
   chopped and 1 cut into fine
   matchsticks
3 onions, peeled, 2 quartered and 1
   chopped
about 900ml (1½ pints) cold water
75g (3oz) dried pasta shapes
75g (3oz) butter, plus extra to
   grease
2 garlic cloves, crushed
1 cos lettuce, finely shredded
2 tbsp freshly chopped parsley
4 thick slices white bread
3 tbsp freshly grated Parmesan
   cheese

PER SERVING
340 cals
16g fat (of which 9g saturates)
26g carbohydrate

METHOD

1 Put the chicken pieces into a pan in which they fit snugly. Add the wine, peppercorns, chillies, bay leaves, rosemary and celery. Add the roughly chopped carrots, quartered onions and cold water, which should almost cover the chicken. Bring to the boil, reduce the heat, cover and simmer gently for 1 hour.

2 Leave to cool slightly, then transfer the chicken to a plate and sieve the stock. When cool enough to handle, remove the chicken from the bone and tear into bite-size pieces. Put to one side.

3 Preheat the oven to 200°C (180°C fan oven) mark 6. Pour the stock into the pan. Bring back to the boil, add the pasta and cook for 5 minutes.

4 Heat 25g (1oz) butter in a clean pan. Add the chopped onion and one garlic clove and cook for 5 minutes until softened. Add the carrot matchsticks and cook for 2 minutes. Add the stock and pasta and cook for 5 minutes. Stir in the chicken, lettuce and parsley. Heat gently, stirring, until the lettuce has wilted. Season to taste with salt and pepper.

5 Meanwhile, lightly grease a baking sheet. Mix together 50g (2oz) softened butter and the remaining garlic in a small bowl. Remove the crusts from the bread, and spread the slices with the garlic butter, then sprinkle with Parmesan cheese. Cut into squares and put on the prepared baking sheet, spacing them a little apart. Cook in the oven for 8–10 minutes until crisp and golden brown.

6 Serve the chicken soup with the hot garlic and Parmesan croutons.

GLAZED CHICKEN WITH ROAST LEMONS

🖐 **HANDS-ON TIME:** 20 MINUTES   🍲 **COOKING TIME:** 1 HOUR 5 MINUTES   ✖ **SERVES:** 6

METHOD

1   Put the caster sugar and water in a large pan and dissolve slowly over a low heat. Bring to the boil and bubble for 2 minutes. Pierce the skin of the lemons with a fork, put them in the sugar syrup, then cover and cook for 20 minutes.

2   Remove the lemons, bubble the liquid over a medium heat for about 12 minutes or until reduced by half and a golden caramel colour. Cut the lemons in half.

3   Preheat the oven to 230°C (210°C fan oven) mark 8. Season the chicken quarters with salt and pepper and put, skin-side down, in a roasting tin that is just large enough to hold them in a single layer with the lemon halves. Pour the sugar syrup over the chicken and lemons.

4   Put the tin on the middle shelf of the oven and cook for 30–35 minutes until cooked through. Baste the chicken from time to time and turn it over halfway through cooking.

5   Serve each piece of chicken with a lemon half (eat the flesh only, not the skin) and garnish with parsley.

INGREDIENTS

250g (9oz) caster sugar
600ml (1 pint) water
3 large lemons
6 chicken breast quarters (breast and wing) about 300g (11oz) each
fresh flat-leafed parsley to garnish

PER SERVING

340 cals
5g fat (of which 2g saturates)
44g carbohydrate

COD STEAKS WITH FENNEL

✋ **HANDS-ON TIME:** 10 MINUTES, PLUS MARINATING 🍲 **COOKING TIME:** 30 MINUTES ✗ **SERVES:** 4

INGREDIENTS

1 tbsp hoisin sauce
4 tbsp light soy sauce
4 tbsp dry vermouth
4 tbsp orange juice
½ tsp Chinese five-spice powder
½ tsp ground cumin
1 garlic clove, crushed
4 × 150g (5oz) thick cod fillets or
   steaks (see Cook's Tip)
1 tbsp vegetable oil
2 fennel bulbs, about 700g (1½lb),
   thinly sliced and tops put to one
   side
2 tsp sesame seeds

PER SERVING
210 cals
6g fat (of which 1g saturates)
8g carbohydrate

METHOD

1   For the marinade, combine the hoisin sauce, soy sauce, vermouth, orange juice, five-spice powder, cumin and garlic. Put the cod in a shallow dish and pour over the marinade. Cover and leave to marinate in a cool place for at least 1 hour.

2   Preheat the grill or a lightly oiled griddle. Remove the fish and put the marinade to one side. Put under the hot grill or on the hot griddle and cook for 4 minutes, then turn over and cook for 3–4 minutes until cooked.

3   Heat the oil in sauté pan. Add the fennel and cook briskly for 5–7 minutes or until brown and beginning to soften. Add the marinade, bring to the boil and bubble until reduced and sticky. Put the fish on a bed of fennel, spoon any pan juices around it and sprinkle over the sesame seeds. Garnish with the reserved fennel tops.

COOK'S TIP

Ask your fishmonger to remove the scales from the skin. When grilled, it will be crisp and delicious to eat.

BAKED COD WITH HORSERADISH CRUST AND TARTARE SAUCE

HANDS-ON TIME: 20 MINUTES   **COOKING TIME:** 15–20 MINUTES, PLUS REHEATING   **SERVES:** 4

INGREDIENTS

50g (2oz) wholemeal bread, crusts
  removed and discarded
grated zest of 1 lemon
3 tbsp freshly chopped parsley
4 cod steaks, about 150g (5oz) each
8 tsp creamed horseradish
4 medium gherkins, finely chopped
150g (5oz) reduced-fat crème
  fraîche
1 tbsp freshly chopped dill
2–3 tsp lemon juice
lemon slices to garnish
fresh dill sprigs to garnish

PER SERVING
230 cals
8g fat (of which 4g saturates)
9g carbohydrate

METHOD

1 Preheat the oven to 200°C (180°C fan oven) mark 6. Put the bread in a food processor and whiz to make fine breadcrumbs. Put in a large bowl and stir in the grated lemon zest and 2 tbsp chopped parsley. Season with salt and pepper.

2 Put the cod steaks in a shallow roasting tin, spread with horseradish and season. Divide the breadcrumb mixture among the steaks, pressing it on firmly. Cook in the oven for 15–20 minutes until tender.

3 Meanwhile, prepare the tartare sauce. Stir the gherkins, 1 tbsp chopped parsley and the dill into the crème fraîche. Flavour the sauce with the lemon juice and mix well.

4 Put the cod steaks on warm serving plates and garnish with lemon slices and dill sprigs. Serve with a spoonful of tartare sauce and seasonal vegetables.

MUSTARD ROAST RIB OF BEEF

HANDS-ON TIME: 5 MINUTES   **COOKING TIME:** 2½ HOURS, PLUS RESTING   **SERVES:** 8–10

METHOD

1 Preheat the oven to 230°C (210°C fan oven) mark 8. Put the rib of beef, fat-side up, in a roasting tin just large enough to hold the joint.

2 Mix the flour and mustard powder together in a small bowl and season with salt and pepper. Rub the mixture over the joint.

3 Put the joint in the centre of the oven and roast for 30 minutes.

4 Lower the beef to a shelf at the bottom of the oven. Turn down the heat to 220°C (200°C fan oven) mark 7 and continue to roast for a further 2 hours, basting occasionally.

5 Put the beef on a carving dish, cover loosely with foil and leave to rest (see Cook's Tips) while you make the gravy.

6 Skim any fat off the sediment in the roasting tin. Pour in the wine and boil vigorously until very syrupy. Pour in the stock and boil until syrupy. Add the vegetable water in the same way. Season with salt and pepper. There should be about 450ml (15fl oz) gravy (see Cook's Tips).

7 Remove the rib bone and carve the beef. Serve with the gravy, Golden Roast Vegetables (page 237), Yorkshire pudding and a green vegetable.

COOK'S TIPS

- Cabernet Sauvignon wine retains a good red colour when cooked.
- Leaving the joint to rest allows the juices that have risen to the surface of the meat during cooking to seep back into the flesh and 'set'. There is now space in the oven for making Yorkshire pudding and the roast vegetables.
- Making the gravy in the roasting tin ensures a rich flavour, using any juices that have escaped from the joint during roasting.

INGREDIENTS

- 2-bone rib of beef, about 2.5–2.7kg (5½–6lb)
- 1 tbsp plain flour
- 1 tbsp mustard powder
- 150ml (5fl oz) red wine (see Cook's Tip)
- 600ml (1 pint) beef stock
- 600ml (1 pint) water from parboiled potatoes

PER SERVING
330–260 cals
9–7g fat (of which 4–3g saturates)
trace–1g carbohydrate

SPICED ROAST LEG OF LAMB

👋 **HANDS-ON TIME:** 20 MINUTES, PLUS MARINATING 🍲 **COOKING TIME:** 2¼ HOURS ✗ **SERVES:** 6

INGREDIENTS

1.6–1.8kg (3½–4lb) leg of lamb, fat
  and parchment-like white skin
  (also known as the fell) trimmed
  and discarded
2 tbsp cumin seeds
2 tbsp coriander seeds
50g (2oz) blanched or flaked
  almonds
1 medium onion, peeled and
  chopped
6 garlic cloves, roughly chopped
2.5cm (1in) piece of fresh root
  ginger, peeled and grated
4 hot green chillies, deseeded and
  roughly chopped
500g carton natural yogurt
½ tsp cayenne pepper
3½ tsp salt
½ tsp garam masala
4 tbsp vegetable oil
½ tsp whole cloves
16 cardamom pods
1 cinnamon stick
10 black peppercorns
fresh flat-leafed parsley sprigs to
  garnish (optional)

PER SERVING

420 cals
22g fat (of which 7g saturates)
9g carbohydrate

METHOD

1 Put the lamb into a large, shallow ceramic dish and put to one side.

2 Put the cumin and coriander seeds in a pan and cook over a high heat until they begin to release their aromas. Put into a pestle and mortar and grind to a fine powder. Set aside.

3 Put the almonds, onion, garlic, ginger, chillies and 3 tbsp of the yogurt into a food processor and whiz to a paste. Put the remaining yogurt in a bowl, stir well and add the paste, ground cumin and coriander, cayenne pepper, salt and garam masala. Stir well to combine.

4 Spoon the yogurt mixture over the lamb and use a brush to encourage it into all the nooks and crannies. Turn the lamb over, making sure the leg is well coated, then cover with clingfilm, put in the fridge and leave to marinate for 24 hours.

5 Remove the lamb from the fridge about 45 minutes before you want to cook it, to allow it to come up to room temperature. Preheat the oven to 200°C (180°C fan oven) mark 6. Transfer the lamb and all of the marinade to a roasting tin. Heat the oil in a small frying pan. Add the cloves, cardamom pods, cinnamon and peppercorns, and fry until they begin to release their aromas. Pour over the lamb.

6 Cover the roasting tin with foil and roast for 1½ hours. Remove the foil, put back in the oven and roast for a further 45 minutes, basting occasionally.

7 Put the lamb on a serving plate and press the sauce through a fine sieve into a bowl. Garnish the lamb with flat-leafed parsley, if you like, and serve with the sauce on the side.

BONED AND STUFFED SHOULDER OF LAMB

HANDS-ON TIME: 20 MINUTES   **COOKING TIME:** 1¾ HOURS   **SERVES:** 6

METHOD

1   Put the bread, the leaves from the thyme and parsley and the nuts into a food processor and whiz for about 1 minute or until finely chopped. Transfer to a bowl. Put 50g (2oz) of the prunes into the processor with the apricots and chop finely. Stir into the crumb mixture.

2   Heat the butter in a small pan. Add the onion and sauté until soft and transparent, stirring from time to time. Stir into the crumb mixture with the nutmeg and seasoning. Mix well and cool.

3   Preheat the oven to 200°C (180°C fan oven) mark 6. Unroll the shoulder of lamb. Spoon the stuffing into the lamb, roll up again and tie at regular intervals. Don't worry if a little of the stuffing begins to ooze out.

4   Put the lamb in a dry roasting tin and cook in the oven for about 1½ hours, basting occasionally. Test with a fine skewer. If the meat juices are pink, the lamb is slightly underdone. Cook for a little longer if you prefer it well done. Put the lamb in a warm serving dish, cover and keep warm.

5   Drain off most of the fat from the roasting tin, then add the wine and water. Bring to the boil, scraping all sediment off the bottom of the pan. Sieve into a small pan. Add the remaining prunes and simmer for about 5 minutes. Adjust the seasoning and serve with the sliced lamb. Garnish with fresh herbs.

COOK'S TIP

Boned shoulders of lamb are available in most supermarkets, or ask your butcher to bone the meat for you.

INGREDIENTS

2 large slices white bread, crusts removed and discarded
a few fresh thyme sprigs
a few fresh parsley sprigs
50g (2oz) shelled pistachio nuts
175g (6oz) ready-to-eat pitted prunes
50g (2oz) ready-to-soak dried apricots
50g (2oz) butter
225g (8oz) onions, peeled and finely chopped
¼ tsp ground nutmeg
1.4kg (3lb) boned shoulder or leg of lamb
150ml (5fl oz) red wine
300ml (10fl oz) water
fresh herbs to garnish

PER SERVING
600 cals
28g fat (of which 12g saturates)
24g carbohydrate

PERFECT ROAST CHICKEN

✋ **HANDS-ON TIME:** 5 MINUTES   🍲 **COOKING TIME:** 1 HOUR–1¼ HOURS, PLUS RESTING   ✗ **SERVES:** 4

METHOD

1 Preheat the oven to 220°C (200°C fan oven) mark 7. Put the chicken in a roasting tin just large enough to hold it comfortably. Spread the butter all over the chicken, then drizzle with the oil and season with salt and pepper.

2 Squeeze the lemon juice over it, then put one lemon half inside the chicken. Put the other half and the garlic into the tin.

3 Put the chicken into the oven for 15 minutes then turn the heat down to 190°C (170°C fan oven) mark 5 and for a further 45 minutes–1 hour until the leg juices run clear when pierced with a skewer or sharp knife. While the bird is cooking, baste from time to time with the pan juices. Add a splash of water to the tin if the juices dry out.

4 Take the chicken out, put on a warm plate and cover with foil. Leave for 10 minutes before carving, so the juices that have risen to the surface soak back into the meat. This will make it more moist and easier to slice. Mash some of the garlic into the pan juices and serve the gravy with the chicken. Serve with boiled new potatoes and freshly cooked seasonal vegetables such as green beans or mangetout.

VARIATIONS

- Push sprigs of fresh tarragon under the breast skin before roasting.
- Pour a glass of dry white wine into the roasting tin instead of the lemon juice.
- Whisk 1 tbsp Dijon mustard into the roasting juices before serving.

INGREDIENTS

1.8kg (4lb) free-range chicken
25g (1oz) butter, softened
2 tbsp olive oil
1 lemon, cut in half
1 small head of garlic, cut in half
  horizontally

PER SERVING
373 cals
29g fat (of which 10g saturates)
0g carbohydrate

GARLIC AND ROSEMARY ROAST CHICKEN

🖐 **HANDS-ON TIME:** 10 MINUTES   🍲 **COOKING TIME:** 1¼ HOURS   ✗ **SERVES:** 4–6

INGREDIENTS

1.4kg (3lb) oven-ready chicken
4 tbsp freshly chopped rosemary or
   1 tbsp dried
450g (1lb) each red and yellow
   peppers, quartered and
   deseeded
450g (1lb) courgettes, trimmed and
   cut into wedges or halved
   lengthways if small
125g (4oz) pitted black olives
2 tbsp capers
2 garlic cloves
50ml (2fl oz) olive oil
125g (4oz) streaky bacon or
   pancetta
2 tsp cornflour
300ml (10fl oz) white wine
300ml (10fl oz) chicken stock
fresh flat-leafed parsley to garnish

PER SERVING
700–470 cals
47–31g fat (of which 13–9g saturates)
18–12g carbohydrate

METHOD

1   Preheat the oven to 200°C (180°C fan oven) mark 6. Fill the chicken cavity with half the rosemary.

2   Put the peppers, courgettes, black olives, capers, garlic, oil and seasoning in a roasting tin. Cover the chicken with the remaining rosemary, streaky bacon or pancetta and sit it on the vegetables. Season and cover the chicken with foil.

3   Cook in the oven for about 1¼ hours, removing the foil halfway through the cooking time.

4   When cooked, put the chicken and vegetables on a warm serving plate, and cover with foil to keep warm. Leave the garlic in the roasting tin with the cooking juices.

5   Mix the cornflour to a paste with 2 tbsp white wine. Add to the roasting tin with the remaining wine, the stock and seasoning, mashing the garlic into the liquid with a fork. Bring to the boil, stirring, then bubble gently for 5 minutes or until lightly thickened. Adjust the seasoning and serve with the chicken. Garnish with parsley.

VARIATION

Make with chicken breasts: prepare peppers and courgettes as step 1; put with the olives, capers, garlic and oil in a roasting tin. Cook at 200°C (180°C fan oven) mark 6 for 30–35 minutes. Add six chicken pieces. Snip the bacon and sprinkle it over the portions with the rosemary. Roast at 200°C (180°C fan oven) mark 6 for 25–30 minutes. Remove the chicken and vegetables. Complete the gravy as steps 4 and 5.

LOIN OF PORK WITH HOT VINAIGRETTE

✋ **HANDS-ON TIME:** 25 MINUTES, PLUS SOAKING   🍲 **COOKING TIME:** ABOUT 3 HOURS   ✗ **SERVES:** 6

METHOD

1. Preheat the oven to 190°C (170°C fan oven) mark 5. Put the dried mushrooms in a bowl, pour in the boiling water, then cover and leave to soak.
2. Brush the meat with the oil and rub in the salt. Put in a roasting tin and roast in the oven for 2¼–2½ hours.
3. Remove the pork from the tin, cover with foil and put to one side. Pour the juices and dark sediment from the tin into a jug. Let the fat and the cooking juices separate, then spoon off the fat and put the juices to one side.
4. Pour 2 tbsp of the fat into the tin. Add the bacon and fry for 10 minutes or until golden brown. Add the fresh mushrooms and crushed garlic and fry for 2 minutes or until the mushrooms start to soften.
5. Stir in the porcini mushrooms and their soaking liquor, the vinegar and sugar. Bring to the boil and simmer gently for 2 minutes. Take the pan off the heat and stir in the reserved pork juices. Add the chopped parsley just before serving.
6. To serve, remove the crackling and carve the pork. Spoon the warm vinaigrette over it.

INGREDIENTS

- 20g pack dried porcini mushrooms
- 450ml (15fl oz) boiling water
- 125g (4oz) fresh brown-cap mushrooms, sliced
- 275g (10oz) rindless streaky bacon, roughly chopped
- 2.5kg (5½lb) boned loin of pork
- 1 tbsp sunflower oil
- 1 tsp salt
- 2 garlic cloves, crushed
- 3 tbsp balsamic vinegar
- 2 tbsp dark muscovado sugar
- 3 tbsp freshly chopped parsley

PER SERVING
840 cals
40g fat (of which 16g saturates)
7g carbohydrate

ROAST PORK LOIN WITH ROSEMARY AND MUSTARD

👋 **HANDS-ON TIME:** 5 MINUTES 🍲 **COOKING TIME:** 1 HOUR 35 MINUTES ✕ **SERVES:** 6–8

INGREDIENTS
2 tbsp freshly chopped rosemary
4 tbsp Dijon mustard
50ml (2fl oz) lemon juice
50g (2oz) light muscovado sugar
175g (6oz) honey
1 tbsp soy sauce
1.4kg (3lb) loin of pork, chine bone
    (backbone) removed, rib bones
    cut off and separated into
    individual ribs (ask the butcher to
    do this for you)

PER SERVING
370–280 cals
14–10g fat (of which 5–4g saturates)
21–16g carbohydrate

METHOD
1 Preheat the oven to 200°C (180°C) mark 6. Mix together the rosemary, mustard, lemon juice, sugar, honey and soy sauce and set aside.
2 Put the loin in a roasting tin and cook in the oven for 40 minutes.
3 Add the ribs to the roasting tin and cook the pork for a further 40 minutes.
4 Drain off any fat and brush the pork with the mustard glaze. Put back in the oven for about 15 minutes, basting occasionally with the glaze until well browned and tender. Serve hot or cold, garnished with rosemary and lemon.

COOK'S TIP
The sweetness of buttered parsnips makes them an ideal accompaniment to pork. Cut about 700g (1½lb) scrubbed, unpeeled parsnips into chunky lengths from the stalk to the root end. Melt 50g (2oz) butter in a deep frying pan and add the parsnips. Stir over the heat for 5–7 minutes, shaking the pan occasionally, until the parsnips are tender and have a wonderful sticky glaze.

ROAST SALMON WITH A PEANUT CRUST

✋ **HANDS-ON TIME:** 5 MINUTES   ♨ **COOKING TIME:** 20 MINUTES   ✗ **SERVES:** 4

INGREDIENTS

1 red chilli, finely chopped
2.5cm (1in) piece fresh root ginger,
   peeled and grated
175g (6oz) unsalted butter,
   softened
3 tbsp freshly chopped parsley
finely grated zest of 1 lime
75g (3oz) salted roasted peanuts
125g (4oz) fresh white breadcrumbs
3–4 spring onions, trimmed and
   finely chopped
4 salmon fillets, about 175g (6oz)
   each, skinned (optional)
boiled jacket potatoes to serve

PER SERVING

830 cals
67g fat (of which 31g saturates)
17g carbohydrate

METHOD

1 Preheat the oven to 200°C (180°C fan oven) mark 6. Beat the chilli and ginger into the butter with the fresh parsley and lime zest. Roughly whiz the peanuts in a food processor.

2 Heat 50g (2oz) of the flavoured butter in a pan. Add the breadcrumbs, spring onions and peanuts and fry until golden, stirring to prevent the breadcrumbs from sticking together. Season with salt and pepper.

3 Arrange the salmon fillets, skin-side uppermost, in a roasting tin. Spoon the fried breadcrumb mixture on top and cook in the oven for 10–15 minutes until the salmon is just cooked.

4 Heat the remaining flavoured butter and serve with the roast salmon and boiled jacket potatoes.

COOK'S TIPS

■ To save cooking time, make up a batch of the spicy flavoured butter and the fried peanut and breadcrumb topping, and freeze ahead. Both of these mixtures can be used direct from the freezer: just allow an extra 2–3 minutes cooking time at step 3.

■ For a simple starter, serve roasted garlic tomatoes. Halve 6 tomatoes and arrange them, cut-side uppermost, in a roasting tin. Season with salt, pepper and crushed garlic, to taste. Drizzle with olive oil and cook at 200°C (180°C fan oven) mark 6 for 10–12 minutes until softened. Serve the garlic tomatoes warm on a bed of mixed salad leaves.

BAKED SALMON WITH WALNUTS AND HERBS

HANDS-ON TIME: 10 MINUTES, PLUS CHILLING   **COOKING TIME:** ABOUT 20 MINUTES   **SERVES: 4**

METHOD

1   Put four even-size pieces of salmon fillet in a shallow, non-metallic dish. Mix together the wine, walnut oil, herbs, garlic, paprika and seasoning. Spoon over the fish, cover and chill for at least 4 hours or overnight, turning from time to time.

2   Preheat the oven to 220°C (200°C fan oven) mark 7 and lightly oil a shallow ovenproof dish. Blanch the celery and turnips in a pan of boiling salted water for 1 minute, then drain under cold running water to cool quickly.

3   Arrange the celery and turnips in a single layer in the dish and season well. Lift the salmon out of the marinade and put on top of the vegetables. Put the marinade to one side.

4   Cook in the oven for 15–20 minutes until the fish is cooked.

5   Meanwhile, put marinade and cream in a small pan and boil until reduced by about half. Take the pan off the heat and quickly whisk in the seasoning and lime juice to taste.

6   To serve, arrange the salmon and vegetables on individual serving plates. Spoon the sauce over the top and garnish with shrimps or prawns.

COOK'S TIP

Just a little walnut oil gives an unusually rich flavour to the sauce.

INGREDIENTS

575g (1¼lb) salmon fillet, skinned
100ml (3½fl oz) white wine
50ml (2fl oz) walnut oil
4 tbsp freshly chopped mixed herbs
   such as parsley and chives
2 garlic cloves, crushed
a large pinch paprika
olive oil
4 celery sticks, cut into fine
   matchsticks
225g (8oz) turnips, cut into fine
   matchsticks
6 tbsp double cream
lime juice to taste
cooked shrimps or prawns to
   garnish

PER SERVING
490 cals
39g fat (of which 13g saturates)
3g carbohydrate

BAKING

These recipes are for those wonderful days when the rest of the family are out doing their own thing and you can indulge yourself by doing some baking, potting some preserves and stocking the freezer with home-made ice creams.

10 DOS AND DON'TS OF BAKING

- Weigh out all the ingredients carefully before starting the recipe so you have everything to hand when you begin to make the cake.
- Check that you have the correct cake tin for the job. The tin sizes quoted in this book refer to the base measurement of the tin.
- Take care to line the tin properly where necessary. For ease, try baking parchment liners. You just pop them in the tin – you don't even have to grease the tin or the paper.
- Allow 15 minutes to preheat the oven to the correct temperature.
- After it has come out of the oven, leave the cake in the tin to cool for 10 minutes and then turn out on to a wire rack to cool completely.
- Let the tins cool completely before washing them in warm, soapy water with a non-abrasive sponge.
- Always work in metric or imperial – never mix the two measurements.
- Try not to be heavy handed – when folding in flour, use light strokes so the air doesn't get knocked out.
- Don't let a cake mixture sit around once you've made it: pop it straight into the cake tin and into the oven, otherwise the raising agents will start to react.

SUGARS

Unrefined brown sugars really do make a difference to the taste of a dish. They contain the natural molasses of the sugar cane so have a distinctive flavour. To taste the flavours, put a little white caster sugar on your tongue and let it dissolve, then repeat with golden caster sugar. You'll notice that the white sugar tastes of nothing other than sweetness, while the golden caster has a subtle caramel flavour. Here is a guide to the other types.

Golden caster
Use for sponge cakes, meringues, pastry, crumbles and for making sugar syrups when poaching fruit.

Light muscovado
Use in sweet sauces such as toffee or butterscotch, savoury barbecue sauce, meringues and mincemeat.

Dark muscovado
A soft, crumbly texture and a flavour similar to black treacle. Try it in gingerbread or chocolate cake.

Golden icing
This gives a toffee flavour to icing and is good in buttercream fillings or for dusting mince pies.

Molasses
The richest sugar of all. Use this in your Christmas pudding or cake for a greater depth of flavour.

Sugar crystals
These dissolve slowly; use to subtly sweeten coffee. Also sprinkle on top of cakes, scones and sweet breads.'

CHOCOLATE BROWNIES

🖐 **HANDS-ON TIME:** 25 MINUTES   🍲 **COOKING TIME:** 55 MINUTES   ✕ **MAKES:** 9

METHOD

1 Preheat the oven to 180°C (160°C fan oven) mark 4. Grease and line a tin 18cm (7in) square.
2 Melt the chocolate and coffee in a bowl set over a pan of simmering water. Leave to cool slightly.
3 Cream the butter and sugar together, then beat in the egg yolks, one at a time. Fold in the almonds, walnuts, cornflour and melted chocolate mix. Whisk the egg whites in a bowl until soft peaks form, and fold in gently. Pour the mixture into the tin and bake in the oven for about 55 minutes. It is cooked when a skewer inserted into the centre comes out clean. Cover with greaseproof paper after 30 minutes. Leave in the tin for 10 minutes, then leave to cool on a wire rack. The brownies will keep for two to three days.

INGREDIENTS

150g (5oz) butter, plus a little extra to grease
150g (5oz) plain chocolate
1½ tsp instant coffee granules
150g (5oz) caster sugar
3 eggs, separated
65g (2½oz) ground almonds
75g (3oz) walnuts
65g (2½oz) cornflour

PER BROWNIE

422 cals
30g fat (of which 13g saturates)
35g carbohydrate

GINGER AND FRUIT TEA BREAD

🖐 **HANDS-ON TIME:** 15 MINUTES, PLUS SOAKING   🍲 **COOKING TIME:** 1 HOUR   ✕ **MAKES:** 12 SLICES

METHOD

1 Cover the dried fruit with tea and leave for at least 2 hours, stirring from time to time. Grease and baseline a 900g (2lb) loaf tin.
2 Preheat the oven to 180°C (160°C fan oven) mark 4. Put all the ingredients except the water in a bowl and mix thoroughly.
3 Turn the mixture into the tin, smooth the surface and brush lightly with the cold water. Bake in the oven for 1 hour or until cooked through. If necessary, cover after 30 minutes to prevent over-browning.
4 Leave the tea bread in the tin for 10–15 minutes, then take out and cool on a wire rack.

TO FREEZE

▪ Complete to the end of step 4. Wrap and freeze.
▪ To use, thaw for 4 hours at cool room temperature.

INGREDIENTS

125g (4oz) ready-to-eat dried apricots, roughly chopped
125g (4oz) dried apples, roughly chopped
125g (4oz) pitted prunes, roughly chopped
about 300ml (10fl oz) strong fruit tea
butter to grease
25g (1oz) stem ginger, chopped
225g (8oz) plain flour
2 tsp baking powder
125g (4oz) dark muscovado sugar
1 egg
2 tbsp cold water

PER SERVING

170 cals
1g fat (of which trace saturates)
40g carbohydrate

ORANGE SYRUP CAKE

HANDS-ON TIME: 20 MINUTES, PLUS SOAKING   **COOKING TIME:** 30–40 MINUTES   **MAKES:** 10 SLICES

METHOD

1 Preheat the oven to 190°C (170°C fan oven) mark 5. Grease and baseline a shallow 20cm (8in) round tin.
2 Cream the butter and 75g (3oz) sugar, then beat in the eggs gradually. Fold in the rice flour, baking powder and ground almonds. Stir in the zest and juice of the orange and 8 tbsp orange juice. The mixture should be of a soft, dropping consistency.
3 Bake in the oven for 40 minutes or until firm. Leave to cool in the tin for 10 minutes, then turn out on to a wire rack.
4 Just before serving, combine the remaining sugar and orange juice plus the lemon juice in a small pan. Add the orange slices, bring to the boil and cook for 1–2 minutes. Take the pan off the heat and leave to cool for 5 minutes. Remove the orange slices from the syrup and set aside. Put the cake on a serving plate and, with a cocktail stick, prick the cake in a number of places. Drizzle over the syrup and leave to soak for 30 minutes. Serve with the orange slices and blueberries.

TO FREEZE

■ Complete to end of step 3, wrap and freeze.
■ To use, thaw at a cool room temperature for 2–3 hours. Complete the recipe.

INGREDIENTS

175g (6oz) butter, plus extra to grease
225g (8oz) caster sugar
2 eggs, beaten
200g (7oz) rice flour
2 tsp baking powder
75g (3oz) ground almonds
grated zest and juice of 1 large orange
250ml carton orange juice
2 large oranges, peeled and thickly sliced
2 tbsp lemon juice
blueberries to serve

PER SLICE

380 cals
20g fat (of which 11g saturates)
47g carbohydrate

WHITE FARMHOUSE LOAF

✋ **HANDS-ON TIME:** 20 MINUTES, PLUS RISING 🍞 **COOKING TIME:** 30–35 MINUTES, PLUS COOLING

✗ **MAKES:** 16 SLICES

WEEKEND COOKING 152

INGREDIENTS

575g (1¼lb) strong plain white flour,
plus extra to dust
125g (4oz) strong plain wholemeal
flour
1 tbsp salt
1 tsp golden caster sugar
1½ tsp fast-action dried yeast
(see Cook's Tip)
25g (1oz) butter, diced
vegetable oil, to oil

PER SERVING

160 cals
2g fat (of which 1g saturates)
32g carbohydrate

METHOD

1 Sift the white flour into a large bowl and stir in the wholemeal flour, salt, sugar and yeast. Rub in the butter with your fingertips. Make a well in the middle and add about 450ml (15fl oz) warm water. Work to a smooth, soft dough, adding a little extra water if necessary.

2 Knead for 10 minutes until smooth, then shape the dough into a ball and put into an oiled bowl. Cover and leave to rise in a warm place for 1–2 hours until doubled in size.

3 Knock back the dough on a lightly floured surface and shape into a large oval loaf. Transfer the dough to a floured baking sheet, cover loosely and leave to rise for a further 30 minutes.

4 Slash the top of the loaf with a sharp knife, dust with flour and bake at 230°C (210°C fan oven) mark 8 for 15 minutes. Lower the oven setting to 200°C (180°C fan oven) mark 6 and bake for a further 15–20 minutes or until the bread is risen and sounds hollow when tapped underneath. Cool on a wire rack.

COOK'S TIP

If available, use 25g (1oz) fresh yeast instead of dried. Crumble into a bowl, add the sugar, 150ml (5fl oz) of the warmed water and 4 tbsp of the white flour. Stir well to dissolve the yeast, then leave in a warm place for 20 minutes until very frothy. Continue as above, adding the frothy yeast to the dry ingredients with the rest of the water.

WHOLEMEAL LOAF

HANDS-ON TIME: 15 MINUTES, PLUS RISING   **COOKING TIME:** 30–35 MINUTES, PLUS COOLING

MAKES: 16 SLICES

METHOD

1 Sift the white flour into a large bowl and stir in the wholemeal flour, salt, sugar and yeast. Make a well in the middle and add about 450ml (15fl oz) warm water. Work to a smooth, soft dough, adding a little extra water if necessary.

2 Knead for 10 minutes until smooth, then shape the dough into a ball and put into an oiled bowl. Cover and leave to rise in a warm place for about 2 hours until doubled in size.

3 Knock back the dough on a lightly floured surface and shape into an oblong. Press into an oiled 900g (2lb) loaf tin, cover and leave to rise for a further 30 minutes.

4 Bake the loaf at 230°C (210°C fan oven) mark 8 for 15 minutes. Lower the oven setting to 200°C (180°C fan oven) mark 6 and bake for a further 15–20 minutes or until the bread is risen and sounds hollow when tapped underneath. Leave in the tin for 10 minutes, then turn out and cool on a wire rack.

COOK'S TIP

If available, use 40g (1½oz) fresh yeast instead of dried. Proceed as for the White Farmhouse Loaf, opposite.

INGREDIENTS

225g (8oz) strong plain white flour, plus extra to dust
450g (1lb) strong plain wholemeal flour
2 tsp salt
1 tsp golden caster sugar
2 tsp fast-action dried yeast (see Cook's Tip)
vegetable oil, to oil

PER SERVING

140 cals
1g fat (of which trace saturates)
29g carbohydrate

OATMEAL SODA BREAD

✋ **HANDS-ON TIME:** 15 MINUTES　🍲 **COOKING TIME:** 25 MINUTES　✖ **MAKES:** ABOUT 10 SLICES

INGREDIENTS
25g (1oz) butter
275g (10oz) plain wholemeal flour
175g (6oz) coarse oatmeal
2 tsp cream of tartar
1 tsp salt
about 300ml (10fl oz) milk and
　　water, mixed

PER SLICE
160 cals
2g fat (of which trace saturates)
31g carbohydrate

METHOD
1　Preheat the oven to 220°C (200°C fan oven) mark 7. Grease and baseline a 900g (2lb) loaf tin.
2　Mix together all the dry ingredients in a bowl. Rub in the butter.
3　Add the milk and water to bind to a soft dough. Spoon into the tin.
4　Bake in the oven for about 25 minutes or until golden brown and well risen. Turn out and leave to cool slightly on a wire rack. It is best eaten on the day of making.

QUICK CHEESE AND APPLE BREAD

✋ **HANDS-ON TIME:** 15 MINUTES　🍲 **COOKING TIME:** 40–45 MINUTES　✖ **MAKES:** ABOUT 8 SLICES

INGREDIENTS
25g (1oz) butter
225g (8oz) self-raising flour, plus
　　extra to dust
¼ tsp pepper
1 small, crisp eating apple, about
　　125g (4oz), peeled, cored and
　　finely chopped
125g (4oz) mature Cheddar cheese,
　　coarsely grated
50g (2oz) roast, salted peanuts,
　　chopped
1 egg
4–5 tbsp milk
apple slice, to decorate

PER SLICE
240 cals
12g fat (of which 6g saturates)
24g carbohydrate

METHOD
1　Preheat the oven to 190°C (170°C fan oven) mark 5. Rub the butter into the flour and pepper. Stir the apple, cheese and peanuts into the dry ingredients.
2　Whisk together the egg and milk, and beat into the mixture to form a soft dough.
3　Turn out onto a lightly floured worksurface and knead quickly into a small, neat round about 15–18cm (6–7in) in diameter. Mark a lattice on the top. Press an apple slice into the centre.
4　Put on a baking sheet and bake in the oven for about 40 minutes or until well risen and golden brown. Turn the bread over and cook for a further 5 minutes. Leave to cool on a wire rack. It is best eaten on the day of making.

RUSTIC BLACKBERRY AND APPLE PIE

👋 **HANDS-ON TIME:** 25 MINUTES 🍲 **COOKING TIME:** 40 MINUTES, PLUS CHILLING ✕ **SERVES:** 6

INGREDIENTS

200g (7oz) plain flour
125g (4oz) chilled unsalted butter,
  cut into dice
1 egg, beaten
3 tbsp golden caster sugar
500g (1lb 2oz) eating apples,
  quartered, cored and cut into
  chunky wedges
300g (11oz) blackberries
75g (3oz) golden caster sugar,
  plus 3 tbsp
¼ tsp ground cinnamon
juice of 1 small lemon

PER SLICE

440cals
19g fat (of which 12g saturates)
66g carbohydrate per serving

METHOD

1 Put the flour into a processor, add the butter and pulse to form crumbs. Add the egg, 2 tbsp sugar and a pinch of salt and pulse again to combine. Wrap in clingfilm and chill while preparing the filling.

2 Preheat the oven to 200°C (180°C fan oven) mark 6. Grease a 25cm (10in) enamel or metal pie plate. Put the apples, blackberries, 75g (3oz) sugar, cinnamon and lemon juice together in a bowl and gently toss together, making sure the sugar dissolves in the juice.

3 Roll out the pastry, using a lightly floured rolling pin, on a large sheet of baking parchment (this will stop it sticking to the surface) to a 30.5cm(12in) circle. Lift up the paper, upturn the pastry onto the pie plate and peel away the paper.

4 Put the prepared fruits in the centre of the dish and fold the pastry edges up and over the fruit. Sprinkle with the remaining sugar and bake for 40 minutes until the fruit is tender and the pastry golden. Serve with vanilla ice cream.

SUMMER PUDDING

🖐 **HANDS-ON TIME:** 5 MINUTES 🍰 **COOKING TIME:** 10 MINUTES, PLUS CHILLING ✕ **SERVES:** 6-8

METHOD

1 Put the redcurrants and blackcurrants in a medium pan. Add the sugar and cassis. Bring to a simmer and cook for around 3-5 minutes until the sugar has dissolved. Add the raspberries and cook for 2 minutes.
2 Meanwhile, line 1 litre (1¾ pint) bowl with clingfilm. Put the base of the bowl on one piece of bread and cut around it. Put it in the bowl.
3 Line the inside of the bowl with more bread slices, slightly overlapping so there are no spaces.
4 Spoon the fruit into the bowl, making sure the juice soaks into the bread. Cut the remaining bread to fit the top of the pudding. Drizzle with any juice. Trim any excess bread from around the edges. Wrap in clingfilm, weight down with a saucer and a can and chill for 2 hours or overnight.
5 To serve, unwrap the clingfilm and upturn the pudding onto a plate.

INGREDIENTS

700g (1½lb) mixed summer fruit (eg 250g (9oz) each redcurrants and blackcurrants, 300g (11oz) raspberries)
125g (4oz) golden caster sugar
3tbsp cassis
9 thick slices of slightly stale white bread, crusts removed

PER SLICE

270-200cals
1-1g fat (of which trace saturates)
60-45g carbohydrate per serving

RHUBARB AND OATMEAL CRUMBLE

🖐 **HANDS-ON TIME:** 15 MINUTES 🍰 **COOKING TIME:** 25-30 MINUTES ✕ **SERVES:** 6

METHOD

1 Put the rhubarb into a medium pan with 100g (3½oz) of the sugar. Mix in half the cinnamon, lemon rind and juice. Cook over a medium heat for 10min, until the rhubarb is just tender but has still kept it's shape. Spoon into a 1.1 litre (2 pint) ovenproof dish, and sit on a baking sheet. Preheat the oven to 220°C (200°C fan oven) mark 7.
2 Make the crumble. Mix together the flour and oatmeal (or oats) in a bowl. Add the butter and rub in until it resembles fine breadcrumbs. Stir in the remaining sugar and cinnamon, then sprinkle over the rhubarb.
3 Bake for 15-20 minutes, until the crumble is golden and the rhubarb is bubbling hot. Serve with plenty of hot custard.

INGREDIENTS

900g (2lb) rhubarb, cut into cubes (discard leaves)
175g (6oz) golden caster sugar
1 tsp ground cinnamon
rind and juice of ½ lemon
75g (3oz) plain flour
75g (3oz) medium oatmeal or porridge oats
75g (3oz) chilled butter, cubed
fresh custard to serve

PER SLICE

310cals
11g fat (of which 7g saturates)
51g carbohydrate per serving

REFRIGERATOR CAKE

✋ **HANDS-ON TIME:** 10 MINUTES ♨ **COOKING TIME:** 4 MINUTES ✗ **SERVES:** 12

INGREDIENTS

175g (6oz) butter, cut into eight
 pieces, plus extra for greasing
200g packet natural glacé cherries,
 halved
2tbsp Kirsch
150g dark chocolate with fruit,
 broken into pieces
200g (7oz) plain chocolate, broken
 into pieces
100g (3½oz) golden syrup
200g (7oz) packet digestive biscuits

PER SLICE
400cals
25g fat (of which 16g saturates)
42g carbohydrate

METHOD

1 Grease and base-line a 20cm (8in) round tin. Put the cherries into
 a bowl and add the Kirsch. Leave to soak.

2 Put all the chocolate, butter and golden syrup in a large
 microwave-proof bowl. Cook on medium (in a 900W oven) for 2
 minutes, stir and cook for a further 2 minutes until chocolate has
 melted. Alternatively put the chocolate in a bowl and melt over a
 pan of simmering water, making sure the bottom of the bowl
 doesn't touch the water.

3 Put the biscuits into a food processor and whiz to roughly crush.

4 Add half the soaked cherries and all the biscuits to the chocolate,
 then stir together. Spoon into a baselined 20cm (8in) loose-based
 round tin and level over.

5 Arrange the remaining cherries around the edge of the cake. Chill
 for at least 15 minutes before serving. Will keep for up to two
 weeks, covered, in the fridge. Serve in chunky wedges.

CHERRY CHOCOLATE PUDDING

HANDS-ON TIME: 15 MINUTES ▪ **COOKING TIME:** 55 MINUTES ▪ **SERVES:** 6

METHOD

1 Grease a 18cm (7in) square cake tin and line the base with greaseproof paper. Preheat the oven to 190°C (170°C fan oven) mark 5.

2 Put the reserved cherry syrup in a small pan with 25g (1oz) sugar. Bring to the boil and simmer until reduced by half. Leave to cool.

3 Put the butter in a small heatproof bowl with 75g (3oz) chocolate and melt over a pan of simmering water, making sure the base doesn't touch the water. Remove from the heat and cool.

4 Put the eggs in a bowl with the remaining sugar and vanilla extract and beat together until thick and pale. Fold in the cooled chocolate, flour and remaining chocolate.

5 Arrange the cherries in the bottom of the cake tin and pour over the chocolate mixture. Bake for 45 minutes, covering with foil after 30 minutes. Leave to cool for 5 minutes in the tin then turn out by carefully inverting onto a large plate or board. Pour over the reserved cherry syrup while the cake is still warm. Serve with ready-made fresh vanilla custard.

INGREDIENTS

425g can pitted black cherries in syrup, drained and syrup reserved, halved
125g (4oz) golden caster sugar
125g (4oz) butter
250g (9oz) plain chocolate, roughly chopped
2 eggs
1 tsp vanilla extract
75g (3oz) self-raising flour

PER SLICE
600cals
31g fat (of which 19g saturated fat)
77g carbohydrate per serving

TOFFEE CRUNCH ICE CREAM

🖐 **HANDS-ON TIME:** 20 MINUTES, PLUS FREEZING 🍰 **COOKING TIME:** 5 MINUTES ✖ **SERVES:** 8

INGREDIENTS

3 chocolate-covered fudge finger
  bars, about 100g (3½oz) total
  weight
284ml carton double cream
2 eggs, separated
50g (2oz) icing sugar
5 chocolate bars with a butter
  almond centre, 175g (6oz) total
  weight, broken into pieces
500g carton chilled ready-made
  custard

PER SERVING

440 cals
29g fat (of which 17g saturates)
40g carbohydrate

METHOD

1 Break the fudge bars into a bowl. Add 2 tbsp double cream and
   heat slowly over a pan of simmering water. Leave to cool until
   tepid but still liquid.

2 Whisk together the egg yolks and icing sugar until pale and fairly
   thick and mousse-like.

3 Whip the remaining cream and egg whites in separate bowls until
   they both form soft peaks.

4 Fold together the whipped cream, custard, egg yolk mixture, fudge
   bar mixture and most of the chocolate bar pieces. Finally, fold in
   the egg whites.

5 Pour the mixture into a shallow freezerproof container to a depth
   of about 5cm (2in), and freeze overnight. Before serving, leave to
   soften for about 40 minutes in the fridge, then stamp out into
   shapes, if you like . Decorate with the remaining chocolate bar
   pieces.

COOK'S TIP

Young children, the elderly, pregnant women and people with
immune-deficiency diseases should not eat raw eggs, due to the
risk of salmonella.

EASY VANILLA ICE CREAM

👋 **HANDS-ON TIME:** 15 MINUTES, PLUS FREEZING 🍲 **COOKING TIME:** 35–45 MINUTES ✕ **SERVES:** 10

INGREDIENTS

6 eggs, separated
125g (4oz) golden syrup
568ml carton double cream, chilled
seeds from 2 split vanilla pods, or
   2 tbsp vanilla paste

PER SERVING

350 cals
31g fat (of which 18g saturates)
11g carbohydrate

METHOD

1   Put the egg yolks and syrup into a large bowl. Using an electric hand whisk or freestanding mixer, whisk together for 4–5 minutes until the mixture leaves a ribbon-like trail when you lift the whisk. Pour the cream into a separate bowl and whisk until it starts to thicken and hold its shape, then use a large metal spoon to fold it into the egg mixture. Whisk briefly to combine. Leave to chill.

2   Wash the whisk well. Put the egg whites in a clean, grease-free bowl and whisk until they form soft peaks. Using a large metal spoon, add one spoonful of egg white to the chilled egg yolk, syrup and cream mixture, and stir thoroughly. Add the remaining egg white and the vanilla seeds or paste, and fold in, taking care not to knock out the air.

3   Pour the mixture into a large, shallow, freezerproof container with a capacity of 1 litre (1¾ pints), then freeze for at least 6 hours until firm. Leave to soften in the fridge for up to 20 minutes before serving.

COOK'S TIPS

■   Don't over-whip the cream or over-whisk the egg whites. They need to be a similar texture to the whisked egg and syrup mixture.
■   Young children, the elderly, pregnant women and people with immune-deficiency diseases should not eat raw eggs, due to the risk of salmonella.

APRICOT ICE CREAM

METHOD

1 Put the apricots in a bowl. Pour the water over them, cover and leave to soak overnight.

2 Put the apricots and soaking liquid in a pan with the lemon zest. Bring to the boil, cover and cook over a low heat for 20–30 minutes, stirring from time to time. Uncover and cook until all the liquid has evaporated. Leave to cool a little and remove the lemon zest. Put the apricots in a food processor with the orange juice and whiz for 20 seconds or until roughly chopped. Set aside to cool.

3 Put the eggs and sugar in a large, heatproof bowl. Using an electric whisk, whisk the mixture over a pan of simmering water for about 10 minutes until a thick mousse forms. Whisk away from the heat until cool.

4 Whip the cream into soft peaks. Fold in the cooled egg mixture, apricots, vanilla essence and Cointreau or Grand Marnier. Put in an ice-cream maker and freeze until stiff, then transfer to a freezerproof container until ready to use.

5 Remove the ice cream from the freezer 15 minutes before serving. Serve in tall glasses with deep-fried orange zest and a squeeze of fresh orange juice on top (not suitable for children due to the alcohol content).

INGREDIENTS

225g (8oz) no-soak dried apricots
450ml (15fl oz) water
pared zest of 1 large lemon
3 tbsp orange juice
2 eggs
50g (2oz) caster sugar
284ml carton double cream
1 tsp vanilla essence
2 tbsp Cointreau or Grand Marnier
deep-fried orange zest to decorate
fresh orange juice to serve

PER SERVING

320 cals
25g fat (of which 15g saturates)
17g carbohydrate

SHORT CUTS

EASY SUPPERS

QUICK ONION GRAVY FOR SAUSAGES

✋ **HANDS-ON TIME:** 5 MINUTES   🍲 **COOKING TIME:** 30 MINUTES   ✗ **SERVES:** 4   **MAKES:** 450ml (15fl oz)

INGREDIENTS
1 tbsp oil
1 red onion, peeled and finely sliced
1 tbsp plain flour
½ tsp tomato purée
415g can beef consommé
150ml (5fl oz) water
2 bay leaves

PER SERVING
120 cals
8g fat (of which trace saturates)
7g carbohydrate

METHOD
1 Heat the oil in a pan. Add the onion and fry for 10 minutes until soft. Stir in the flour and tomato purée and cook for 1 minute.
2 Add the beef consommé, water and bay leaves. Bring to the boil, then reduce the heat and simmer for 15 minutes. Season to taste with salt and pepper, remove the bay leaves and serve with sausages and mash.

CREAMY MUSHROOM CHICKEN

✋ **HANDS-ON TIME:** 5 MINUTES   🍲 **COOKING TIME:** 25–30 MINUTES   ✗ **SERVES:** 4

INGREDIENTS
280g jar mushrooms in olive oil, drained and 1 tbsp oil put to one side
4 small skinless chicken breasts
2 celery sticks, trimmed and thinly sliced diagonally
150ml (5fl oz) dry white wine
200ml tub half-fat crème fraîche
2 tbsp freshly chopped tarragon

PER SERVING
300 cals
18g fat (of which 7g saturates)
3g carbohydrate

METHOD
1 Heat the reserved oil in a large frying pan with a lid, or a flameproof casserole, and fry the chicken for 5 minutes until browned all over. Remove from the pan and set aside. Add the celery and mushrooms to the frying pan and cook for a further 2 minutes. Pour in the white wine and bring the sauce to the boil, then reduce the heat to a simmer.
2 Put the chicken back into the pan. Cover and cook for 15 minutes until it's cooked to the centre and the juices run clear. Mix in the crème fraîche and tarragon, and season well with salt and pepper. Cook for a further 5 minutes until the sauce is piping hot. Serve with boiled new potatoes and French beans.

CRABCAKES

✋ **HANDS-ON TIME:** 15 MINUTES   🍲 **COOKING TIME:** 18 MINUTES   ✗ **SERVES:** 4

METHOD

1 Heat a frying pan to medium hot. Add the onion seeds and stir for 1–2 minutes to release the aroma. Set aside to cool. Scoop out the crabmeat and any garnish of chopped parsley and egg, into a bowl. Add the potato, lemon zest, onion seeds and breadcrumbs, and mix together, seasoning to taste with salt and pepper.

2 Lightly flour your hands, then shape the mixture into eight cakes. Dust each one with a little flour, put on a plate and leave to chill for 15 minutes or overnight.

3 Preheat the oven to 140°C (120°C fan oven) mark 1. Heat the oil in a frying pan. Add half the crabcakes and cook over a medium heat for 4 minutes, then turn over and cook for a further 4 minutes until golden brown and heated through. Keep the cooked crabcakes warm in the oven while you fry the remainder. Serve with a dressed mixed salad, a dollop of mayonnaise and lemon wedges to squeeze over the crabcakes.

TO PREPARE AHEAD

To make the crabcakes a day in advance, follow the recipe to the end of step 2, cover and leave to chill overnight, then complete the recipe.

COOK'S TIP

If you've got leftover mash from another meal, use that instead of buying ready-made mash.

INGREDIENTS

1 tsp black onion seeds
2 dressed crab
400g pack chilled mashed potato
grated zest of 1 small lemon
40g (1½oz) fresh white
breadcrumbs
a little plain flour to dust
2 tbsp vegetable oil

PER SERVING
270 cals
11g fat (of which 1g saturates)
25g carbohydrate

WARM PRAWN AND PEANUT NOODLES

🖐 **HANDS-ON TIME:** 10 MINUTES   🍲 **COOKING TIME:** 2 MINUTES   ✕ **SERVES:** 4

INGREDIENTS

300g pack straight-to-wok noodles
360g pack stir-fry vegetables
4 tbsp coconut cream
4 tbsp smooth peanut butter
1 tbsp red or green Thai curry paste
juice of ½ lime
225g (8oz) cooked, peeled king
    prawns
a small handful freshly chopped
    coriander
25g (1oz) chopped peanuts to serve

PER SERVING

420 cals
20g fat (of which 7g saturates)
38g carbohydrate

METHOD

1 Put the noodles and stir-fry vegetables in a large bowl and cover with boiling water. Cover with clingfilm and leave to stand for 5 minutes.
2 Meanwhile, mix together the coconut cream, peanut butter, curry paste and lime juice.
3 Drain the noodles and vegetables. Put them in a wok to warm through and toss with the king prawns, the coriander and half the dressing. Serve sprinkled with the peanuts and a little more of the dressing.

OVEN-ROAST COD AND CHIPS

🖐 **HANDS-ON TIME:** 15 MINUTES   🍲 **COOKING TIME:** 25–30 MINUTES   ✕ **SERVES:** 2

INGREDIENTS

450g (1lb) large potatoes, peeled
    and cut into chips
3 tbsp olive oil
2 thick cod fillets, about 200g (7oz)
    each
350g (12oz) frozen peas
2 tbsp crème fraîche
2 tbsp freshly chopped mint
sea salt flakes to sprinkle
lemon wedges to serve

PER SERVING

670 cals
29g fat (of which 7g saturates)
55g carbohydrate

METHOD

1 Rest a wire rack over a roasting tin and put into the oven. Preheat it to 200°C (180°C fan oven) mark 6. Put the chips on the rack and drizzle with 1 tbsp oil, then roast for 25–30 minutes, turning once, until cooked through and golden.
2 Meanwhile, dry the cod fillets with kitchen paper and season with salt and pepper. Heat the remaining oil in a large frying pan and cook the cod skin-side down until skin is crisp. Transfer to a baking tray and cook in the oven for 15–20 minutes until the fish is tender and flaking.
3 Cook the frozen peas in a pan of boiling salted water for 8–10 minutes until very tender. Drain well and put back in the pan, then add the crème fraîche and mint. Whiz to a purée with a hand-held stick blender until almost smooth.
4 Season the chips with sea salt and divide the pea purée between two plates. Top each with a portion of cod, then serve with the chips and a wedge of lemon to squeeze over the fish.

STIR-FRIED PRAWNS AND PAK CHOI WITH RICE

✋ HANDS-ON TIME: 2 MINUTES　　**🫕 COOKING TIME:** 25 MINUTES　　**✗ SERVES:** 4

INGREDIENTS

300g (11oz) mixed American long grain rice and wild rice, mixed
750ml (1¼ pints) water
1 tbsp sesame oil
2 heads pak choi, chopped
250g (9oz) cooked, peeled king prawns
1–2 tbsp teriyaki sauce

PER SERVING

360 cals
4g fat (of which 1g saturates)
61g carbohydrate

METHOD

1 Put the rice into a pan with the water and bring to the boil. Simmer for 15–18 minutes until the water has been absorbed and the rice is tender.

2 Meanwhile, heat the oil in a large pan. Add the pak choi and stir-fry for 2–3 minutes until beginning to soften. Add the king prawns and heat through for 2–3 minutes until piping hot. Stir in the teriyaki sauce.

3 Divide the rice among four bowls and top with the pak choi, prawns and any sauce. Serve immediately.

COOK'S TIP

Pak choi is a member of the cabbage family. It's full of nutrients and delicious stir fried.

PRAWN AND SPINACH PANCAKES

✋ **HANDS-ON TIME:** 10 MINUTES   🍲 **COOKING TIME:** 20 MINUTES   ✗ **SERVES:** 6

METHOD

1 Preheat the oven to 200°C (180°C fan oven) mark 6. Squeeze the thawed spinach in your hands to remove as much excess liquid as possible, then chop roughly and season with just a little salt but plenty of pepper.

2 Lightly oil a medium-size ovenproof dish, about 20cm (8in) square. Open out each pancake and spread a little of the mayonnaise in the centre, leaving a 2.5cm (1in) clear edge. Sprinkle on a little of the Cheddar and the Parmesan into each pancake, then top with spring onion, spinach and prawns. Gather the edges of the pancakes loosely together and tuck side by side in the dish, leaving the filling exposed. There should be just enough space in the dish to hold all the pancakes in a single layer.

3 Spoon the cream over the pancakes and sprinkle with the remaining cheese. Cook in the oven for 20 minutes or until the tops are crisp and golden and everything is heated through. Serve immediately with a green salad.

COOK'S TIP

Stock the freezer with ready-made pancakes – supper can be on the table in no time.

INGREDIENTS

- 100g (3½oz) frozen leaf spinach, thawed
- 1 tbsp olive oil
- 200g pack ready-made pancakes
- 3 tbsp light mayonnaise
- 200g (7oz) low-fat mature Cheddar cheese, grated
- 25g (1oz) freshly grated Parmesan cheese
- 3 spring onions, trimmed and finely chopped
- 300g (11oz) large cooked, peeled prawns
- 142ml carton double cream

PER SERVING

390 cals

25g fat (of which 13g saturates)

17g carbohydrate

SALMON AND WATERCRESS SALAD

✋ **HANDS-ON TIME:** 10 MINUTES 🍲 **COOKING TIME:** 0 MINUTES ✗ **SERVES:** 4

INGREDIENTS

1 ripe mango, peeled and cut into
  bite-size pieces
a small bunch of freshly chopped
  watercress
1 red onion, peeled and finely sliced
2 tbsp extra-virgin olive oil
2 tsp white wine vinegar
juice of 1 small orange
1 tbsp freshly chopped parsley
2 × 150g packs hot-smoked salmon
  fillets

PER SERVING

270 cals
16g fat (of which 3g saturates)
17g carbohydrate

METHOD

1 Put the mango into a large bowl with the watercress and onion.
2 Whisk together the olive oil, wine vinegar, orange juice and parsley
  in a small bowl. Season with salt and pepper,
  then toss the dressing through the salad.
3 Divide the hot-smoked salmon fillets among four plates. Add the
  salad and serve immediately.

HOT NOODLE SALAD

✋ **HANDS-ON TIME:** 10 MINUTES 🍲 **COOKING TIME:** 5–7 MINUTES ✗ **SERVES:** 4 ✓

INGREDIENTS

250g pack of medium egg noodles
2 tsp groundnut oil
2 × 300g packs stir-fry vegetables
1 tsp crushed chilli flakes
4 eggs, beaten

PER SERVING

350 cals
8g fat (of which 2g saturates)
51g carbohydrate

METHOD

1 Put the egg noodles in a bowl of boiling water and leave to soak for
  5 minutes. Drain well.
2 Meanwhile, heat the oil in a large wok over a high heat. Add the
  vegetables and chilli flakes and stir-fry for 3–4 minutes. Season
  the eggs with salt and pepper and pour over the vegetables. Cook
  for 1–2 minutes to let the egg set on the bottom, then stir in the
  noodles.
3 Serve with roughly chopped peanuts, freshly chopped coriander
  and lime wedges to squeeze over the top.

CARAMELISED ONION AND TWO-CHEESE TART

HANDS-ON TIME: 10 MINUTES   **COOKING TIME:** 50 MINUTES–1 HOUR   **SERVES:** 4   V

METHOD

1 Preheat the oven to 200°C (180°C fan oven) mark 6. Line the pastry case with greaseproof paper, fill with baking beans and bake blind for 10 minutes. Remove the paper and beans, prick the pastry base all over with a fork and cook for a further 15–20 minutes until golden.

2 Spoon the onion confit into the pastry case. Beat the goat's cheese and egg together until smooth, and season well with salt and pepper. Spoon on top of the onions and smooth the surface with a knife.

3 Scatter over the Parmesan cheese and cook in the oven for 25–30 minutes until the filling is set and just beginning to brown.

4 Leave to cool for 15 minutes, then cut away the sides of the foil case. Very carefully slide the tart on to a serving plate and arrange the rocket on top just before serving. Serve warm with sliced tomatoes, seasoned and drizzled with balsamic vinegar and extra-virgin olive oil.

INGREDIENTS

230g ready-made shortcrust pastry case
275g jar onion confit
300g tub soft, mild goat's cheese
1 egg, beaten
25g (1oz) freshly grated Parmesan cheese
50g (2oz) bag rocket

PER SERVING

520 cals
35g fat (of which 16g saturates)
32g carbohydrate

MOZZARELLA, PARMA HAM AND ROCKET PIZZA

HANDS-ON TIME: 10 MINUTES   **COOKING TIME:** 15–18 MINUTES   **SERVES:** 4

METHOD

1 Preheat the oven to 200°C (180°C fan oven) mark 6 and lightly flour a baking sheet. Mix up the pizza base according to the pack instructions. Divide the dough into two and knead each ball on a lightly floured surface for about 5 minutes, then roll them out to make two 23cm (9in) rounds. Put each on to the prepared baking sheet and put to one side in a warm place while you assemble the toppings.

2 Divide the tomato sauce between the pizza bases and spread it over them, leaving a small border around each edge. Scatter over the mozzarella pieces, then tear the ham into strips and spread over the cheese. Season well with salt and pepper.

3 Bake the pizzas for 15–18 minutes until golden. Slide on to a wooden board, top with rocket leaves and drizzle with olive oil. Cut in half to serve.

COOK'S TIP

If you're very short of time, buy two ready-made pizza bases.

INGREDIENTS

a little plain flour to dust
290g pack pizza base mix
350g (12oz) fresh tomato and chilli pasta sauce
2 × 125g (4oz) tubs buffalo mozzarella cheese, drained and roughly chopped
6 slices Parma ham
50g (2oz) wild rocket leaves
a little extra-virgin olive oil to drizzle

PER SERVING
580 cals
26g fat (of which 10g saturates)
57g carbohydrate

EASY LASAGNE

✋ **HANDS-ON TIME:** 5 MINUTES   🍲 **COOKING TIME:** 45 MINUTES   ✗ **SERVES:** 4

INGREDIENTS

1 tbsp oil
1 large onion, peeled and finely
    chopped
450g (1lb) minced beef
2 garlic cloves, crushed
290g jar condiverde (marinated
    vegetables in a seasoned
    dressing)
2 × 400g cans chopped tomatoes
1 tsp dried marjoram
375g (12oz) fresh garlic and herb
    tagliatelle
salt
330g jar ready-made cheese sauce
4 tbsp milk
75g (3oz) Cheddar cheese, grated

PER SERVING
740 cals
30g fat (of which 13g saturates)
70g carbohydrate

METHOD

1   Heat the oil in a pan. Add the onion and fry until soft. Add the beef and fry, stirring, until the meat is brown. Add the crushed garlic, condiverde, tomatoes and marjoram. Simmer for 25 minutes until the meat is tender.

2   Cook the tagliatelle in a pan of boiling salted water. Drain, put back into the pan and stir in the cheese sauce and milk. Heat through for 3 minutes.

3   Preheat the grill. Put alternate layers of mince and pasta in a heatproof dish and top with the cheese. Cook under the hot grill until bubbling.

SPINACH AND AUBERGINE LASAGNE

HANDS-ON TIME: 10 MINUTES   **COOKING TIME:** 40–45 MINUTES   **SERVES:** 4   V

METHOD

1. Put the spinach into a large pan and stir over a medium heat for 1–2 minutes until it has just wilted. Drain and squeeze out any liquid, then set aside. Put the aubergines on kitchen paper to soak up any excess oil.

2. Preheat the oven to 200°C (180°C fan oven) mark 6. Spread half the tomato sauce over the base of a 1.7 litre (3 pint) ovenproof dish, then put half the grilled aubergines in a single layer over the top. Top with three lasagne sheets, which will overlap, then spread half the cheese sauce evenly over the surface.

3. Put the cooked spinach on top of the cheese sauce, then season with salt and pepper. Repeat the layers with the remaining tomato sauce, aubergines, lasagne and cheese sauce, then sprinkle over the grated Parmesan cheese and a scattering of pepper.

4. Put the dish on a baking sheet and cook in the oven for 35–40 minutes until the topping is golden brown and bubbling. Serve with a mixed salad and crusty bread.

INGREDIENTS

- **150g (5oz) baby spinach leaves, washed**
- **310g jar grilled aubergines in olive oil, drained**
- **500g tub fresh tomato and basil sauce**
- **200g tub fresh four-cheese sauce**
- **6 sheets fresh lasagne**
- **40g (1½oz) freshly grated Parmesan cheese**

PER SERVING

360 cals

20g fat (of which 7g saturates)

33g carbohydrate

VERY EASY FOUR CHEESE GNOCCHI

✋ **HANDS-ON TIME:** 3 MINUTES   🍲 **COOKING TIME:** 10 MINUTES   ✗ **SERVES:** 2 √

INGREDIENTS

350g pack fresh gnocchi
300g tub fresh four cheese sauce
240g pack sunblush tomatoes
2 tbsp freshly torn basil leaves
**1 tbsp freshly grated Parmesan
   cheese**
15g (½oz) butter, chopped

PER SERVING

630 cals
28g fat (of which 15g saturates)
77g carbohydrate

METHOD

1 Bring a large pan of water to the boil, then add 1 tsp salt and the gnocchi and cook according to the pack instructions or until all the gnocchi have floated to the surface. Drain well and put the gnocchi back into the pan.

2 Preheat the grill. Add the four cheese sauce and tomatoes to the gnocchi and heat gently, stirring, for 2 minutes.

3 Season with salt and pepper, then add the basil and stir again. Spoon into individual heatproof bowls, sprinkle the Parmesan over each and dot with butter.

4 Cook under the grill for 3–5 minutes until golden and bubbling.

PEPPER AND GOAT'S CHEESE PASTA

✋ **HANDS-ON TIME:** 5 MINUTES   🍲 **COOKING TIME:** 15–20 MINUTES   ✗ **SERVES:** 4 √

INGREDIENTS

350g (12oz) dried pasta shapes
**320g jar roasted red peppers,
   drained and chopped**
500g carton passata
120g pack soft goat's cheese
**a small handful of fresh basil
   leaves or rocket**

PER SERVING

400 cals
7g fat (of which 3g saturates)
73g carbohydrate

METHOD

1 Cook the pasta shapes in a large pan of boiling water until *al dente*. Drain well and set aside.

2 Add the peppers and passata to the pasta pan (no need to wash the pan) and heat gently for 2–3 minutes until the sauce is hot. Tip the pasta back into the pan, crumble in the goat's cheese, add the basil leaves or rocket and toss together.

SWEET TREATS

JAM TARTS

👋 **HANDS-ON TIME:** 10 MINUTES, PLUS CHILLING 🍰 **COOKING TIME:** 12–15 MINUTES ✗ **SERVES:** 25

INGREDIENTS
½ × 500g pack shortcrust pastry
a little plain flour to dust
jam

PER SERVING
70 cals
3g fat (of which 1g saturates)
12g carbohydrate

METHOD
1 Roll out the pastry to a thickness of 5mm (¼in) on a lightly floured worksurface. Using a 5 × 5cm (2 × 2in) heart-shaped cutter, cut out 25 hearts. Put on a non-stick baking sheet. Put a smaller heart-shaped cutter on top of each to use as a mould and spread jam inside. Leave to chill for 30 minutes.
2 Preheat the oven to 200°C (180°C fan oven) mark 6. Bake the tarts for 12–15 minutes until golden. Leave to cool for 10 minutes. The tarts will keep in an airtight container for up to three days.

COOK'S TIP
Use jams in several different flavours to give a colourful array of tarts.

LEMON VODKA JELLY

👋 **HANDS-ON TIME:** 5 MINUTES, PLUS CHILLING 🍰 **COOKING TIME:** NONE ✗ **SERVES:** 4

INGREDIENTS
135g pack of lemon jelly, broken
  into pieces
300ml (10fl oz) boiling water
175ml (6fl oz) cold water
100ml (3½fl oz) lemon-flavoured
  vodka

PER SERVING
140 cals
0g fat
21g carbohydrate

METHOD
1 Chill four 150ml (5fl oz) wine glasses. Put the lemon jelly into a jug and pour over the boiling water. Stir until the jelly pieces dissolve.
2 Top up with the cold water and lemon-flavoured vodka. Stir, then divide among the chilled glasses and leave to chill overnight.
3 Leave the jellies to stand at room temperature for 30 minutes before serving (not suitable for children due to the alcohol content).

COOK'S TIP
Try this using different flavours of jelly and vodka.

EXOTIC BOOZY PANCAKES

✋ **HANDS-ON TIME:** 33 MINUTES   🍲 **COOKING TIME:** 14–20 MINUTES   ✖ **SERVES:** 6

METHOD

1   Put the fruit into a large frying pan. Add the rum, butter and sugar and cook over a low heat for 7–10 minutes until the fruit has thawed but isn't too soft. Remove the fruit with a slotted spoon, cover and set aside.
2   Bring the juice in the pan to the boil, then cook for 7–10 minutes until reduced to a syrupy consistency.
3   Meanwhile, heat the pancakes in the microwave on High for 1 minute (based on a 900W oven) or according to the pack instructions. Alternatively, wrap the pancakes in foil and steam over a pan of boiling water for 5 minutes until heated through.
4   Serve each pancake topped with fruit and drizzled with the syrup. Add a generous dollop of crème fraîche, then sprinkle a little nutmeg on top (not suitable for children due to the alcohol content).

INGREDIENTS

2 × 500g packs frozen tropical fruit
6 tbsp rum
50g (2oz) butter
2 tbsp golden caster sugar
6 ready-made pancakes
200ml tub crème fraîche
freshly grated nutmeg to serve

PER SERVING
470 cals
30g fat (of which 18g saturates)
39g carbohydrate

CHEAT'S RASPBERRY ICE CREAM

✋ **HANDS-ON TIME:** 5 MINUTES, PLUS FREEZING (OPTIONAL)   🍲 **COOKING TIME:** NONE   ✖ **SERVES:** 6

METHOD

1   Put six ramekins or freezerproof glasses into the freezer to chill. Put the still-frozen raspberries into a food processor with the icing sugar and whiz for 3–4 seconds until the raspberries look like large crumbs.
2   Add the double cream and whiz again for 10 seconds. Spoon into the ice-cold dishes and serve immediately or spoon into a small freezerproof container and freeze for 20–30 minutes. Serve with summer fruit, if you like.

COOK'S TIP

Depending on the sweetness of the raspberries, you may need to add a little more icing sugar – taste the mixture before you spoon the ice cream into the dishes.

INGREDIENTS

300g (11oz) frozen raspberries
5–6 tbsp golden icing sugar
284ml carton extra-thick double cream
summer fruit to serve (optional)

PER SERVING
410 cals
34g fat (of which 21g saturates)
26g carbohydrate

WHITE CHOCOLATE AND BERRY CREPES

HANDS-ON TIME: 2 MINUTES **COOKING TIME:** 10 MINUTES **SERVES:** 4

METHOD

1 Put the thawed berries into a large pan and cook over a medium heat for 5 minutes until heated through.

2 Meanwhile, put the chocolate and cream into a heatproof bowl, and set over a pan of simmering water, making sure the bottom of the bowl doesn't touch the hot water. Heat gently, stirring, for 5 minutes or until the chocolate has just melted. Remove the bowl from the pan and mix the chocolate and cream to a smooth sauce. Alternatively, microwave the chocolate and the cream together on High for 2–2½ minutes (based on a 900W oven), then stir until smooth.

3 Meanwhile, heat the crêpes according to the pack instructions.

4 To serve, put each crêpe on a warm plate and fold in half. Spoon a quarter of the berries into the middle of each, then fold the crêpe over the filling and pour the hot chocolate sauce over the top.

COOK'S TIP

Instead of mixed berries, try using just one type of berry.

INGREDIENTS

500g bag frozen mixed berries, thawed
100g (3½oz) good-quality white chocolate, broken into pieces
142ml carton double cream
4 thin ready-made pancakes

PER SERVING

480 cals
34g fat (of which 19g saturates)
40g carbohydrate

FOOD FOR FRIENDS

FILLET OF BEEF WITH ROQUEFORT AND CHESTNUTS

HANDS-ON TIME: 15 MINUTES **COOKING TIME:** 30 MINUTES **SERVES:** 6

INGREDIENTS

75g (3oz) Roquefort cheese, crumbled
75g (3oz) unsalted butter, softened
900g (2lb) fillet of beef
2 tbsp olive oil
50g (2oz) onions, chopped
5 tbsp port
300ml (10fl oz) beef stock
439g can whole chestnuts in water, drained
3 tbsp chopped fresh parsley
fresh flat-leafed parsley to garnish
green lentils tossed with baked shallots or button onions to serve

PER SERVING

470 cals
27g fat (of which 13g saturates)
21g carbohydrate

METHOD

1 Preheat the oven to 220°C (200°C fan oven) mark 7. Beat together the cheese and butter. Cover and leave to chill.

2 Tie the beef with fine string. Heat the oil in a frying pan, preferably non-stick. Add the beef and fry until well browned.

3 Put the beef on a wire rack standing over a roasting tin and roast in the oven for 30 minutes for rare, 35 minutes for medium rare and 40 minutes for well done.

4 Meanwhile, discard the fat from the frying pan. Add the onion, port and stock to the pan and boil until reduced by half.

5 Whisk in the Roquefort butter over a low heat until smooth. Adjust the seasoning and keep warm.

6 Toast the chestnuts for a few minutes until browned, then mix with the parsley.

7 Slice the beef to serve. Garnish with chestnuts and serve with the Roquefort sauce and green lentils tossed with baked shallots or button onions.

COOK'S TIP

The sweetness of port complements the tender fillet of beef better than red wine.

ROAST FILLET OF PORK WITH APRICOT AND ONION

HANDS-ON TIME: 10 MINUTES, PLUS MARINATING   **COOKING TIME:** 1 HOUR   **SERVES:** 4

METHOD

1 Put the pork in a non-metallic dish. Combine the soy sauce, wine, sherry, honey and thyme, season with pepper and spoon over the pork. Cover with clingfilm and leave to marinate in the fridge for at least 2 hours, preferably overnight.

2 Meanwhile, put the apricots and wine in a pan. Bring to the boil, cover and simmer for 20 minutes or until the apricots have softened. Strain, putting the liquid aside, and chop the apricots roughly.

3 Preheat the oven to 200°C (180°C fan oven) mark 6. Lift the pork from the marinade and set aside. Heat 1 tbsp oil in an ovenproof casserole. Add the meat and fry over a high heat until browned. Roast in the oven for 20 minutes or until cooked through.

4 Heat 1 tbsp oil in a sauté pan. Add the onion and cook, stirring, for 10–12 minutes until softened. Add the apricots. Keep warm.

5 When the meat is cooked, remove from the oven and keep warm. Add the marinade and reserved apricot juices to the meat juices in the casserole dish. Blend the cornflour with the cold water and stir into the sauce. Bring to the boil and cook over a medium heat, stirring, for 2 minutes until the sauce thickens.

6 Cut each pork fillet into slices 1cm (½in) thick. To serve, spoon a little apricot and onion mixture on to plates. Put the sliced pork fillet on top and pour a little sauce over it.

COOK'S TIPS

- There's no need to season with salt as the soy sauce is salty
- Serve a selection of green vegetables to accompany this dish - sugarsnap peas, broccoli and green beans would be a perfect combination.

INGREDIENTS

700g (1½lb) pork tenderloin, trimmed of excess fat
4 tbsp light soy sauce
150ml (5fl oz) red wine
4 tbsp dry sherry
1 tbsp runny honey
1 fresh thyme sprig or a pinch of dried thyme
75g (3oz) dried apricots
100ml (3½fl oz) white wine
2 tbsp olive oil
175g (6oz) onions, peeled and sliced
2 tsp cornflour
1 tbsp cold water

PER SERVING

430 cals
19g fat (of which 6g saturates)
18g carbohydrate

LEMON-ROASTED PORK WITH GARLIC AND BASIL

INGREDIENTS

2 pork tenderloins, about 350g (12oz) each, trimmed
finely grated zest and juice of 2 lemons, sieved
6 tbsp freshly chopped basil or parsley
12 garlic cloves, blanched and halved if large
2–3 bay leaves
2 tbsp oil
sautéed shallots to serve
fresh herbs and lemon slices to garnish

PER SERVING

180 cals
9g fat (of which 3g saturates)
trace carbohydrate

METHOD

1   Split the pork lengthways without cutting right through, and open each piece out flat. Sprinkle with the lemon zest and basil. Lay the garlic cloves evenly along the middle of each fillet and season with salt and pepper.

2   Close the pork and tie loosely at 2.5cm (1in) intervals with string. Put in a shallow, non-metallic dish with the bay leaves and sieved lemon juice. Cover and leave to marinate in the fridge overnight.

3   Preheat the oven to 200°C (180°C fan oven) mark 6. Remove the pork and put the marinade aside. Heat the oil in a sauté pan. Add the meat and fry until browned. Transfer to a shallow roasting tin with the marinade. Season the pork and cook in the oven for 35 minutes, basting frequently. Serve sliced, garnished with herbs and lemon slices, and with sautéed shallots.

MARINATED LAMB FILLETS WITH HONEY AND LEMON COUSCOUS

HANDS-ON TIME: 40 MINUTES, PLUS MARINATING   **COOKING TIME:** 1 HOUR 20 MINUTES   **SERVES:** 4–6

INGREDIENTS

4 best end of neck lamb fillets,
   about 1kg (2¼lb) total weight
   (see Cook's Tip), trimmed of
   any fat
2 fresh rosemary sprigs
454g tub thick Greek yogurt
3 garlic cloves
300g (11oz) soft goat's cheese
6 tbsp freshly chopped mint
250ml (8fl oz) olive oil
1 aubergine, about 300g (11oz),
   chopped
275g (10oz) onions, chopped
2 fennel bulbs, 300g (11oz) total
   weight, chopped
1 cucumber, halved, deseeded and
   chopped
275g (10oz) plum tomatoes, peeled
   (optional) and chopped
4 tbsp runny honey
4 tbsp white wine vinegar
3 tbsp lemon juice
225g (8oz) couscous
450ml (15fl oz) water
6 tbsp freshly chopped parsley

PER SERVING
1310–880 cals
81–54g fat (of which 30–20g saturates)
67–47g carbohydrate

METHOD

1 Put the lamb in a bowl with the rosemary. Whiz the yogurt, garlic and cheese in a food processor until smooth. Season with salt and pepper and stir in the mint. Mix 4 tbsp yogurt mixture with 6 tbsp oil and spread over the lamb. Leave to marinate in the fridge for at least 6 hours or overnight. Put the remaining yogurt mixture in the fridge.

2 Heat 6 tbsp oil in a non-stick frying pan. Add the aubergine and onion and cook over a high heat, stirring, for 10 minutes or until soft and golden. Leave to cool in a bowl. Add the fennel to a pan of boiling salted water, bring back to the boil and cook for 1 minute. Drain, refresh in cold water and drain again. Stir into the aubergine mixture.

3 Put the honey in a small pan, bring to the boil and cook for 2 minutes or until caramelized. Add the vinegar, bring to the boil and bubble for 1 minute. Take the pan off the heat, and stir in the remaining oil, lemon juice and seasoning. Put the couscous and 2 tsp salt in a bowl, add the water and leave to stand for 15–20 minutes. Break up any lumps, put in a steamer lined with a J-cloth set over a pan of boiling water. Cover and steam for 10 minutes, then stir into the aubergine mixture together with the honey dressing.

4 Stir the tomatoes, cucumber and parsley into the couscous and adjust the seasoning.

5 Preheat the grill. Put the lamb (at room temperature) on a foil-lined grill pan and cook for 6–7 minutes on each side. Pour over any cooking juices then leave to rest for 10 minutes. Carve into thin slices and serve with couscous and the reserved yogurt sauce.

COOK'S TIP
If you can't find fillet, buy 4 racks of lamb and cut out the eye of the meat in four long strips.

RABBIT BAKED WITH WINE AND PRUNES

HANDS-ON TIME: 20 MINUTES, PLUS SOAKING   **COOKING TIME:** 1¼ HOURS   **SERVES:** 6

METHOD

1 Put the prunes and wine in a bowl. Cover and leave to soak for about 4 hours.

2 Preheat the oven to 170°C (150°C fan oven) mark 3. Heat 3 tbsp oil in a flameproof casserole and fry the rabbit joints in batches until browned, then remove from the casserole. Add the onion and garlic, with a little more oil if you need to, and cook until lightly browned.

3 Put all the rabbit back in the casserole, add the Armagnac and warm. Light carefully with a taper or long match. Shake the pan gently until the flames subside.

4 Strain the prunes and put to one side. Add the wine and the stock to the casserole and bring to the boil. Tie the sprigs of thyme together and add to casserole with the bay leaves and plenty of seasoning. Cover with a tight-fitting lid and cook in the oven for about 1 hour or until tender.

5 Lift the rabbit out of the juices and keep warm. Boil the cooking juices until reduced by about half. Add the cream and mushrooms and continue boiling for 2–3 minutes. Stir in the prunes and warm through. Adjust the seasoning and spoon the sauce over the rabbit to serve. Garnish with fresh thyme sprigs.

TO FREEZE

■ Cool, pack and freeze at end of step 3. Pack and freeze the prunes separately.

■ To use, thaw both overnight at a cool room temperature. Bring to the boil then simmer for about 15 minutes or until piping hot. Complete the recipe.

INGREDIENTS

175g (6oz) pitted prunes
300ml (10fl oz) red wine
olive oil
1 large onion, peeled and chopped
2 large garlic cloves, crushed
about 2.3kg (5lb) rabbit joints
75ml (2½fl oz) Armagnac
450ml (15fl oz) light stock
a few fresh thyme sprigs or 1 tsp
   dried thyme
2 bay leaves
125g (4oz) brown-cap mushrooms,
   sliced
142ml carton double cream
fresh thyme sprigs to garnish

PER SERVING
410 cals
19g fat (of which 10g saturates)
15g carbohydrate

DUCK TERRINE WITH APPLE, APRICOT AND BRANDY

HANDS-ON TIME: 1½ HOURS, PLUS MARINATING   **COOKING TIME:** 2¼ HOURS, PLUS CHILLING   **SERVES:** 15

INGREDIENTS

50g (2oz) pitted prunes, roughly chopped (see Cook's Tips)

50g (2oz) ready-to-eat dried apricots, roughly chopped (see Cook's Tips)

6 tbsp brandy

350g (12oz) turkey breast fillet, cut into 2.5cm (1in) cubes

800g (1¾lb) duck breasts, skinned – there should be 500g (1lb 2oz) meat

a few fresh thyme sprigs

225g (8oz) shallots or onions, peeled and roughly chopped

350g (12oz) eating apples, peeled, cored and chopped

50g (2oz) butter

225g (8oz) minced pork

2 tbsp freshly chopped thyme

1 egg, beaten

50g (2oz) shelled pistachio nuts

PER SLICE

190 cals

10g fat (of which 6g saturates)

11g carbohydrate

METHOD

1   The day before, put the prunes and apricots in a bowl with 4 tbsp brandy, cover and leave to soak overnight. Put the turkey and duck in a roasting tin with the thyme sprigs and remaining brandy, then cover and leave to marinate in the fridge overnight.

2   Heat the butter in a pan. Add the shallots and cook for 10 minutes or until soft. Stir in the apple, then cover and cook for 5–10 minutes until soft. Set aside to cool.

3   Preheat the oven to 180°C (160°C fan oven) mark 4. Remove the turkey from the marinade and put in a food processor with the minced pork and the apple mixture. Whiz to a rough purée, then combine with the chopped thyme, egg, marinated fruits and pistachio nuts. Season well with salt and pepper (see Cook's Tips).

4   Remove the duck from the marinade and put between sheets of greaseproof paper. Flatten gently with a rolling pin until 1cm (½in) thick.

5   Baseline a 1.2 litre (2 pint) terrine or loaf tin with greaseproof paper or foil. Put a duck breast in the base of the terrine to cover it evenly with no gaps. Spread over half of the stuffing, then repeat the process, finishing with a layer of duck.

6   Cover with foil and put in a roasting tin. Add enough hot water to come three-quarters of the way up the sides of the terrine and cook in the oven for 2–2¼ hours until the juices run clear when tested with a skewer. Transfer to a wire rack, cover with a weighted board and, when cool, leave to chill for 6 hours or overnight.

7   Run a knife around the terrine and turn out on to a board. Remove the greaseproof paper and carve into thin slices. Serve with a red onion chutney.

COOK'S TIPS

■   Try this with other dried fruit, such as dried cherries. You'll need 125g (4oz) in lace of the prunes and apricots.

■   Season the stuffing with ½ tsp salt to ensure it has a really good flavour.

VENISON AND CHESTNUT CASSEROLE

✋ **HANDS-ON TIME:** 20 MINUTES　🍲 **COOKING TIME:** 2¾ HOURS　✗ **SERVES:** 8

METHOD

1　Preheat the oven to 170°C (150°C fan oven) mark 3. Heat the oil and butter in a large flameproof casserole and fry the meat in batches until browned, adding more oil if you need to. Lift the meat out of the casserole using a slotted spoon.

2　Add the carrots, onions, celery and garlic to the casserole and cook until lightly browned. Mix in the flour and cook for 1 minute, then stir in the stock, sherry, pared lemon zest and sieved juice, and the bay leaves. Bring to the boil, put the meat back into the casserole and season with salt and pepper. Cover tightly and cook in the oven for 1½ hours.

3　Stir in the apricots, re-cover and cook for a further 1 hour or until the meat is quite tender.

4　Stir in the chestnuts and brandy and simmer for 5 minutes. Adjust the seasoning and garnish with chopped parsley.

TO FREEZE

- Cool, pack and freeze at the end of step 3.
- To use, thaw overnight at a cool room temperature. Bring the casserole to the boil. Complete the recipe.

COOK'S TIPS

- Casserole venison comes from the shoulder, while haunch is cut from the leg.
- Trim off any fat from the venison as it has an unpleasant taste.

INGREDIENTS

about 3 tbsp oil
50g (2oz) butter
700g (1½lb) lean casserole or haunch of venison, trimmed and cut into 4cm (1½in) chunks
700g (1½lb) lean stewing beef, trimmed and cut into 4cm (1½in) chunks
350g (12oz) carrots, peeled and sliced
450g (1lb) onions, peeled and chopped
350g (12oz) celery, trimmed and sliced
2 large garlic cloves, crushed
4 tbsp plain flour
1.2 litres (2 pints) beef stock
300ml (10fl oz) dry sherry
pared zest and sieved juice of 1 lemon
2 bay leaves
75g (3oz) ready-to-eat dried apricots
439g can whole chestnuts in water, drained
2 tbsp brandy
freshly chopped parsley to garnish

PER SERVING

470 cals
17g fat (of which 7g saturates)
31g carbohydrate

SALMON EN CROUTE

✋ **HANDS-ON TIME:** 30 MINUTES, PLUS MARINATING   🍲 **COOKING TIME:** 1 HOUR   ✖ **SERVES:** 8

METHOD

1 Mix 3 tbsp orange juice with the pepper and the chopped dill. Rub the mixture into the salmon flesh. Sandwich the two salmon fillets together and put in a non-metallic dish. Cover and leave to marinate for at least 1 hour.

2 Preheat the oven to 200°C (180°C fan oven) mark 6. Roll out half the pastry, thinly, to a rectangle measuring 38 × 20cm (15 × 8in) on a lightly floured worksurface. Put on a large baking sheet and prick all over with a fork. Bake in the oven for about 15 minutes or until golden brown and cooked through. Leave to cool on a wire rack.

3 Meanwhile, squeeze all the excess liquid from the thawed spinach. Mix the spinach with the soft cheese and season to taste with salt and pepper. Heat the butter in a small pan. Add the spring onions and sauté for 3–4 minutes until just beginning to soften. Leave to cool, then stir in the prawns and orange zest. Season to taste.

4 Preheat the oven again to 200°C (180°C fan oven) mark 6. Put the cooked pastry back on the baking sheet and put a fish fillet on top, skinned-side down. Trim the pastry, allowing a border of 1cm (½in) all round. Spread the spinach mixture over the fish, then spoon the prawn mixture on top. Cover with the remaining fillet of salmon, skinned-side up. Instead of making one large Salmon en Croute you can make smaller parcels as shown in the picture.

5 Brush the cooked pastry edge with egg. Roll out the remaining pastry thinly and put over the fish to enclose completely. Trim off most of the excess pastry and set aside, leaving about 2.5cm (1in) to tuck under all round. Decorate with a pastry lattice cut from the trimmings.

6 Glaze all over with egg. Make two small holes in the pastry to allow steam to escape and bake in the oven for 40–45 minutes until the pastry is well-risen and golden brown. Serve warm, garnished with dill sprigs and orange slices.

INGREDIENTS

- coarsely grated zest and juice of 1 orange
- 1 tsp coarsely ground pepper
- 1 tbsp freshly chopped dill or 2 tsp dried
- 1 salmon or sea trout, about 1.6–1.8kg (3½–4lb), cleaned, skinned and filleted, about 900g (2lb) filleted weight
- 700g (1½lb) puff pastry, thawed if frozen
- a little plain flour to dust
- 350g (12oz) frozen chopped spinach, thawed
- 125g (4oz) full-fat soft cheese
- 25g (1oz) butter or margarine
- 125g (4oz) spring onions, trimmed and chopped
- 125g (4oz) cooked, peeled prawns
- 1 egg, beaten
- fresh dill sprigs to garnish
- orange slices to garnish

PER SERVING
670 cals
46g fat (of which 19g saturates)
35g carbohydrate

GRILLED TURBOT WITH CHERVIL AND TOMATO SAUCE

HANDS-ON TIME: 20 MINUTES   **COOKING TIME:** 10–12 MINUTES   **SERVES:** 4

INGREDIENTS

300ml (10fl oz) milk
1 onion slice
1 mace blade
4–6 black peppercorns
2 tomatoes
25g (1oz) butter
15g (½oz) plain flour
1 tsp tomato purée
about 4 tbsp freshly chopped
   chervil
4 turbot steaks, about 175g (6oz)
   each
lemon juice to taste
fresh chervil to garnish

PER SERVING

230 cals
8g fat (of which 4g saturates)
8g carbohydrate

METHOD

1 Put the milk in a small pan with the onion, mace and peppercorns and bring to the boil. Remove from the heat and leave to infuse for 10 minutes. Sieve.

2 Immerse the tomatoes in boiling water for 15–30 seconds, then remove and peel away the skins. Cut the flesh into strips, discarding the seeds.

3 Heat 15g (½oz) butter in a small pan. Stir in the flour and cook for 1 minute. Take the pan off the heat and gradually stir in the sieved milk. Season with salt and pepper.

4 Put the pan back on the heat and bring to the boil, stirring all the time, then simmer gently for a few minutes. Whisk in the tomato purée and the chervil.

5 Meanwhile, preheat the grill. Heat the remaining butter. Halve the turbot steaks, brush with melted butter and cook under the grill for 5–6 minutes on each side.

6 Add the tomato strips to the sauce. Reheat gently, stirring in some lemon juice to taste. Garnish the turbot with chervil and serve with the tomato sauce.

EXOTIC CHICKEN

✋ **HANDS-ON TIME:** 20 MINUTES   🍲 **COOKING TIME:** 1¾ HOURS   ✗ **SERVES:** 6

METHOD

1 Preheat the oven to 200°C (180°C fan oven) mark 6. Cut two pieces of non-stick baking parchment, each measuring about 75 × 40cm (30 × 16in). Sprinkle each with water to dampen slightly, then put one on top of the other.

2 Combine the chilli, ginger, lemongrass, kaffir lime leaves, some grated lime zest and the garlic with the coriander. Pile in the centre of the baking parchment. Season inside the chicken generously with salt and pepper, scatter over the rest of the grated lime zest and put the chicken on top of the fresh spices.

3 Mix the chilli sauce with 1 tbsp oil and brush all over the chicken. Bring the edges of the baking parchment together and tie at the top with string to encase the chicken completely. Put in a roasting tin just large enough to hold the parcel and cook in the oven for 1 hour 40 minutes.

4 Mix the remaining oil with the turmeric and potatoes in a roasting tin and toss well to coat evenly. Put on a tray above the chicken for the last 40 minutes of the cooking time. Roast until golden and tender. Add the desiccated coconut to the potatoes and stir to coat evenly. Put back in the oven and cook for a further 5 minutes or until the coconut has turned golden. Keep warm.

5 Untie the parchment and allow any juices inside the chicken to run into a pan. Lift the chicken out and add as much of the flavouring ingredients as possible to the pan. Cover the chicken with foil and keep warm in a low oven. Add the lime juice to the pan and bring to the boil. Bubble furiously for 1 minute. Keep hot.

6 Carve the chicken and serve with the roast potatoes and cooking juices. Garnish with fresh coriander.

INGREDIENTS

1 large red chilli, deseeded and finely chopped
2.5cm (1in) piece fresh root ginger, peeled and thinly sliced
10cm (4in) piece lemongrass, cut into thin matchstick strips
2 kaffir lime leaves (or a little extra grated lime zest), cut into thin matchstick strips
grated zest of 1 lime
2 garlic bulbs, halved
2 tbsp freshly chopped coriander
1.8kg (4lb) oven-ready chicken
1 tbsp chilli sauce
3 tbsp oil, such as grapeseed
1 tsp ground turmeric
800g (1¾lb) baby new potatoes
3 tbsp desiccated coconut
juice of 2 limes
fresh coriander to garnish

PER SERVING
370 cals
17g fat (of which 6g saturates)
22g carbohydrate

CHICKEN TABBOULEH WITH TOMATO DRESSING

HANDS-ON TIME: 50 MINUTES, PLUS MARINATING AND SOAKING   **COOKING TIME:** 45 MINUTES   **SERVES:** 4

METHOD

1   Put the chilli in a non-metallic bowl with the garlic, 3 tbsp lime juice, turmeric and lightly scored chicken. Toss and leave to marinate in the fridge for at least 3 hours.

2   Mix the tomatoes with the capers, 2 tbsp lime juice, the sugar and seasoning.

3   Put the bulgur wheat in a bowl, then cover with the boiling water. Leave to soak for 30 minutes. Drain, then stir in the cucumber, pinenuts, herbs, raisins, remaining lime juice and 3 tbsp oil. Season.

4   Preheat the oven to 240°C (220°C fan oven) mark 9. Drain the chicken, putting the marinade to one side. Put, skin-side up, in a roasting tin with the remaining oil and onions. Cook in the oven for 30–35 minutes until done. Set aside. Add the tomato mixture and remaining marinade to the roasting tin and put back in the oven for 5 minutes.

5   Spoon the dressing over the chicken. Garnish with lime slices and parsley, if you like, and serve at room temperature with the tabbouleh.

COOK'S TIP

Bulgur wheat is grains of wheat that have been boiled until they crack, and then dried. It is reconstituted in water.

INGREDIENTS

1 large red chilli, deseeded and
   finely chopped
3 garlic cloves, crushed
juice of 4 limes: about 8 tbsp juice
½ tsp ground turmeric
4 chicken breast quarters (breast
   and wing), about 300g (11oz)
   each, lightly scored
125g (4oz) cucumber, chopped
450g (1lb) tomatoes, preferably
   plum, chopped
2 tbsp capers
1 tbsp sugar
225g (8oz) bulgur wheat
600ml (1 pint) boiling water
225g (8oz) onions, peeled and thinly
   sliced
50g (2oz) pinenuts, toasted
3 tbsp freshly chopped parsley
3 tbsp freshly chopped chives
50g (2oz) raisins
5 tbsp olive oil
lime slices to garnish
fresh flat-leafed parsley to garnish

PER SERVING

800 cals
34g fat (of which 6g saturates)
64g carbohydrate

PEPPERED CHICKEN WITH ORANGE

✋ **HANDS-ON TIME:** 5 MINUTES   🍲 **COOKING TIME:** 25 MINUTES   ✗ **SERVES:** 6

INGREDIENTS

6 chicken breast fillets with skin
1 tbsp olive oil
125g (4oz) butter, chilled
125g (4oz) onions, peeled and finely
   chopped
2 tsp peppercorns in brine
200ml (7fl oz) brandy
450ml (15fl oz) chicken stock
pared zest and juice of 1 large
   orange
fresh flat-leafed parsley sprigs to
   garnish
freshly cooked potatoes of your
   choice to serve

PER SERVING OF SAUCE ONLY

500 cals
38g fat (of which 18g saturates)
3g carbohydrate

METHOD

1   Preheat the oven to 180°C (160°C fan oven) mark 4. Season the chicken with plenty of pepper.

2   Heat the oil in a non-stick frying pan. Add the chicken breasts and cook for about 5 minutes until golden. Put the chicken in an ovenproof dish and cook in the oven for about 20 minutes until done.

3   Meanwhile, heat 25g (1oz) of the butter in the pan. Add the onion and peppercorns and cook, stirring, for 10 minutes until golden and soft. Add the brandy and bubble to reduce by half. Add the stock, pared orange zest and juice. Bubble again to reduce by half (about 7 minutes).

4   Dice the remaining butter and add a little at a time, whisking after each addition. Season with salt and pepper and keep warm.

5   Pour the sauce over the cooked chicken, garnish with parsley and serve with potatoes.

COOKING FOR A CROWD

PLANNING A PARTY

- Whatever type of party you're going to have, make sure your plans are feasible for the space available.
- Set a budget, including food, drink and all the little extras.
- Is it better to serve a cold buffet, a sit-down meal or just canapés?
- If you opt for a buffet, consider the age of your guests. Elderly people who find balancing plates and glasses difficult will prefer to sit down. Ensure that you have enough seats.
- When selecting the food, think about how you will cook, store and reheat it. Are your pans or casseroles big enough? Is your fridge/oven big enough? Ask neighbours and friends for the use of theirs if practical.
- Check that you have enough crockery, cutlery, glasses, serving dishes, etc.
- Enlist the help of all the family: give everyone a task both before and during the event.

After you've decided what type of party you're having, here are ways to ensure the party goes without a hitch:

- Make a work plan for the day and try to keep to it – for example, which drinks to serve and the time the food is to be served, what time the cake will be cut.
- On the day, allow yourself plenty of time to cook or reheat food, and to arrange platters of cold food. Always recruit plenty of helpers to avoid a last-minute panic.
- Keep cold food tightly covered until it's served.
- Never leave food in a hot room or marquee before serving – keep it chilled for as long as possible.

DRINKS TIPS

- Order wine online.
- If you're serving a welcoming glass of fizz, try a sparkling wine. Top up with cassis for Kir Royale.
- Put wine bottles in bin liners (to protect labels) and chill in buckets of ice and water – this is quicker than using the fridge.
- To check for corked wine, pour some into a glass, swirl and inhale. If it smells musty and 'off', pop the cork back in and return the wine to the shop.
- Buy a selection of fruit juices and fizzy water to make a non-alcoholic fruit punch.

CANAPES

Home-made canapés taste so much better than those from a shop – and they cost less, too. Your guests will notice the difference and really appreciate your efforts. Nibbles look best on large serving dishes with no more than two varieties on each. Hand round napkins at the same time.

For pre-supper canapés with drinks, allow about five bites per head. If serving canapés throughout the evening, allow at least ten per person, including two or three sweet ones. However, if you want to make only a few canapés, you can bulk things out with these simple additions:

FLAVOURED OLIVES Serve with cocktail sticks so they are easy to eat.
MINI PRETZELS These are really moreish.
SLICES OF PARMA HAM Wrap round the end of breadsticks; serve with extra-virgin olive oil for dipping.
FRENCH STICK Slice, then spread with black olive paste and top with a slice of goat's cheese.

SAUSAGE AND SAGE ROLLS

HANDS-ON TIME: 20 MINUTES **COOKING TIME:** 25 MINUTES **MAKES:** 24

INGREDIENTS

6 good-quality pork sausages
a little plain flour to dust
375g pack ready-rolled shortcrust
  pastry
1 egg, beaten with a pinch of salt
36–48 fresh sage leaves

PER SERVING

120 cals
9g fat (of which 3g saturates)
9g carbohydrate

METHOD

1 Slit the sausage skins and remove the meat. Put it into a bowl and mix it well, using your hands.

2 Dust a clean worksurface with a little flour and roll out the pastry slightly, until it's about 1cm (½in) bigger. Cut in half lengthways to make two long strips. Position one strip so that the longest edge is nearest to you.

3 Dust your hands with flour. Take half the sausagemeat and roll it into a long sausage, then lay it down the middle of one pastry strip. Brush a little egg along the long edge of the pastry furthest away from you. Take the near edge and roll it over the sausagemeat to give a neat roll. Trim the long and short edges with a sharp knife, then cut the roll into 5cm (2in) pieces. Repeat with the rest of the pastry and sausagemeat.

4 Brush each roll with egg, put one or two sage leaves on top, then brush again. Put on a baking sheet and leave to chill for 15 minutes. Preheat the oven to 200°C (180°C fan oven) mark 6.

5 Bake the sausage rolls for 25 minutes until they're crispy and golden.

RED PEPPER PESTO CROUTONS

HANDS-ON TIME: 20 MINUTES ⚫ **COOKING TIME:** 15–20 MINUTES ✖ **MAKES:** 24 ✓

METHOD

1 Preheat the oven to 200°C (180°C fan oven) mark 6. Brush both sides of the bread with olive oil and put on a baking sheet. Cook in the oven for 15–20 minutes.
2 Spread 1 tsp pesto on each crouton, top with a pepper strip and a pinenut.

COOK'S TIP

To make pesto, roughly chop 75g (3oz) basil, 50g (2oz) Parmesan cheese, 25g (1oz) pinenuts, and ½ crushed garlic clove in a food processor. With the motor running, add 50–75ml (2–3fl oz) extra-virgin olive oil to make a paste. Season well with salt and pepper.

INGREDIENTS

1 thin French stick, sliced into
   24 rounds
ready-made pesto (see Cook's Tip)
4 pepper pieces (from a jar of
   marinated peppers), each sliced
   into 6 strips
24 pinenuts to garnish

PER SERVING
80 cals
4g fat (of which 1g saturates)
9g carbohydrate

BEEF AND PARMA HAM BITES

HANDS-ON TIME: 15 MINUTES, PLUS RESTING ⚫ **COOKING TIME:** 11–13 MINUTES ✖ **MAKES:** 24

METHOD

1 Brush a little oil over the surface of the griddle pan, then heat until hot. Season the steak all over with salt and pepper and cook for 3 minutes on each side to seal in all the juices. Leave to rest for 5 minutes. Preheat the oven to 200°C (180°C fan oven) mark 6 and lightly oil a baking sheet.
2 Slice the steak into four lengths, then cut each into six pieces. Put a small basil leaf on top of each piece, then wrap a strip of ham around each bit of steak. Put the bites on the prepared baking sheet and roast for 5–7 minutes until just cooked through.
3 Meanwhile, push a basil leaf and one of the sunblush tomatoes on each cocktail stick. Take the baking sheet out of the oven and push a cocktail stick halfway into each piece of beef, making sure the sharp end of the stick doesn't protrude. Put on to platters and serve warm.

INGREDIENTS

a little olive oil
350g (12oz) fillet steak, about 2cm
   (1¾in) thick
48 fresh basil leaves
6 slices Parma ham, cut into
   4 strips lengthways
24 sunblush tomatoes

PER SERVING
40 cals
2g fat (of which 1g saturates)
2g carbohydrate

MINI POPPADUMS WITH AUBERGINE PURÉE

HANDS-ON TIME: 5 MINUTES, PLUS COOLING   **COOKING TIME:** ABOUT 1 HOUR   **SERVES:** 8   V

METHOD

1 Preheat the oven to 200°C (180°C) mark 6. Pierce the aubergines several times with a small, sharp knife, put on a baking sheet and cook in the oven for about 1 hour or until very soft. Leave to cool.

2 Peel the aubergines. Wrap the flesh in a clean cloth and squeeze to remove any excess juice. Add the garlic, tahini and lemon juice and mash well with a fork or whiz in a processor. Stir in the chopped coriander and enough water to give a dipping consistency. Season with salt and pepper.

3 Put a little purée on each of the poppadums and garnish with paprika and coriander sprigs. For fewer calories, serve the purée with crudités instead.

COOK'S TIP

Tahini is a thick creamy paste that is made from ground sesame seeds. Look out for it in good supermarkets and healthfood shops.

INGREDIENTS

2 large aubergines
1–2 garlic cloves, crushed
1 tbsp tahini (see Cook's Tip)
juice of ½ lemon
3 tbsp freshly chopped coriander, plus extra sprigs to garnish
1 pack mini poppadums (40 in pack)
paprika to garnish

PER SERVING

160 cals
2g fat (of which trace saturates)
25g carbohydrate

SPICY RED PEPPER DIP

HANDS-ON TIME: 5 MINUTES, PLUS CHILLING   **COOKING TIME:** 20 MINUTES   **SERVES:** 8   V

METHOD

1 Preheat the grill. Put the peppers under the hot grill until the skin has blackened and the flesh becomes soft. Cover the peppers with a clean wet cloth or put them in a polythene bag to allow them to steam for 5 minutes. This helps loosen the skin.

2 Peel and deseed the peppers, then put the flesh in a food processor or blender with all the remaining ingredients. Whiz until smooth. Cover and leave to chill for at least 2 hours to let the flavours develop. Adjust the seasoning, if you need to. Serve with a selection of crudités.

INGREDIENTS

3 large red peppers, about 450g (1lb) total weight, halved
200g tub reduced-fat soft cheese
½ tsp hot pepper sauce
a selection of vegetable crudités to serve

PER SERVING

60 cals
4g fat (of which 2g saturates)
3g carbohydrate

GRAVADLAX ON RYE BREAD

HANDS-ON TIME: 15 MINUTES   **COOKING TIME:** NONE   **MAKES:** 32   V

INGREDIENTS
4 slices rye bread
2 x 140g packs gravadlax with
    mustard and dill sauce (minimum
    4 large slices)
juice of 1 lemon
fresh dill sprigs to garnish

PER SERVING
30 cals
1g fat (of which trace saturates)
2g carbohydrate

METHOD
1   Spread the bread with the mustard and dill sauce. You may not
    need it all. Cut each slice lengthways into four strips, then
    widthways in half to make eight pieces.
2   Cut the gravadlax into strips and crumple a strip over each piece
    of rye bread. Cover with clingfilm. Just before serving, squeeze
    over a little lemon juice on top, season with pepper and garnish
    with a dill sprig.

MINI YORKSHIRES WITH STEAK AND HORSERADISH

HANDS-ON TIME: 20 MINUTES   **COOKING TIME:** 10 MINUTES   **MAKES:** 24

INGREDIENTS
1 tbsp sunflower oil
300g (11oz) rump steak
2 x 120g packs mini Yorkshire
    puddings
6 tbsp crème fraîche
1 tbsp horseradish
watercress sprigs to garnish

PER SERVING
60 cals
4g fat (of which 2g saturates)
3g carbohydrate

METHOD
1   Preheat the oven to 200°C (180°C fan oven) mark 6. Heat the oil in
    a frying pan. Add the steak and sear over a medium-high heat to
    brown on both sides. For rare steak, slice into 24 pieces now; for
    medium rare, reduce the heat and cook for a further 3 minutes
    (5 minutes for well done) before slicing. These timings are only a
    rough guide.
2   Meanwhile, put the Yorkshire puddings in a roasting tin and heat in
    the oven for 10 minutes.
3   Mix together the crème fraîche and horseradish. Arrange the steak
    on the puddings and top with the horseradish cream. Season with
    pepper and garnish each pudding with a watercress sprig.

AMARETTI WITH LEMON MASCARPONE

👋 **HANDS-ON TIME:** 15 MINUTES 🍰 **COOKING TIME:** 5 MINUTES ✕ **MAKES:** 12

METHOD

1 Put the lemon juice in a small pan. Add the sugar and dissolve over a low heat. Add the lemon peel and cook for 1–2 minutes. It will curl up. Lift out, using a slotted spoon, and put on a sheet of baking parchment, setting aside the syrup. Sprinkle with golden caster sugar to coat.

2 Beat the mascarpone in a bowl to soften, then stir in the sugar syrup.

3 Crush one of the amaretti biscuits and put to one side, ready to dust.

4 Put a blob of mascarpone on each remaining amaretti biscuit, then top with a couple of strips of the crystallized lemon zest. Sprinkle over the crushed amaretti crumbs.

COOK'S TIP

If you're short of time, buy a pack of crystallized lemon slices and use these to decorate the amaretti biscuits. Alternatively, you can simply decorate each biscuit with a little finely grated lemon zest.

INGREDIENTS

juice of ¼ lemon
pared peel of ¼ lemon, white skin removed, finely sliced into long strips
1 tbsp golden caster sugar, plus a little extra to sprinkle
50g (2oz) mascarpone cheese
13 single amaretti biscuits

PER SERVING

50 cals
2g fat (of which 1g saturates)
7g carbohydrate

CHOCOLATE AND GINGER TRUFFLES

👋 **HANDS-ON TIME:** 10 MINUTES, PLUS CHILLING 🍰 **COOKING TIME:** 3 MINUTES ✕ **MAKES:** 12

METHOD

1 Pour the cream into a small pan and bring to the boil. Turn off the heat and add the chocolate. Stir to mix everything together. Pour into a bowl and leave to cool, then chill for 2 hours.

2 Put a 1cm (½in) nozzle into a piping bag and spoon in the chocolate ganache. Arrange 12 ginger slices on a tray and pipe a blob of ganache on to each. Put to one side. You can freeze any leftover ganache and use to make more truffles.

3 Thinly slice the remaining pieces of ginger and use to decorate the top of each chocolate truffle. Leave to chill overnight. Remove from the fridge 10–15 minutes before serving.

INGREDIENTS

142ml carton double cream
125g (4oz) plain chocolate, roughly chopped
15 slices crystallized ginger

PER SERVING

120 cals
9g fat (of which 5g saturates)
10g carbohydrate

BISTRO BEEF IN BEER

🖐 **HANDS-ON TIME:** 30–40 MINUTES   ♨ **COOKING TIME:** 3–4 HOURS   ✕ **SERVES:** 10

INGREDIENTS

4 tbsp olive oil
1.5kg (3lb 3½oz) chuck steak, cut
    into bite-size pieces
450g (1lb) button onions or
    shallots, peeled and left whole
3 fat garlic cloves, crushed
2 tbsp demerara sugar
350g (12oz) shiitake mushrooms
2 tbsp each plain flour and English
    mustard powder
450ml (15fl oz) Continental-style
    beer
a few fresh thyme sprigs
2 bay leaves

For the gremolata topping

80g pack flat-leafed parsley,
    chopped
coarsely grated rind of 2 oranges,
    plus juice of 1 orange
50g (2oz) walnut pieces, toasted
    and roughly chopped
2 red onions, peeled and very finely
    chopped

PER SERVING
300 cals
15g fat (of which 4g saturates)
14g carbohydrate

METHOD

1   Preheat the oven to 150°C (130°C fan oven) mark 2. Heat half the olive oil in a large flameproof casserole until sizzling. Brown the meat, a few pieces at a time, adding the remaining oil if needed. Be careful not to overcrowd the pan or the meat will stew rather than brown. Every piece should be dark brown – the colour adds richness to the final flavour. Transfer each batch of meat to a plate while you brown the remainder.

2   Add the onions to the pan and cook over a medium heat, stirring constantly, for 5 minutes or until they're beginning to soften and colour. Add the garlic and sugar and fry for 4–5 minutes or until the onions are soft and caramelized. Add the mushrooms and cook for 2–3 minutes.

3   Turn the heat down and return all the meat and any juices to the casserole. Add the flour, mustard and plenty of seasoning, and stir in with a wooden spoon. Gradually pour in the beer, stirring as you go. Bring slowly to a gentle simmer, add the thyme and bay leaves and cover with a tight-fitting lid.

4   Put the casserole in the oven and cook for 3–3½ hours. The beef should be tender and the sauce dark and rich. Season to taste.

5   Mix all the gremolata ingredients. Serve separately to scatter over the stew.

OVEN-BAKED CRUSTY POTATOES

✋ **HANDS-ON TIME:** 15 MINUTES ♨ **COOKING TIME:** 1 HOUR–1¼ HOURS ✗ **SERVES:** 10

METHOD

1 Preheat the oven to 180°C (160°C fan oven) mark 4. Drain the potatoes, put back into the bowl and add the onions.

2 Add all but a tablespoonful of the rosemary leaves to the potatoes and onions and stir to mix well. Season with salt and pepper.

3 Use a little of the melted butter to brush over the bottom and sides of two large shallow gratin dishes, then divide the potato mixture between the two.

4 Whisk together the stock and mustard and pour over the potatoes. Mix the cheese with the breadcrumbs, reserved rosemary and remaining melted butter. Scatter over the potatoes, then season.

5 Cook on the highest oven shelf for 1–1¼ hours until the top is crisp and golden.

INGREDIENTS

8 large baking potatoes, unpeeled, thinly sliced into rounds and dropped into a bowl of cold water

3 medium onions, peeled and cut into thin wedges

20g pack fresh rosemary, leaves only, roughly chopped

50g (2oz) butter, melted

600ml (1 pint) light stock

2 tsp Dijon mustard

50g (2oz) Gruyère cheese, finely grated

50g (2oz) fresh white breadcrumbs

PER SERVING

240 cals

6g fat (of which 4g saturates)

42g carbohydrate

LEAF AND OLIVE SALAD

✋ **HANDS-ON TIME:** 10 MINUTES ♨ **COOKING TIME:** NONE ✗ **SERVES:** 10 V

METHOD

1 Stir the olives into the vinaigrette and set aside until needed.

2 When ready to serve, toss all the salad ingredients with the vinaigrette dressing and put in a bowl, ready to serve.

INGREDIENTS

25g (1oz) pitted black olives, chopped

5 tbsp vinaigrette dressing

5 small hearts round lettuce, core removed, then quartered, or Little Gem lettuce, quartered

100g bag watercress leaves, roughly chopped

PER SERVING

40 cals

4g fat (of which 1g saturates)

trace carbohydrate

ROASTED STUFFED PEPPERS

👋 **HANDS-ON TIME:** 20 MINUTES   🍲 **COOKING TIME:** 45 MINUTES   ✗ **SERVES:** 10   V

INGREDIENTS

40g (1½oz) butter
4 Romano peppers, halved, with
   stalks on and deseeded
3 tbsp olive oil
350g (12oz) chestnut mushrooms,
   roughly chopped
4 tbsp finely chopped fresh chives
100g (3½oz) feta cheese
50g (2oz) fresh white breadcrumbs
25g (1oz) Parmesan cheese, grated

PER SERVING

320 cals
26g fat (of which 12g saturates)
12g carbohydrate

METHOD

1. Preheat the oven to 180°C (160°C fan oven) mark 4. Use a little of the butter to grease a shallow ovenproof dish and put the peppers in it side by side, ready to be filled.
2. Heat the remaining butter and 1 tbsp olive oil in a pan. Add the mushrooms and fry until they're golden and there's no excess liquid left in the pan. Stir in the chives, then spoon the mixture into the pepper halves.
3. Crumble the feta over the mushrooms. Mix the breadcrumbs and Parmesan in a bowl, then sprinkle over the peppers.
4. Season with salt and pepper and drizzle with the remaining oil. Roast in the oven for 45 minutes or until golden and tender. Serve warm.

TO PREPARE AHEAD

Make up to the end of step 4, up to one day ahead. Cover and chill. Reheat under the grill for 5 minutes.

PLUMS IN PORT

👋 **HANDS-ON TIME:** 10 MINUTES, PLUS CHILLING   🍲 **COOKING TIME:** ABOUT 1 HOUR   ✗ **SERVES:** 10

INGREDIENTS

2kg (4½lb) firm plums
1 cinnamon stick
2.5cm (1in) piece fresh root ginger,
   peeled and finely sliced
600ml (1 pint) ruby port or chilled
   fresh juice
300ml (10fl oz) fresh smooth
   orange juice
125g (4oz) golden caster sugar
1 tbsp arrowroot
3 tbsp cold water

PER SERVING

220 cals
0g fat
41g carbohydrate

METHOD

1. Preheat the oven to 180°C (160°C fan oven) mark 4. Put the whole plums into a large, shallow, flameproof casserole and add the cinnamon stick, ginger, port, orange juice and sugar. Cook, uncovered, for 40 minutes, gently turning the plums halfway through.
2. Remove the cinnamon stick and ginger. Mix the arrowroot with the cold water and stir into the plum liquid. Put the casserole on the hob and bring to a slow simmer, stirring all the time. Cook gently for 5 minutes or until the liquid is slightly thickened and clear.
3. Serve the plums warm or chilled.

COOK'S TIPS

- Turn the plums gently when cooking, so they don't break up.
- If you can't buy arrowroot, use cornflour instead.

WHITE CHOCOLATE AND ORANGE CAKE

👋 **HANDS-ON TIME:** 35 MINUTES, PLUS CHILLING　🍲 **COOKING TIME:** 35–40 MINUTES　✗ **SERVES:** 14

INGREDIENTS
butter to grease
6 large eggs, separated
250g (9oz) golden caster sugar
150g (5oz) self-raising flour
150g (5oz) ground almonds
grated zest of 2 oranges

For the syrup
100g (3½oz) golden granulated
　sugar
250ml (8fl oz) sweet white wine
juice of 3 large oranges

For the white chocolate ganache
225g (8oz) white chocolate, chopped
568ml carton double cream
350g (12oz) strawberries, thinly
　sliced

PER SERVING
530 cals
34g fat (of which 17g saturates)
49g carbohydrate

METHOD

1　Grease a deep 23cm (9in) round cake tin and line the base with greaseproof paper. Preheat the oven to 180°C (160°C fan oven) mark 4.

2　Put the egg whites in a clean, grease-free bowl and whisk until they form soft peaks. Gradually beat in 50g (2oz) sugar. Whisk until the mixture stands in stiff peaks and looks glossy.

3　Put the egg yolks and remaining sugar in another bowl. Whisk until soft and moussey. Carefully stir in the flour to make a paste.

4　Using a clean metal spoon, add a third of the egg white to the paste and fold in carefully. Put the remaining egg white, ground almonds and orange zest in the bowl and fold in, taking care not to knock too much volume out of the egg white. You should end up with a smooth batter.

5　Spoon into the tin and bake in the oven for 35 minutes or until a skewer inserted the centre comes out clean. Leave to cool in the tin for 10 minutes, then turn out on to a wire rack to cool completely.

6　Put the syrup ingredients in a small pan and stir over a gentle heat until the sugar has dissolved. Bring to the boil and bubble for 5 minutes or until syrupy. Cool and set aside.

7　To make the ganache, put the chocolate in a heatproof bowl with half the cream. Set over a pan of simmering water, making sure that the bottom of the bowl doesn't touch the water, and leave until the chocolate has melted, then stir. Don't stir the chocolate until it has completely melted. Leave to cool until beginning to thicken, then beat with a wooden spoon until cold and thick. Put the remaining double cream in a bowl and whip lightly. Beat a large spoonful of the whipped cream into the chocolate cream to loosen it, then fold in the remainder. Cover and leave to chill for 2 hours.

8　Cut the cake in half horizontally, pierce all over with a skewer and put it, cut-sides up, on an edged tray or baking sheet. Spoon over the syrup and leave to soak in.

9　Spread a quarter of the ganache over the base cake and scatter with 225g (8oz) strawberries. Cover with the top half of the cake and press down lightly. Using a palette knife, smooth the remaining ganache over the top and sides of the cake. Cover loosely and leave to chill for up to 4 hours. Decorate with the remaining strawberries and serve. (See page 263 for the quantities for the two smaller tiers.)

CREAMY WATERCRESS SOUP

HANDS-ON TIME: 20 MINUTES   **COOKING TIME:** 30–35 MINUTES   **SERVES:** 8   V

INGREDIENTS
75g (3oz) butter
175g (6oz) watercress
10–12 trimmed spring onions
700g (1½lb) baking potatoes, peeled and roughly chopped
225g (8oz) frozen petits pois
1.7 litres (3 pints) hot vegetable stock
142ml carton single cream

PER SERVING
170 cals
12g fat (of which 7g saturates)
12g carbohydrate

METHOD
1 Heat the butter in a large pan, then add the watercress and spring onions, snipping them into rough pieces with scissors as you drop them into the pan. Cook gently over a low heat for 10 minutes.
2 Add the potatoes to the pan along with the peas and most of the vegetable stock. Cover, bring to the boil, then simmer gently for 20–25 minutes until the potatoes are very tender.
3 Pour in the cream, then season to taste with salt and pepper.
4 Purée the soup in the pan with a hand-held blender, or leave to cool, then purée in a blender. Add a little extra stock if the soup is too thick.
5 Warm the soup through to serve; don't boil or the cream will split.

MUSTARD ROAST NEW POTATOES

HANDS-ON TIME: 5 MINUTES   **COOKING TIME:** 35–40 MINUTES   **SERVES:** 8   V

INGREDIENTS
1.4kg (3lb) small new or salad potatoes
1 tbsp English mustard
4 tbsp olive oil

PER SERVING
150 cals
4g fat (of which 1g saturates)
28g carbohydrate

METHOD
1 Preheat the oven to 220°C (200°C fan oven) mark 7. Put the potatoes in an even layer in one large or two small roasting tins, halving any large ones. Add the mustard. Drizzle with the oil and sprinkle with plenty of salt and pepper. Shake the tin to coat the potatoes in the oil and seasoning.
2 Roast for 35–40 minutes until the potatoes are golden and tender when pierced with a sharp knife. Shake the tin once or twice during cooking to brown the potatoes evenly. Serve immediately.

MASHED PARSNIPS WITH APPLE

HANDS-ON TIME: 10 MINUTES **COOKING TIME:** 10 MINUTES **SERVES:** 8 V

METHOD

1 Put the parsnips into a large pan of cold salted water and bring to the boil. Simmer for 10 minutes or until almost tender.
2 Drop the apples into the parsnips for the last 2–3 minutes of the cooking time. Drain and put back in the pan. Add the sugar and butter and mash together. Stir in the parsley and taste for seasoning before serving.

INGREDIENTS

10–12 medium parsnips, peeled and roughly chopped
salt
1 large cooking apple, peeled, cored and chopped
2 tbsp light brown sugar
50g (2oz) butter
20g pack fresh flat-leafed parsley, roughly chopped

PER SERVING

120 cals
6g fat (of which 4g saturates)
16g carbohydrate

SPECIAL MINT JELLY

HANDS-ON TIME: 5 MINUTES **COOKING TIME:** 5 MINUTES **SERVES:** 8 V

METHOD

1 Finely grate the zest and squeeze the juice from the orange into a small pan. Finely chop the mint and add half to the pan with the redcurrant jelly and balsamic vinegar. Cook on a low heat for 5 minutes until smooth.
2 Strain into a jug and stir in the remaining mint. Serve warm or cold with the lamb (page 216).

INGREDIENTS

1 large orange
20g pack fresh mint
450g jar redcurrant jelly
4 tbsp good-quality balsamic vinegar

PER SERVING

150 calories
0g fat
40g carbohydrate

RACK OF LAMB WITH BALSAMIC GRAVY

HANDS-ON TIME: 5 MINUTES · **COOKING TIME:** 30–45 MINUTES · **SERVES:** 8

INGREDIENTS

4 fat garlic cloves, crushed
2 tbsp Herbes de Provence
6 tbsp balsamic vinegar
12 tbsp olive oil
4 trimmed racks of lamb, each with
about 6 bones

PER SERVING

420 cals
33g fat (of which 9g saturates)
0g carbohydrate

METHOD

1   Preheat the oven to 220°C (200°C fan oven) mark 7. Put the garlic into a bowl along with the herbs, 2 tbsp vinegar and 4 tbsp oil. Season with salt and pepper.
2   Put the racks in a large flameproof roasting tin and rub the garlic mixture into both the fat and meat.
3   Roast for 25–30 minutes if you like your meat pink, or cook for a further 5–10 minutes if you like it well done. Lift the racks from the roasting tin and put to one side on a warm serving dish. Cover with foil and leave to rest.
4   Put the roasting tin on the hob over a medium heat and whisk in the remaining vinegar and oil, scraping up any sediment as the liquid bubbles. Season if needed. Pour into a small heatproof jug.
5   Serve the lamb in cutlets with the hot gravy.

RHUBARB AND PEAR CRUMBLE

HANDS-ON TIME: 25 MINUTES · **COOKING TIME:** 40–45 MINUTES · **SERVES:** 8

INGREDIENTS

450g (1lb) rhubarb, cut into 2.5cm
(1in) pieces
2 ripe pears, peeled, cored and
roughly chopped
75g (3oz) demerara sugar
1 tsp ground cinnamon
50g (2oz) chilled butter
75g (3oz) self-raising flour
2 shortbread fingers, broken into
pieces
50g (2oz) whole hazelnuts
500g carton Greek natural yogurt

PER SERVING

300 cals
18g fat (of which 9g saturates)
28g carbohydrates

METHOD

1   Preheat the oven to 180°C (160°C fan oven) mark 4. Put the fruit into a small, shallow baking dish and sprinkle with 25g (1oz) of the sugar and the cinnamon. Mix well.
2   Next, make the crumble mixture. Put the butter in a food processor, add the flour and remaining sugar and whiz until it looks like rough breadcrumbs.
3   Add the shortbread to the processor with the hazelnuts. Whiz again for 4–5 seconds until the crumble is blended but still looks rough. Sprinkle the crumble over the fruit, spreading it up to the edges and pressing it down with the back of a wooden spoon.
4   Bake in the oven for 40–45 minutes or until the topping is golden brown and crisp. Leave to cool.
5   Divide half the cooled crumble among eight serving dishes or glasses. Spoon the yogurt on top, then finish with the remaining crumble. Using a knife or skewer, draw a figure of eight to swirl the crumble into the yogurt. Serve warm or chilled.

SUMMER BARBECUES

SETTING UP THE BARBECUE

- Barbecues need a draught to get going, so choose a spot that isn't too exposed or too sheltered. Site it on a level area away from children and any fire hazards.
- Line the ash tray with foil, shiny side up, to reflect heat and make cleaning easier afterwards.
- Light the coals an hour before starting to cook to allow the flames to die down to ash. The coals need to turn white, to give an even heat. If the barbecue is too hot the food will burn on the outside before cooking inside.
- To add flavour, sprinkle aromatic herbs such as rosemary or sage, or whole spices, on to the coals, or use flavoured wood chips.
- Open barbecues are fine for foods that cook in less than 30 minutes, but covered barbecues are better for larger cuts of meat, baked potatoes and vegetables that need longer cooking or lower temperatures..
- Brush the grill with a little oil to prevent food sticking.
- Use a fish cage for whole fish – it's easier to turn it over and keep in one piece.
- Start food off in the centre of the grill (where it's hottest), then move it to the outer edges to cook through without burning.
- If using wooden skewers for kebabs, soak them in water for 30 minutes to prevent burning.

COOKING TIPS

- Never leave raw food in the sun, even for a short time. Keep it in the fridge or a cool box.
- Keep raw food separate from cooked to prevent any cross-contamination.
- Thaw frozen food thoroughly before barbecuing.
- Trim excess fat from meat to prevent drips, which cause flames to flare up when cooking.
- Use marinades to help flavour and tenderise meat and poultry – marinate in a non-metallic bowl for at least 20 minutes, or overnight in the fridge.

- Firm fish such as tuna, sardines, monkfish and mackerel are good to use as they hold their shape well.

THE RECIPES

Liven up barbecued chicken, lamb, pork sausages and fish steaks in an instant with easy marinades and butters. The following recipes are for four people.

SAUSAGES

Recipes below are enough for 450g (1lb) sausages. Thread sausages on to skewers with sprigs of rosemary or thyme.

HONEY AND SHERRY MARINADE Combine 4 tbsp soy sauce with 2 tbsp each sherry, runny honey and sesame oil. Brush over the sausages as they're cooking and serve with roasted red onions.

STICKY TOMATO KETCHUP MARINADE Crush 4 garlic cloves and mix with 5 tbsp marmalade and 2 tbsp each red wine vinegar and tomato ketchup. Brush over the sausages as they're cooking.

HONEY AND MUSTARD MARINADE Mix equal quantities of runny honey and grainy mustard with a little freshly chopped rosemary and olive oil. Toss the sausages in the marinade before cooking. Skewer with sprigs of rosemary or thyme.

CHICKEN

Use chicken thighs or breasts.

GINGER AND RED CHILLI MARINADE Grate a 5cm (2in) piece fresh root ginger and 1 small peeled onion. Combine with 1 finely chopped large red chilli, 2 crushed garlic cloves, 1 tbsp soy sauce, 2 tbsp oil and 2 tbsp honey. Spread over chicken and leave to marinate for 30 minutes. Cook for 4–5 minutes on each side until the juices run clear when pierced with a sharp knife.

HOT DEVILLED SAUCE Combine 1 tbsp olive oil with 2 tbsp mango chutney, 1 tbsp tomato ketchup, 1 tsp

Worcestershire sauce, 1 tbsp Dijon mustard, 1 tsp paprika, 2 tbsp dark soft brown sugar and 3 tbsp orange juice. Season with salt and pepper and pour over the chicken. Leave to marinate for 30 minutes. Cook for 4–5 minutes on each side until the juices run clear when pierced with a sharp knife.

YOGURT AND SAFFRON MARINADE Mix 200ml (7fl oz) Greek yogurt with 2 crushed garlic cloves, a pinch of saffron, 1 tbsp freshly chopped mint and 2 tbsp olive oil. Season with salt and pepper and pour over the chicken. Cover and marinate for at least 1 hour. Cook for 4–5 minutes on each side until the juices run clear when pierced with a sharp knife.

PORK

FIVE-SPICE MARINADE Five-spice Marinade Combine 2 crushed garlic cloves with 1 tsp Chinese five-spice powder, 4 tbsp hoisin sauce, 3 tbsp soft brown sugar and 2 tbsp each light soy sauce and orange juice. Marinate 450g (1lb) cubed pork tenderloin for 30 minutes. Thread on to wooden skewers with pieces of yellow pepper and shiitake mushrooms. Cook for 3–4 minutes on each side.

MUSTARD, SAGE AND APPLE MARINADE Stir 1 tbsp freshly chopped sage into 2 tbsp Dijon mustard with 50ml (2fl oz) apple juice and 1 tbsp each cider vinegar and oil. Season with salt and pepper, pour over four chops and marinate for 30 minutes. Cook for 4–5 minutes on each side.

CARAMELISED PEPPERCORN Roughly crush 2 tbsp mixed peppercorns and combine with 4 tbsp each soft brown sugar and wholegrain mustard and 50g (2oz) softened butter. Season with salt and pepper. Cook four chops on one side for 4–5 minutes, turn, spread with the butter and cook the other side.

LAMB

MINT AND GOAT'S CHEESE MARINADE Beat together 200ml (7fl oz) Greek yogurt with 2 garlic cloves and 175g (6oz) soft goat's cheese until smooth. Stir in 3 tbsp freshly chopped mint and 3 tbsp oil. Pour over four lamb steaks or chump chops and marinate for about 30 minutes. Cook for 3–4 minutes on each side for medium-rare. Serve with grilled lemon wedges.

HONEY AND GINGER BUTTER Grate a 5cm (2in) piece fresh root ginger and beat into 125g (4oz) softened butter with 2 crushed garlic cloves, 2 tbsp honey, the grated zest and 2 tbsp juice of a lime and 2 tbsp freshly chopped coriander. Season well with salt and pepper and spread over 450g (1lb) lamb neck fillets. Cook for 3–4 minutes on each side for medium-rare.

SPICED MARINADE Mix 1 small grated onion with 1 crushed garlic clove, ½ tsp each ground cumin and paprika, a pinch of cayenne pepper, 2 tbsp each freshly chopped parsley and coriander, 4 tbsp olive oil and the juice of ½ lemon. Pour over four lamb chump chops and marinate for 30 minutes. Cook for 3–4 minutes on each side for medium-rare.

FISH STEAKS

Use tuna, salmon or swordfish.

SUN-DRIED TOMATO PASTE Mix 50g (2oz) melted butter with 2 tbsp sun-dried tomato paste, 2 tsp lemon juice and salt and pepper. Brush over the fish steaks as they're cooking.

WASABI MAYONNAISE Stir 2 tsp wasabi paste (a green Japanese paste that tastes like horseradish) into 6 tbsp mayonnaise. Serve with barbecued fish steaks or as a dip.

VEGETARIAN

GARLIC HERB VEGETABLES Crush 2 garlic cloves into 6 tbsp olive oil and brush over halved baby fennel, sliced aubergine, large field mushrooms, halved peppers or whole corn-on-the-cob. Scatter over finely chopped thyme, then cook until tender.

HALLOUMI KEBABS Mix 100g (3½oz) natural yogurt, 1 tsp ground cumin, 2 tbsp olive oil and a squeeze of lemon in a bowl. Add 1 large chopped courgette, 1 chopped red pepper, 12 cherry tomatoes, 125g (4oz) cubed halloumi cheese and mix. Push on to skewers and grill until the vegetables are tender.

SALADS Turn the page for four great salads to serve at a barbecue. They're easy to multiply up if you need to serve more.

TOMATO, MOZZARELLA AND BASIL SALAD WITH BALSAMIC DRESSING

✋ **HANDS-ON TIME:** 15 MINUTES   🍲 **COOKING TIME:** NONE   ✗ **SERVES:** 4   ✓

INGREDIENTS
2 tbsp balsamic vinegar
4 tbsp extra-virgin olive oil
25g (1oz) pine nuts
3 ripe beef tomatoes, sliced
125g pack buffalo mozzarella,
     drained and torn into bite-size
     pieces
15 small basil leaves

PER SERVING
260 cals
4g fat (of which 6g saturates)
2g carbohydrate

METHOD
1   Make the dressing: put the balsamic and oil into a small bowl, whisk together and season with salt and pepper.
2   Put the pine nuts into a dry frying pan and toast, stirring, for 3 minutes. Set aside to cool.
3   Arrange the tomatoes and mozzarella on a large plate, season and drizzle with the dressing. Scatter over the pine nuts and basil to serve.

CHICKPEA SALAD WITH LEMON AND PARSLEY DRESSING

✋ **HANDS-ON TIME:** 15 MINUTES   🍲 **COOKING TIME:** NONE   ✗ **SERVES:** 4   ✓

INGREDIENTS
juice of ½ lemon
6 tbsp extra-virgin olive oil
4 tbsp flat-leafed parsley, chopped
2 x 410g tinned chickpeas, drained
     and rinsed
1 small red onion, peeled and finely
     sliced

PER SERVING
350 cals
23g fat (of which 3g saturates)
25g carbohydrate

METHOD
1   Make the dressing: put the lemon juice, oil and parsley in a medium bowl and whisk together. Season with salt and pepper.
2   Tip the chickpeas into a large bowl, add the onion and drizzle with the dressing. Mix well and season to taste.
3   Set aside for 10 minutes to allow the onion to soften in the dressing, then serve.

CRISP GREEN SALAD WITH BLUE CHEESE DRESSING

👋 **HANDS-ON TIME:** 15 MINUTES 🍲 **COOKING TIME:** NONE ✕ **SERVES:** 4 V

METHOD

1 Make the dressing: put half the Roquefort into a food processor, add the yogurt, vinegar and oil and whiz for 1 minute until combined. Season with salt and pepper.
2 Separate the lettuce leaves, wash in cold water and dry on kitchen paper. Arrange on a large plate, tearing any large leaves in two, and scatter over the croutons.
3 Pour over the dressing, crumble over the remaining Roquefort and serve.

INGREDIENTS

100 g (3½oz) Roquefort cheese
2 tbsp low-fat natural yogurt
1 tbsp white wine vinegar
5 tbsp extra-virgin olive oil
2 baby Cos or hearts of Romaine lettuce
50g (2oz) croutons

PER SERVING

310 cals
29g fat (of which 9g saturates)
7g carbohydrate

SPINACH, AVOCADO AND BACON SALAD WITH MUSTARD DRESSING

👋 **HANDS-ON TIME:** 15 MINUTES 🍲 **COOKING TIME:** 5 MINUTES ✕ **SERVES:** 4

METHOD

1 Make the dressing: put the mustard, lemon juice and oil in a small bowl and whisk together. Season with salt and pepper.
2 Preheat the grill. Lay the bacon rashers on a wire rack in a grill pan, and grill for 4–5 minutes until golden and crisp. Drain on kitchen paper and leave to cool, then snip into pieces with scissors.
3 Empty the spinach into a large bowl. Scatter over the bacon and avocado slices and drizzle over the mustard dressing. Carefully toss everything together.

INGREDIENTS

1 tbsp wholegrain mustard
juice of ½ lemon
6 tbsp extra-virgin olive oil
12 smoked streaky bacon rashers
200g (7oz) baby leaf spinach, washed and ready to use
1 large ripe and ready avocado, quartered, peeled and sliced

PER SERVING

530 cals
50g fat (of which 5g saturates)
1g carbohydrate

CHICKEN CHILLI

✋ **HANDS-ON TIME:** 20 MINUTES 🍲 **COOKING TIME:** 40 MINUTES ✖ **SERVES:** 4

FOOD FOR FRIENDS

INGREDIENTS

2 x 20g packs fresh coriander
2 tbsp olive oil
1 large Spanish onion, peeled and
    finely chopped
1 red chilli, deseeded and finely
    chopped
450g (1lb) chicken fillet, diced
1 tbsp plain flour
410g can mixed pulses or mixed
    beans, drained and rinsed?
2 x 400g cans chopped tomatoes
    with garlic
1–2 tbsp light muscovado sugar
juice of 1 small lime

PER SERVING

350 cals
12g fat (of which 3g saturates)
32g carbohydrate

METHOD

1 Preheat the oven to 170ºC (150ºC fan oven) mark 3. Chop the leaves from the coriander stalks and cut the stalks finely. Rewrap the leaves and pop them in the fridge.

2 Heat 1 tbsp oil in a large non-stick casserole and fry the onion, coriander stalks and chilli for 5–7 minutes until the onion is soft and golden. Spoon on to a plate and set aside.

3 Add the remaining oil to the casserole and fry the chicken for 5 minutes or until golden.

4 Return the onion mixture to the casserole and stir in the flour. Add the pulses, tomatoes and sugar, then bring to the boil. Cover the casserole with a tight-fitting lid and cook in the oven for 40 minutes.

5 To serve, finely chop the coriander leaves and stir into the casserole with the lime juice. Serve with warm tortillas and some grated mature Cheddar, chopped green chillies and soured cream.

CAULIFLOWER CHEESE

✋ **HANDS-ON TIME:** 15 MINUTES   🍲 **COOKING TIME:** 25 MINUTES   ✗ **SERVES:** 4

METHOD

1 Break the green leaves off the cauliflower and remove the tough stem. Cut the cauliflower into florets and cook in boiling salted water for 10–12 minutes or until just tender, adding the green leaves for the last 2 minutes.

2 Meanwhile, melt the butter in a pan, then add the flour and cook, stirring, for 1 minute. Gradually stir in the milk over the heat and cook for 3–4 minutes until thickened. Stir in half the cheese and season well.

3 Cook the bacon under a hot preheated grill for 6–8 minutes, turning once, until crisp and golden.

4 Drain the cauliflower, put in a warmed gratin dish and pour over the sauce. Sprinkle with the remaining cheese and grill for 3–4 minutes until bubbling and golden. Cut the bacon into pieces and scatter on top with the sun-dried tomatoes. Serve with baked potatoes.

INGREDIENTS

1 large cauliflower
40g (1½oz) each butter and plain flour
600ml (1 pint) milk
125g (4oz) mature Cheddar cheese, grated
4 streaky bacon rashers
4 pieces sun-dried tomato, drained and sliced

PER SERVING

480 cals
31g fat (of which 17g saturates)
23g carbohydrate

BOSTON BAKED BEANS

✋ **HANDS-ON TIME:** 15 MINUTES   🍲 **COOKING TIME:** 40 MINUTES   ✗ **SERVES:** 6

METHOD

1 Heat the oil in a large flameproof casserole and add the onions and garlic. Fry for 10 minutes over a medium heat until lightly coloured, then add the sausage and bacon. Cook until beginning to brown.

2 Stir in the tomato purée, treacle, mustard, tomatoes and beans. Add enough water to cover, stir well, then bring to the boil. Season with salt and pepper, reduce the heat and simmer, uncovered, for 20 minutes. Add the ham and simmer for 10 minutes.

3 Spoon into bowls and serve with garlic bread and a green salad.

INGREDIENTS

3 tbsp olive oil
2 onions, peeled and chopped
2 garlic cloves, peeled and crushed
200g (7oz) full-flavoured sausages, such as chorizo, thickly sliced
250g (9oz) rindless bacon, diced
2 tbsp each tomato purée and treacle
1 tbsp dry English mustard
400g can chopped plum tomatoes
2 x 400g cans cannellini beans, drained and rinsed
200g (7oz) cooked ham, cubed

PER SERVING

500 cals
34g fat (of which 12g saturates)
27g carbohydrate

SPICED ONE-POT CHICKEN

✋ HANDS-ON TIME: 10 MINUTES, PLUS MARINATING   **🍲 COOKING TIME:** 1 HOUR 10 MINUTES   **✗ SERVES:** 6

METHOD

1 Combine the Thai curry paste, orange juice and garlic in a small bowl. Put the chicken pieces in the marinade and leave to marinate for 15 minutes.
2 Preheat the oven to 220°C (200°C fan oven) mark 7. Put the vegetables in a large roasting tin, then remove the chicken from the marinade and arrange on top of the vegetables. Pour over the marinade and season with salt and pepper. Mix everything together so it's covered with the marinade and scatter with the capers.
3 Cook for 1 hour 10 minutes, turning from time to time, until the chicken is cooked through and the skin is golden.

TO PREPARE AHEAD

■ Complete the recipe to the end of step 2. Cover and chill for up to one day.
■ To use, complete the recipe, but cook for a further 5–10 minutes.

INGREDIENTS

3 tbsp Thai red curry paste
150ml (5fl oz) orange juice
2 garlic cloves, crushed
6 chicken pieces, 2.3kg (5lb) total weight, with bone in
700g (1½lb) squash or pumpkin, peeled and cut into 5cm (2in) cubes
5 red onions, peeled and quartered
2 tbsp capers, drained and chopped

PER SERVING

680 cals
46g fat (of which 15g saturates)
18g carbohydrate

HOT STILTON BITES

✋ HANDS-ON TIME: 15 MINUTES   **🍲 COOKING TIME:** 10 MINUTES   **✗ SERVES:** 6

METHOD

1 Preheat the oven to 220°C (200°C) mark 7 and put in a baking sheet to heat. Roll out the pastry to a thickness of 1cm (½ inch) and cut into 5cm (2in) squares. Scatter the Stilton and Parmesan cheeses, cayenne pepper, poppy seeds and mustard seeds over the pastry.
2 Put the bites on the hot baking sheet and bake in the oven for 10 minutes or until golden.

TO PREPARE AHEAD

■ Complete the recipe to the end of step 1, then cover and chill for up to one day.
■ To use, complete the recipe.

INGREDIENTS

250g (9oz) ready-rolled puff pastry, thawed if frozen
125g (4oz) Stilton cheese, crumbled
25g (1oz) Parmesan cheese, grated
1 tsp cayenne pepper
1 tsp poppy seeds
1 tsp black mustard seeds

PER SERVING

260 cals
19g fat (of which 10g saturates)
16g carbohydrate

ROAST APPLES WITH BUTTERSCOTCH SAUCE

HANDS-ON TIME: 5 MINUTES, PLUS 10 MINUTES SOAKING **COOKING TIME:** 15–20 MINUTES **SERVES:** 6

INGREDIENTS
125g (4oz) sultanas
2 tbsp brandy
6 large Bramley apples, cored
4 tbsp soft brown sugar
2 tbsp apple juice

For the butterscotch sauce
125g (4oz) butter
125g (4oz) soft brown sugar
2 tbsp golden syrup
2 tbsp black treacle
4 tbsp brandy
284ml carton double cream
**125g (4oz) chopped and toasted
   hazelnuts**
ricotta cheese to serve

PER SERVING
800 cals
47g fat (of which 26g saturates)
85g carbohydrate

METHOD

1   Preheat the oven to 220°C (200°C fan oven) mark 7. Put the sultanas in a bowl, pour in the brandy and leave to soak for 10 minutes, then stuff each apple with equal amounts.

2   Put the apples in a roasting tin, sprinkle over the brown sugar and apple juice. Bake for 15–20 minutes until soft.

3   Meanwhile, make the sauce. Heat the butter, soft brown sugar, golden syrup and treacle in a heavy-based pan, stirring all the time. When the sugar has dissolved and the mixture is bubbling, stir in the brandy and cream. Bring back to the boil and put to one side.

4   Remove the apples from the oven. Serve with the sauce, hazelnuts and a dollop of ricotta cheese.

TO PREPARE AHEAD
- Complete step 3 of the recipe, then cool, cover and chill for up to one day. Complete step 1 up to 4 hours in advance.
- To use, complete the recipe and bring the sauce back to the boil to serve.

SPICED PUMPKIN FRITTERS

👋 **HANDS-ON TIME:** 15 MINUTES   🍲 **COOKING TIME:** ABOUT 15 MINUTES   ✖ **SERVES:** 4   V

METHOD

1 Steam the pumpkin for 8–10 minutes until only just tender. Remove from the steamer and cool.
2 To make the batter, whiz the flour, salt, baking powder, cumin seeds and ground cumin with the egg yolk in a blender or food processor. Gradually stir in the water to form a smooth batter. Stir in the onion, garlic, chilli sauce and coriander. Whisk the egg white in a grease-free bowl until stiff and fold lightly into the batter.
3 Fill a deep-fat fryer with oil until it is one-third full, and heat to 180°C (350°F) or until a cube of bread browns in 30 seconds. Using two forks, dip a few slices of pumpkin into the batter to coat evenly, then put in the hot oil. Fry for 1–1½ minutes until the fritters are crisp and golden brown.
4 Drain on crumpled kitchen paper and keep warm while you cook the remaining pumpkin in the same way. Serve hot, sprinkled with coarse salt.

COOK'S TIP

This is an excellent way to use the flesh scooped out of a pumpkin lantern.

INGREDIENTS

700g (1½lb) pumpkin flesh, peeled and cut into thick slices about 10cm (5in) lon g and 1cm (½in) wide
175g (6oz) wholemeal plain flour
½–1 tsp salt
¼ tsp baking powder
½ tsp cumin seeds
½ tsp ground cumin
1 egg, separated
175ml (6fl oz) water
1 small onion, peeled and finely chopped
1–2 garlic cloves, crushed
1½ tsp chilli sauce
2 tbsp freshly chopped coriander
vegetable oil to fry

PER SERVING
340 cals
18g fat (of which 3g saturates)
40g carbohydrate

MINI BAKED POTATOES WITH CARAWAY SEEDS

👋 **HANDS-ON TIME:** 5 MINUTES   🍲 **COOKING TIME:** 35–45 MINUTES   ✖ **SERVES:** 6   V

METHOD

1 Preheat the oven to 220°C (200°C fan oven) mark 7. Toss the small potatoes in the oil and sprinkle over the caraway seeds and sea salt. Season with pepper.
2 Roast the potatoes in the oven for 35–45 minutes until golden and cooked through. Serve with crispy bacon and soured cream.

INGREDIENTS

18 small potatoes
2 tbsp olive oil
1 tbsp caraway seeds
1 tbsp sea salt

PER SERVING
450 cals
5g fat (of which 1g saturates)
95g carbohydrate

CHRISTMAS

PLAN AHEAD

- Make a list of everything you'll need to buy.
- Order the bird well in advance.
- Make the Christmas pudding and cake at least six weeks before Christmas Day.
- Prepare as much ahead of time as you can and use the freezer as an extra storecupboard.

- Clear out the fridge to make room for the extra food.
- Use a cool garage or outhouse to store vegetables.
- Don't forget to thaw items from the freezer in good time.

SMOKED SALMON SALAD WITH MUSTARD AND DILL DRESSING

✋ **HANDS-ON TIME:** 15 MINUTES, PLUS CHILLING   🍲 **COOKING TIME:** NONE   ✖ **SERVES:** 8

INGREDIENTS
For the dressing
4 tbsp extra-virgin olive oil
juice of 1 lemon
½ tsp golden caster sugar
2 tsp wholegrain mustard
4 tsp finely chopped dill

For the salad
1 small head of fennel
110g bag baby leaf salad
75g (3oz) wild rocket
400g (14oz) oak-smoked wild
    salmon

PER SERVING
140 cals
9g fat (of which 1g saturates)
1g carbohydrate

METHOD
1 Pour the olive oil, lemon juice, sugar and mustard into a clean jam jar and season with salt and pepper. Seal, then shake to combine and chill for up to one day.
2 Using a sharp knife, trim and thinly slice the fennel. Wash the fennel, baby leaf salad and rocket, then dry in a salad spinner or drain in a colander and spread out on a clean teatowel to remove excess moisture. (Once dried, the salad can be stored, covered, in the fridge for up to one day.)
3 To serve, place twists of smoked salmon on each plate, then pile the salad leaves and fennel alongside and season with pepper. Add the dill to the dressing and shake well to mix. Drizzle over and around the salad leaves. Serve immediately.

COOK'S TIP
- Keep both separately chilled and covered in the fridge.

ROAST TURKEY WITH SAGE, LEMON AND THYME

👋 **HANDS-ON TIME:** 40 MINUTES, PLUS CHILLING 🍲 **COOKING TIME:** 3¾ HOURS ✕ **SERVES:** 16

INGREDIENTS

For the stuffing
4 tbsp olive oil
2 large onions, peeled and finely
  chopped
4 garlic cloves, crushed
150g (5oz) fresh white breadcrumbs
75g (3oz) medium cornmeal or
  polenta
100g (3½oz) hazelnuts, toasted and
  chopped
finely grated zest of 2 lemons and
  juice of 1 lemon
4 tbsp fresh flat-leafed parsley,
  roughly chopped
4 tbsp fresh sage, roughly chopped
2 eggs, lightly beaten

For the seasoning
1 tbsp whole pink peppercorns
2 tsp sea salt
2 tbsp paprika
2 tbsp celery salt

For the turkey
6.3kg (14lb) turkey, with giblets
2 small red onions, peeled and cut
  into wedges
2 lemons, cut into wedges
6 whole garlic cloves
8 fresh thyme sprigs
8 fresh sage leaves
8 fresh flat-leafed parsley sprigs
trussing needle and 2m fine string
  a skewer
250ml (8fl oz) olive oil
60cm (23½in) square of muslin

PER SERVING
280 cals
10g fat (of which 2g saturates)
11g carbohydrate

METHOD

1 To make the stuffing, heat the oil in a pan. Add the onion and garlic and fry gently for 10 minutes to soften but not brown. Tip into a bowl to cool. Meanwhile, put the breadcrumbs, cornmeal or polenta, hazelnuts, lemon zest, parsley, sage and eggs into a large bowl and squeeze over the lemon juice. Add the cooled onion and garlic and season with salt and pepper. Stir to bind together and leave to cool.

2 For the seasoning, put the peppercorns, sea salt, paprika and celery salt in a pestle and mortar and pound to crush, or whiz in a mini processor.

3 For the turkey, stand it upright on a board, with the parson's nose (the rear end) facing upwards. Sprinkle the inside cavity with 1 tbsp of the peppercorn seasoning, then pack the cavity with half the onion and lemon wedges, garlic cloves, thyme, sage and all the parsley sprigs.

4 Sit the turkey with the parson's nose facing away from you. Lift up the loose skin at the neck end with one hand and, using the other, fill the cavity with handfuls of cold stuffing. Turn the turkey over on to its breast, then lift the neck flap up and over the stuffing to cover and bring the wing tips round on top.

5 Thread the trussing needle with string and sew the neck flap to the turkey to enclose the stuffing. Push the skewer firmly through the wings, twist the string around the ends and pull to tighten so that both wings are snug against the breast. Turn the turkey over, tuck in the parson's nose, cross the legs together, then bring the string up and over the legs and wrap around tightly, finishing with a double knot to secure. Cut off any excess.

6 Pour the olive oil into a large roasting tin. Immerse the muslin in it to coat completely, then stretch it out, with the edges overhanging the tin. Sit the turkey on the muslin and sprinkle with the remaining peppercorn seasoning. Scatter the remaining thyme and sage across the turkey, then arrange the remaining lemon and onion wedges and the garlic cloves around the bird. Bring the muslin up and over the turkey to wrap completely, then turn it over so that it's breast-side down in the roasting tin. Over-wrap with clingfilm and leave to chill overnight in the bottom of the fridge. Remember to take out 30 minutes before cooking so it has time to come to room temperature.

7   Preheat the oven to 200°C (180°C fan oven) mark 6. Weigh the
    stuffed turkey and calculate the cooking time: roast for 15 minutes
    for each 450g (1lb), plus 15 minutes. For the turkey in this recipe, it
    is about 3¾ hours. Halfway through the cooking time, after 1 hour
    50 minutes, turn the turkey over so it's breast-side up (see Cook's
    Tip). Continue roasting for a further 1 hour 55 minutes or until a
    skewer inserted into the thickest part of the thigh for 10 seconds
    comes out piping hot and the juices run clear. There's no need to
    remove the muslin during cooking as the skin will brown naturally.
8   Remove the turkey from the tin and take off the muslin. Put the
    turkey on a serving plate and cover with foil, then leave to rest for
    at least 20 minutes before carving. Carefully pour off as much of
    the visible fat from the tin as you can, leaving the dark brown
    juices behind to make the gravy (see page 25 for gravy recipe).

COOK'S TIP

- Turning the turkey halfway through cooking can be difficult – it will
  be easier and safer if you wear new, clean rubber gloves to do it.
- As well as the vegetables on page 233, serve with Orange-Glazed
  Carrots (page 240) and Roast Parsnips with Sea Salt (page 236).
- Roast turkey wouldn't be the same without Cranberry sauce, see
  page 26 for the recipe.

CRISPY ROAST POTATOES

🖐 **HANDS-ON TIME:** 25 MINUTES 🍲 **COOKING TIME:** 1 HOUR 20 MINUTES ✕ **SERVES:** 8

METHOD

1   Cut two or three small wedges from the top of each potato, then
    cut two or three wedges across to create a grid pattern, which
    helps to make them extra crispy.
2   Put into a pan of cold salted water, bring to the boil and cook for
    6 minutes exactly. Drain well. Spread out the potatoes on a baking
    sheet and leave to cool, then cover with clingfilm and freeze.
3   Preheat the oven to 200°C (180°C fan oven) mark 6. Put the goose
    fat in a roasting tin and heat for 3–4 minutes until sizzling. Add the
    frozen potatoes and roast for 30 minutes, then sprinkle over the
    sea salt. Roast for a further 40 minutes, turning halfway through,
    or until golden.

INGREDIENTS

**1.5kg (3lb) medium even-size
    potatoes, peeled**
50g (2oz) goose fat
2 tsp sea salt

PER SERVING

170 cals
5g fat (of which 2g saturates)
30g carbohydrate

LEEK, MUSHROOM AND ARTICHOKE CROUTE

INGREDIENTS

3 tbsp olive oil
2 garlic cloves, crushed
125g (4oz) shiitake mushrooms, sliced
1 tbsp balsamic vinegar
50g (2oz) whole cooked chestnuts, roughly chopped
fresh thyme sprigs
400g can artichoke hearts, drained then quartered
350g (12oz) leeks, washed and sliced
375g sheet ready-rolled puff pastry
1 egg, lightly beaten to glaze
cranberry sauce to serve
extra-virgin olive oil to serve

PER SERVING
250 calories
16g fat (of which 5g saturates)
22g carbohydrate

METHOD

1   Heat 2 tbsp olive oil in a large pan and fry the garlic for 1 minute. Add the mushrooms and cook over a low heat for 3 minutes to soften. Add the balsamic vinegar, chestnuts, ½ tsp thyme leaves – stripped off the sprigs – and the artichokes, then cook for 1 minute.

2   Heat the remaining oil in a clean pan, add the leeks and cook for 4 minutes to soften slightly. Turn into a bowl and cool for 5 minutes.

3   Unroll the pastry and sprinkle the surface with the remaining thyme sprigs. Roll the leaves slightly into the pastry. Flip the pastry over so that the leaves are on the underside. Roll the pastry into a 38 x 25.5cm (15 x 10in) rectangle. Using a sharp knife, cut the pastry in half vertically to create two long thin rectangles.

4   Spoon half the mushroom mixture down the centre of each piece of pastry. Top with the leeks. Season with salt and freshly ground black pepper. Brush the pastry edges with water, then fold each side of the pastry up over the filling and seal.

5   Cut both rolls in half and put on to a greased baking sheet. Cover and chill overnight, or freeze for up to one month.

6   Preheat the oven to 200°C (180°C fan oven) mark 6. Brush the pastry with egg to glaze. Cook for 20 minutes (25 minutes from frozen) until the pastry is golden. Slice each croute into six and serve three slices per person, topped with a dollop of cranberry sauce and a light drizzle of olive oil.

COOK'S TIP

This is a good vegetarian main course for Christmas Day and gives eight good portions. Should you have any left, you can freeze it for another time. The sliced croute also makes a good alternative to sausage rolls.

PAN-FRIED SPROUTS WITH CHESTNUTS AND SHALLOTS

👋 **HANDS-ON TIME:** 15 MINUTES   🍲 **COOKING TIME:** 10 MINUTES   ✖ **SERVES:** 8   V

METHOD

1 Blanch the sprouts in a large pan of boiling salted water for 2 minutes. Drain and refresh with a little cold water.
2 Heat the oil in a wok, add the shallots and stir-fry for about 5 minutes until almost tender.
3 Add the sprouts to the pan with the chestnuts and stir-fry for 4–5 minutes to heat through.
4 Add the butter and nutmeg to the pan and season generously with salt and pepper. Serve immediately.

COOK'S TIP

The best way to keep Brussels sprouts bright green with a good crunch is to blanch them first, then pan-fry just before you serve.

INGREDIENTS

900g (2lb) small Brussels sprouts, bases trimmed
1 tbsp olive oil
8 shallots, peeled and finely chopped
200g pack chestnuts
15g (½oz) butter
a pinch of freshly grated nutmeg

PER SERVING

140 cals
6g fat (of which 2g saturates)
18g carbohydrate

ROSEMARY ROASTED BACON ROLLS AND CHIPOLATAS

👋 **HANDS-ON TIME:** 15 MINUTES, PLUS CHILLING   🍲 **COOKING TIME:** 30 MINUTES   ✖ **SERVES:** 8

METHOD

1 Use the back of a knife to stretch each rasher slightly, then roll up into bacon rolls. Put into a small roasting tin.
2 Separate the chipolatas with scissors. Take each one, then twist twice in the centre and cut to make two mini chipolatas. Add to the roasting tin and scatter with rosemary. Cover and leave to chill overnight.
3 Preheat the oven to 200°C (180°C fan oven) mark 6. Roast for 30 minutes until cooked through and browned.

COOK'S TIP

For more vegetable recipes see pages 236-243.

INGREDIENTS

10 maple-smoked, traditional-style, rindless streaky bacon rashers, cut in half
10 chipolatas
4 fresh rosemary sprigs

PER SERVING

200 cals
16g fat (of which 6g saturates)
3g carbohydrate

CLASSIC CHRISTMAS CAKE

✋ **HANDS-ON TIME:** 45 MINUTES, PLUS MACERATING FRUIT

🍞 **COOKING TIME:** 2 HOURS ✕ **MAKES:** 2 CAKES, 16 SLICES PER CAKE

INGREDIENTS
275g (10oz) currants
275g (10oz) sultanas
275g (10oz) raisins
200g (7oz) glacé cherries with
    natural colour
100g (3½oz) stem ginger, drained
    and chopped
grated zest and juice of 1 unwaxed
    lemon
2 tsp vanilla extract
150ml (5fl oz) ginger wine
150ml (5fl oz) cognac, plus extra
    cognac to drizzle
350g (12oz) butter, at room
    temperature, plus extra to
    grease
350g (12oz) dark brown sugar
4 medium eggs
350g (12oz) self-raising flour
2 tbsp ground mixed spice
1 tsp ground cinnamon
1 tsp ground ginger
100g pack mixed nuts, such as
    walnuts, Brazil nuts and
    almonds, roughly chopped
125g (4oz) carrots, peeled and
    coarsely grated

PER SERVING
280 cals
12g fat (of which 6g saturates)
42g carbohydrate

METHOD
1   Put the currants, sultanas, raisins, glacé cherries, ginger, lemon zest and juice, and vanilla extract in a container. Pour the ginger wine and cognac over, cover and leave to macerate for 1–5 days in a cool place.
2   Grease two 20cm (8in) tins, line with baking parchment or liner and wrap brown paper around the outside of each, securing with string. Preheat the oven to 170°C (150°C fan oven) mark 3.
3   Using either a freestanding or hand-held mixer, cream together the butter and the dark brown sugar until the mixture is pale and fluffy, then beat in the eggs gradually, one at a time.
4   Sift together the self-raising flour, mixed spice, cinnamon and ground ginger. Fold half the spiced flour into the creamed mixture.
5   Take half the soaked fruit, some of the ginger wine and cognac liquid, and whiz in a food processor until blended. Fold this into the cake mixture with the remaining whole fruits, remaining spiced flour, the nuts, carrots and any leftover liquid.
6   Divide the mixture evenly between the two cake tins and bake for 2 hours or until a skewer inserted into the centre comes out clean. Leave to cool, then remove from the tin and drizzle with 1 tbsp cognac. Wrap and store in an airtight container for up to one month.

COOK'S TIP
When the cake has cooled, wrap it in greaseproof paper and then in foil, making sure the cake is completely covered. Store in an airtight tin in a cool, dark place.

CHRISTMAS PUDDING

✋ **HANDS-ON TIME:** 30 MINUTES, PLUS MACERATING AND MATURING

🍲 **COOKING TIME:** 6–8 HOURS, PLUS REHEATING ✗ **MAKES:** 2 PUDDINGS, EACH SERVES 6

METHOD

1 Put all the dried fruit into a bowl with the grated carrot, Grand Marnier, Guinness and orange juice. Stir to mix and leave to macerate for 1 hour. Meanwhile, grease two 1 litre (1¾ pint) pudding basins and line each with a 40cm (16in) muslin square.

2 Put the butter, sugar and orange zest into a large bowl and cream together, using a hand-held electric whisk or wooden spoon, until pale and fluffy. Gradually beat in the eggs, adding a little flour if the mixture appears to be starting to curdle.

3 Sift together the flour and mixed spice. Put the bread into a food processor and pulse to make crumbs; remove and set aside. Put the nuts into the processor and pulse briefly to chop roughly.

4 Using a large metal spoon, fold the flour, breadcrumbs and nuts into the creamed mixture. Add the macerated fruit and alcohol and stir to combine.

5 Divide the mixture between the two prepared pudding basins and smooth the surface. Gather the muslin up and over the top, then twist and secure with string.

6 To cook each pudding, put in the top of a steamer filled with simmering water and steam for 8 hours, topping up the water as necessary. Or stand the basin on a trivet in a large pan containing boiling water and boil for 6 hours, checking the water level from time to time and topping up as needed.

7 Leave the puddings to cool, then wrap tightly in foil and store in a cool, dark place for at least 1 month (or up to 6 months) to mature.

8 To reheat a pudding, steam as before for 2 hours, topping up the water twice. Once the heat is turned off, the pudding will keep hot for up to 1 hour. To serve, carefully lift out the pudding, cut the string and remove the muslin. Upturn the pudding on to a serving plate and decorate with a sprig of holly.

9 To flambé, warm the Cognac in a ladle, holding it over the hob until the alcohol ignites, then pour over the pudding. Serve immediately, with fresh vanilla custard or brandy butter (not suitable for children due to the alcohol content).

INGREDIENTS

150g (5oz) currants
150g (5oz) raisins
150g (5oz) sultanas
150g (5oz) ready-to-eat dates, chopped
150g (5oz) ready-to-eat prunes, chopped
1 carrot, about 75g (3oz), peeled and grated
100ml (3½fl oz) Grand Marnier
100ml (3½fl oz) Guinness
finely grated zest and juice of 1 orange
175g (6oz) butter, softened, plus extra to grease
175g (6oz) molasses or dark muscovado sugar
3 eggs, beaten
75g (3oz) self-raising flour
1 tbsp ground mixed spice
150g (5oz) crustless fresh white bread
75g (3oz) blanched almonds, toasted
50g (2oz) pecan nuts, toasted
2 tbsp Cognac, to flambé

PER SERVING
480 cals
20g fat (of which 9g saturates)
65g carbohydrate

ROAST PARSNIPS WITH SEA SALT

✋ **HANDS-ON TIME:** 25 MINUTES   🍲 **COOKING TIME:** 45 MINUTES   ✗ **SERVES:** 8

INGREDIENTS
800g (1¾lb) small parsnips, peeled
salt
50g (2oz) goose fat
2 tsp sea salt

PER SERVING
100 cals
6g fat (of which 2g saturates)
11g carbohydrate

METHOD
1   Cut out three small wedges in one side of each parsnip. Put into a pan of cold salted water, bring to the boil and cook for 5 minutes exactly. Drain. Spread the parsnips out on a baking sheet and leave to cool, then pop into a bag and freeze.
2   Preheat the oven to 200°C (180°C fan oven) mark 6. Heat the goose fat in a roasting tin for 3–4 minutes until sizzling. Add the frozen parsnips and roast for 15 minutes, then sprinkle over the sea salt. Roast for a further 25 minutes, turning once, until golden.

VEGETABLES WITH GARLIC AND WALNUT SAUCE

✋ **HANDS-ON TIME:** 15 MINUTES, PLUS CHILLING   🍲 **COOKING TIME:** DEPENDS ON VEGETABLES USED

✗ **SERVES:** ABOUT 12   V

INGREDIENTS
125g (4oz) walnut pieces
3 large garlic cloves
2 tbsp water
100ml (3½fl oz) olive oil
a few fresh parsley sprigs
freshly cooked vegetables, such as
    potatoes, beans, pumpkin, fennel
    and carrots to serve

PER SERVING OF SAUCE ONLY
170 cals
13g fat (of which 2g saturates)
10g carbohydrate

METHOD
1   Put the walnuts, garlic, seasoning and water in a food processor and whiz briefly.
2   With the processor still running, gradually add the oil, then add the parsley and whiz again.
3   Cover the sauce and leave to chill for up to two weeks.
4   Toss freshly cooked vegetables in the sauce.

GOLDEN ROAST VEGETABLES

🖐 **HANDS-ON TIME:** 10 MINUTES   🍲 **COOKING TIME:** 1 HOUR 35 MINUTES   ✖ **SERVES:** 8

METHOD

1 Put the vegetables and lemon in a large pan, cover with cold salted water and bring to the boil. Cook for 5 minutes, drain and put back into the pan. Cover and shake well to roughen the edges, then lift the lid to allow the steam to escape and the vegetables to dry.

2 Pour the hot beef fat into a large roasting tin and turn the vegetables in the hot fat.

3 Put on the top shelf of the oven and cook for 1¼ hours, turn occasionally, or until crisp and cooked through.

4 Sprinkle with salt and serve with roast beef and accompaniments.

INGREDIENTS

700g (1½lb) potatoes, peeled and cut into large chunks
450g (1lb) celeriac, peeled and cut into large chunks
450g (1lb) swede, peeled and cut into large chunks
450g (1lb) parsnips, peeled and cut into large chunks
1 lemon, chopped
salt
6–8 tbsp hot fat from roast meat

PER SERVING

190 cals
11g fat (of which 4g saturates)
23g carbohydrate

RED CABBAGE

🖐 **HANDS-ON TIME:** 7-10 MINUTES   🍲 **COOKING TIME:** 5-10 MINUTES   ✖ **SERVES:** 6   V

METHOD

1 Add the wine vinegar and ginger to a large pan of water and bring to the boil. Add the cabbage, season with salt and cook for 5–10 minutes. Drain and discard the ginger. Serve drizzled with olive oil and fresh thyme.

INGREDIENTS

2 tbsp white wine vinegar
2.5cm (1in) cube of fresh root ginger, peeled
1.4kg (3lb) red cabbage, outer leaves discarded, cored and finely shredded
salt
olive oil to drizzle
fresh thyme to serve

PER SERVING

60 cals
3g fat (of which trace saturates)
5g carbohydrate

CARROT AND PARSNIP PURÉE WITH CORIANDER

✋ **HANDS-ON TIME:** 10 MINUTES 🫕 **COOKING TIME:** 20 MINUTES ✗ **SERVES:** 4 ✓

INGREDIENTS

450g (1lb) carrots, peeled and sliced
450g (1lb) parsnips, peeled and sliced
1 tbsp ground coriander
3 tbsp reduced-fat crème fraîche
4 tbsp freshly chopped coriander

PER SERVING
120 cals
3g fat (of which 1g saturates)
20g carbohydrate

METHOD

1 Put the vegetables in a pan of cold salted water. Bring to the boil and cook for 20 minutes until soft. Drain well.
2 Whiz the vegetables, ground coriander and crème fraîche until puréed. Season with salt and pepper, then stir in the chopped coriander and serve.

LEEKS WITH TOASTED CHEESE SAUCE

✋ **HANDS-ON TIME:** 15 MINUTES 🫕 **COOKING TIME:** 25 MINUTES ✗ **SERVES:** 4 ✓

INGREDIENTS

700g (1½lb) even-size leeks
25g (1oz) butter
25g (1oz) plain flour
125g (4oz) light soft cheese with garlic and herbs
15g (½oz) freshly grated Parmesan cheese

PER SERVING
180 cals
12g fat (of which 7g saturates)
11g carbohydrate

METHOD

1 Put the leeks in a pan of cold salted water, bring to the boil and bubble for 2–3 minutes until just tender. Drain and put 300ml (10fl oz) cooking liquid to one side.
2 Heat the butter in a pan. Add the flour and mix until smooth. Blend in the reserved liquid and bring to the boil, stirring all the time. Add the soft cheese, season with salt and pepper and bring back to the boil.
3 Preheat the grill. Arrange the leeks in a shallow flameproof dish, then spoon the sauce over the top and sprinkle with Parmesan cheese. Cook under the grill until golden and bubbling. Serve immediately.

COURGETTE BATONS

HANDS-ON TIME: 10 MINUTES **COOKING TIME:** 5 MINUTES **SERVES:** 4 V

METHOD
1 Cook the courgettes in a pan of boiling salted water for 3–5 minutes until just tender but with a good bite.
2 Drain and serve immediately, garnished with flat-leafed parsley.

COOK'S TIP
You can prepare the courgettes ahead of time and keep them in a plastic bag in the fridge.

INGREDIENTS
900g–1.1kg (2–2½lb) courgettes, trimmed and cut into fat sticks
fresh flat-leafed parsley sprigs to garnish

PER SERVING
50 cals
1g fat (of which trace saturates)
5g carbohydrate

BRAISED GARLIC CABBAGE

HANDS-ON TIME: 4 MINUTES **COOKING TIME:** 6 MINUTES **SERVES:** 8 V

METHOD
1 Heat the oil in a heavy-based pan. Add the garlic and cook for 30 seconds.
2 Add the cabbage and cook, stirring, for 5 minutes. Season with salt and pepper, then stir in the chopped parsley and serve.

INGREDIENTS
2 tbsp olive oil
2 garlic cloves, crushed
1 small Savoy cabbage, quartered and shredded
2 tbsp chopped fresh parsley

PER SERVING
60 cals
4g fat (of which 1g saturates)
4g carbohydrate

BUBBLE AND SQUEAK CAKES

✋ **HANDS-ON TIME:** 15 MINUTES　　🍲 **COOKING TIME:** 45 MINUTES, PLUS COOLING　　✗ **SERVES:** 12　V

INGREDIENTS
575g (1¼lb) old potatoes
125g (4oz) butter
175g (6oz) leeks, finely shredded
175g (6oz) green cabbage, finely
　　shredded
plain flour to dust
1 tbsp oil

PER SERVING
130 cals
10g fat (of which 6g saturates)
10g carbohydrate

METHOD
1　Cook the potatoes in a large pan of boiling salted water until tender, then drain and mash.
2　Heat 50g (2oz) of the butter in a large non-stick frying pan. Add the leeks and cabbage and fry for 5 minutes, stirring, until soft and beginning to colour. Combine the leeks and cabbage with the potatoes and season well with salt and pepper. Leave to cool. When cool enough to handle, mould into 12 cakes and dust with flour.
3　Heat the oil and remaining butter in a non-stick frying pan and cook the cakes for 4 minutes on each side or until they are golden, crisp and hot right through.

ORANGE-GLAZED CARROTS

✋ **HANDS-ON TIME:** 15 MINUTES　　🍲 **COOKING TIME:** 10–15 MINUTES　　✗ **SERVES:** 8　V

INGREDIENTS
700g (1½lb) carrots, peeled and cut
　　into thin matchsticks
50g (2oz) butter
50g (2oz) light brown sugar
150ml (5fl oz) orange juice
150ml (5fl oz) dry white wine
2 tbsp balsamic vinegar
2 tbsp freshly chopped flat-leafed
　　parsley

PER SERVING
110 cals
6g fat (of which 3g saturates)
14g carbohydrate

METHOD
1　Put the carrots, butter, sugar, juice, wine and vinegar into a pan, season with salt and pepper and bring to the boil. Reduce the heat and simmer, uncovered, for 10–15 minutes until the carrots are tender and liquid has evaporated enough to form a glaze.
2　Keep warm, then scatter with parsley just before serving.

CRISPY POTATO SKINS

HANDS-ON TIME: 5 MINUTES   **COOKING TIME:** 1¾ HOURS   **SERVES:** 4–6   V

INGREDIENTS
900g (2lb) baking potatoes
coarse sea salt
oil, to deep-fry
soured cream to garnish
roughly chopped fresh chives
   to garnish

PER SERVING
190–130 cals
7-4g fat (of which 1-1g saturates)
30-20g carbohydrate

METHOD
1   Preheat the oven to 200°C (180°C fan oven) mark 6. Prick the potato skins and rub with salt. Put in a roasting tin and cook in the oven for 1½ hours.
2   Quarter the potatoes and scoop out the insides, leaving a good 1cm (½in) flesh attached to the skins. Deep-fry the potato skins in hot oil for 2–3 minutes until crisp and golden, then drain on kitchen paper and toss in salt. Pile into a serving dish and garnish with soured cream and roughly chopped chives.

242

CREAMY BAKED POTATOES WITH MUSTARD SEEDS

HANDS-ON TIME: 15–20 MINUTES   **COOKING TIME:** 1¼ HOURS   **SERVES:** 6   V

INGREDIENTS
6 baking potatoes, about 1.4kg (3lb)
2 tbsp sunflower oil
1 tbsp coarse sea salt
4–5 large garlic cloves, unpeeled
50g (2oz) butter
6 tbsp crème fraîche
2 tbsp mustard seeds, toasted and
   lightly crushed
fresh oregano sprigs to garnish

PER SERVING
330 cals
16g fat (of which 7g saturates)
42g carbohydrate

METHOD
1   Preheat the oven to 200°C (180°C fan oven) mark 6. Prick the potato skins, rub with the oil and sprinkle with salt. Cook in the oven for 40 minutes. Add the garlic and cook for 20 minutes.
2   Slice the tops off the potatoes, scoop the flesh into a warm bowl, squeeze the garlic out of its skin and add to the potato with the butter, crème fraîche and mustard seeds. Mash and season with salt and pepper. Spoon the mixture back into the hollowed-out skins.
3   Put back in the oven and cook for 15 minutes or until golden brown. Garnish with oregano and serve.

TO FREEZE
Complete to the end of step 2, cool quickly, wrap and freeze.
To use, thaw at cool room temperature overnight. Cook at 200°C (180°C fan oven) mark 6 for 20–25 minutes until hot to the centre.

POTATO GRATIN

👋 **HANDS-ON TIME:** 10 MINUTES, PLUS STANDING   🍲 **COOKING TIME:** 1¼ HOURS   ✕ **SERVES:** 8   𝒱

METHOD

1 Push the clove into the onion. Put in a large pan with the milk, cream and bay leaf. Slowly bring to the boil, then take the pan off the heat and leave to infuse for 30 minutes.

2 Preheat the oven to 180°C (160°C fan oven) mark 4. Discard the clove and bay leaf and finely chop the onion. Put the chopped onion back into the milk and season with salt and pepper.

3 Add the potato slices to the milk and bring to boil, then immediately take the pan off the heat.

4 Using a slotted spoon, transfer the potato slices to a large, shallow ovenproof dish. Pour the milk over and sprinkle with the breadcrumbs. Cook in the oven for about 1¼ hours or until the potatoes are tender and golden brown. Garnish with bay leaves and serve.

INGREDIENTS

1 clove
1 small onion, peeled
600ml (1 pint) milk
300ml (10fl oz) double cream
1 bay leaf, plus extra to garnish
1.1kg (2½lb) potatoes, peeled and
  thickly sliced
50g (2oz) fresh white breadcrumbs

PER SERVING

320 cals
20g fat (of which 12g saturates)
31g carbohydrate

ROAST POTATOES WITH GARLIC

👋 **HANDS-ON TIME:** 15 MINUTES   🍲 **COOKING TIME:** 1¼ HOURS   ✕ **SERVES:** 8   𝒱

METHOD

1 Preheat the oven to 180°C (160°C fan oven) mark 4. Put the potatoes in a pan of cold salted water and bring to the boil. Boil for 2 minutes, then drain thoroughly.

2 Heat the oil in a roasting tin in the oven. Add the potatoes and baste with the oil until the potatoes are coated on all sides. Separate the garlic bulbs into cloves, leaving the papery skins attached. Scatter the garlic over the potatoes. Cook in the oven for about 45 minutes, turning occasionally.

3 Turn the oven up to 220°C (200°C fan oven) mark 7 and continue cooking the potatoes and garlic for a further 20–25 minutes until they go crisp and golden brown. Season the potatoes with salt and pepper and serve sprinkled with the garlic and chopped parsley.

COOK'S TIP

Once the garlic has been roasted, it's deliciously mild and creamy. Encourage your guests to slip the cloves from their skins and mash them into the gravy or sauce.

INGREDIENTS

1.8kg (4lb) potatoes, peeled and cut
  into large, even-sized pieces
olive oil, to baste
2 whole garlic bulbs, unpeeled
chopped fresh parsley, to garnish

PER SERVING

280 cals
8g fat (of which 1g saturates)
49g carbohydrate

GLAZED PEARS

👋 **HANDS-ON TIME:** 15 MINUTES 🍲 **COOKING TIME:** 10 MINUTES ✕ **SERVES:** 6

INGREDIENTS
butter to grease
1 small, shop-bought Madeira cake
about 4 tbsp Kirsch
3 small Williams pears, thinly
  sliced
about 25g (1oz) butter, melted
1 tbsp caster sugar
good-quality almond-flavoured ice
  cream to serve (see Cook's Tip)

PER SERVING WITHOUT ICE CREAM
240 cals
9g fat (of which 5g saturates)
35g carbohydrate

METHOD
1   Preheat the grill and lightly grease a baking sheet. Cut the Madeira cake lengthways into six thin 5mm (¼in) slices, then stamp out six 7cm (2¾in) rounds. Put on the prepared baking sheet and drizzle with the Kirsch.
2   Arrange the pears in an overlapping spiral on the Madeira cake. Brush lightly with butter and sprinkle with caster sugar. Put the cake under the hot grill for 10 minutes or until pale golden.
3   Serve warm with scoops of almond-flavoured ice cream.

COOK'S TIP
If you are serving ice cream at a party, it is a good idea to scoop portions on to a foil-lined baking sheet and return to the freezer to firm. When ready to serve, simply lift a portion on to each plate.

CHOCOLATE ORANGES

👋 **HANDS-ON TIME:** 15 MINUTES 🍲 **COOKING TIME:** NONE ✕ **SERVES:** 6

INGREDIENTS
25g (1oz) dark chocolate
1–2 tsp Cointreau
1 tbsp cold water
3 large oranges, peeled and pith
  removed

PER SERVING
50 cals
1g fat (of which 1g saturates)
9g carbohydrate

METHOD
1   Melt the chocolate in a bowl over a pan of simmering water. Cool for 5 minutes, then stir in the Cointreau and water.
2   Slice each orange into rounds and arrange on a plate.
3   Drizzle with the chocolate sauce and serve (not suitable for children due to the alcohol content).

FAST FRUIT TART

METHOD

1 Preheat the oven to 220°C (200°C fan oven) mark 7. Put a flat baking sheet into the oven to heat.
2 Unroll the pastry on a lightly floured worksurface and pile the plums in the centre. Scatter over the blueberries. Roughly fold up the edges of the pastry to enclose but not cover the fruit.
3 Use an oven glove to take the baking sheet out of the oven, then slide the tart on to it. Brush the edges with the egg, then sprinkle the demerara sugar over the fruit.
4 Bake on the top shelf of the oven for 20–25 minutes until golden and crisp. Dust generously with icing sugar and serve with vanilla ice cream.

VARIATIONS

- Add a good pinch of ground cinnamon to the sugar.
- Sprinkle the centre of the pastry with 2 tbsp ground almonds before adding the fruit.
- Mix 1–2 tbsp chopped toasted hazelnuts with the demerara sugar.

INGREDIENTS

375g pack ready-rolled shortcrust pastry
a little plain flour to dust
4 ripe plums, cut in half and pitted, or any seasonal fruit
about 150g (5oz) blueberries
1 small egg, beaten
3 tbsp demerara sugar
icing sugar to dust
vanilla ice cream to serve

PER SERVING

480 cals
26g fat (of which 11g saturates)
57g carbohydrate

NECTARINES IN SPICED HONEY AND LEMON

METHOD

1 Put the honey, star anise and lemon juice in a heatproof bowl. Stir in the boiling water and leave until just warm.
2 Add the nectarines or peaches to the bowl and leave to cool.
3 Transfer to a glass serving dish. Serve with a scoop of good-quality vanilla ice cream.

INGREDIENTS

4 tbsp runny honey
2 star anise
1 tbsp freshly squeezed lemon juice
150ml (5fl oz) boiling water
4 ripe nectarines or peaches, halved and pitted
good-quality vanilla ice cream

PER SERVING

80 cals
0g fat
20g carbohydrate

CINNAMON PANCAKES

👋 **HANDS-ON TIME:** 20 MINUTES, PLUS STANDING   🍲 **COOKING TIME:** 12 MINUTES   ✕ **SERVES:** 6

INGREDIENTS
125g (4oz) plain flour
½ tsp ground cinnamon
1 egg
300ml (10fl oz) skimmed milk
1 tsp olive oil
fruit compote to serve

PER SERVING
120 cals

1g fat (of which trace saturates)

24g carbohydrate

METHOD
1   In a large bowl, whisk together the flour, cinnamon, egg and skimmed milk to make a smooth batter. Leave to stand for 20 minutes.
2   Heat the olive oil in a heavy-based frying pan over a medium heat. Pour in a ladleful of batter and tilt the pan to coat the base with an even layer. Cook for 1 minute or until golden. Flip over and cook for 1 minute. Repeat with the remaining batter, adding more oil if necessary to make six pancakes.
3   Serve filled with a fruit compote, with a sprinkling of sugar.

APPLE AND CRANBERRY STRUDEL

👋 **HANDS-ON TIME:** 20 MINUTES   🍲 **COOKING TIME:** 40 MINUTES   ✕ **SERVES:** 6

INGREDIENTS
700g (1½lb) red apples
1 tbsp lemon juice
2 tbsp golden caster sugar
100g (3½oz) dried cranberries
1 tbsp olive oil
6 sheets filo pastry
1 tbsp golden caster sugar

PER SERVING
140 cals

3g fat (of which trace saturates)

29g carbohydrate

METHOD
1   Preheat the oven to 190ºC (170ºC fan oven) mark 5. Quarter, core and thickly slice the apples.
2   Put the apples into a bowl and mix with the lemon juice, 1 tbsp sugar and the cranberries.
3   Warm the oil. Lay 3 sheets of filo side by side, overlapping the long edges, and brush with the oil. Cover with the remaining filo sheets. Brush again with oil, then tip the apple mix on to the pastry and roll up from a long edge.
4   Put on a non-stick baking sheet, brush with the remaining oil and sprinkle with the remaining sugar. Bake for 40 minutes or until the pastry is golden and the apples are soft.

HOT FUDGE PUDDING

🖐 **HANDS-ON TIME:** 30 MINUTES, PLUS SOAKING 🍲 **COOKING TIME:** 1 HOUR ✖ **SERVES:** 6

METHOD
1 Soak the apricots in a bowl of boiling water for at least 2 hours. Stir together the fresh custard and milk.
2 Spread the bread thinly with the butter, then cut into quarters.
3 Grease a shallow 2 litre (3½ pint) ovenproof dish and pour a thin layer of the custard over the base of the dish.
4 Drain the apricots and then roughly chop. Mix with the grated orange zest. Layer up the bread, apricots, fudge and custard, finishing with a layer of custard. Leave to soak for about 1 hour.
5 Preheat the oven to 180°C (160°C fan oven) mark 4. Dust the top of the pudding with caster sugar. Put the dish in a roasting tin and pour in enough hot water to come at least halfway up the sides.
6 Bake in the oven for 1 hour or until the custard has set properly and the top has turned a rich deep brown colour. Cover with foil after 40 minutes to prevent the top from burning.
7 Leave the pudding to cool for about 10 minutes before serving.

INGREDIENTS
175g (6oz) ready-to-eat dried apricots
2 × 500g cartons fresh custard (about 900ml/1½ pints)
568ml carton milk
300g (11oz) sweet bread, such as brioche, cut into slices 5mm (¼in) thick
75g (3oz) softened butter, plus extra to grease
grated zest of 1 orange
200g (7oz) bought fudge, roughly chopped
caster sugar to dust

PER SERVING
660 cals
29g fat (of which 17g saturates)
91g carbohydrate

CARAMELIZED PINEAPPLE

🖐 **HANDS-ON TIME:** 15 MINUTES 🍲 **COOKING TIME:** 10 MINUTES ✖ **SERVES:** 6

METHOD
1 Slice the pineapple into rounds, then cut each in half and remove the core.
2 Put the sugar and rum into a bowl with the pineapple and toss to coat.
3 Heat the oil in a non-stick frying pan until hot. Add the pineapple, reserving the liquid, and fry on each side over a medium heat for 4–5 minutes until golden and caramelized. Divide among six plates.
4 Add the reserved rum and sugar to the pan and bubble for 1 minute. Drizzle the sauce over the pineapple and serve.

INGREDIENTS
1 large ripe pineapple, peeled
6 tbsp each brown sugar and rum
2 tbsp olive oil

PER SERVING
140 cals
5g fat (of which trace saturates)
23g carbohydrate

BANOFFEE PIE

HANDS-ON TIME: 15 MINUTES, PLUS CHILLING   **COOKING TIME:** 2–3 MINUTES   **SERVES:** 14

METHOD

1 Grease the base and sides of a 23cm (9in) loose-based tart tin. Whiz the biscuits in a food processor until they resemble breadcrumbs. Pour in the melted butter and whiz briefly to combine. Press the mixture into the prepared tart tin and leave to chill for 2 hours.

2 Arrange the banana slices evenly over the biscuit base and spoon the dulce de leche on top. Whip the cream until thick and spread it over the top. Dust with a sprinkling of cocoa powder and serve.

VARIATIONS

- Top with a handful of toasted flaked almonds instead of the cocoa powder.
- Whiz 25g (1oz) chopped pecan nuts into the biscuits with the butter.
- Scatter grated plain dark chocolate over the cream.

INGREDIENTS

100g (3½oz) butter, melted, plus extra to grease
200g (7oz) digestive biscuits, roughly broken
2 small bananas, peeled and sliced
8 tbsp dulce de leche
284ml carton double cream
1 tbsp cocoa powder to dust

PER SERVING

250 cals
19g fat (of which 10g saturates)
18g carbohydrate

CHOCOLATE CHERRY ROLL

HANDS-ON TIME: 15 MINUTES, PLUS COOLING   **COOKING TIME:** 25 MINUTES   **SERVES:** 6–8

METHOD

1 Preheat the oven to 180ºC (160ºC fan oven) mark 4. Line a 30.5 x 20.5cm (12 x 8in) Swiss roll tin with baking parchment.

2 Mix the cocoa and 3 tbsp of the milk in a bowl. Heat the remaining milk in a pan until almost boiling. Stir into the cocoa mix, then cool for 10 minutes.

3 Whisk the egg yolks and sugar until pale and thick, then gradually whisk in the cooled milk. Fold in the egg whites. Spoon into the tin and level the surface.

4 Bake for 25 minutes or until just firm. Turn out on to a board lined with parchment. Peel off the baking parchment and cover with a damp teatowel.

5 Spread the jam over the roulade and top with the cherries. Roll up from the shortest end, then dust with cocoa and icing sugar. Cut into slices and serve.

INGREDIENTS

4 tbsp cocoa, plus extra to dust
100ml (3½fl oz) milk plus 3 tbsp
5 eggs, separated
125g (4oz) golden caster sugar
400g can pitted cherries, drained and chopped
1–2 tbsp cherry jam
icing sugar to dust

PER SERVING

190 cals
6g fat (of which 2g saturates)
27g carbohydrate

8

COOKING WITH CHILDREN

GETTING STARTED

Teaching children an interest in food at an early age is the easiest way to ensure a healthy attitude towards food for life.

HOW TO FRY AN EGG

1 Crack an egg into a cup, so that if some of the shell falls in you can scoop it out with a teaspoon.
2 Heat 1tbsp vegetable or sunflower oil in a non-stick frying pan for 1 minute.
3 Turn the heat down low and carefully pour the egg into the hot fat. (If the heat is too high, the white will burn before the yolk is cooked.) Tilt the pan and use a large spoon to scoop fat up and pour it over the yolk – this cooks the yolk at the same time as the white.
4 Cook until the yolk is just set

HOW TO BOIL AN EGG

1 Bring a small pan of water to the boil. Once the water is boiling, add a medium egg. For a soft-boiled egg, cook for 6 minutes; for a salad egg, cook for 8 minutes; and for hard-boiled, cook for 10 minutes.
2 Using a slotted spoon, remove the egg from the hot water and serve.

HOW TO POACH AN EGG

1 Fill a deep frying pan two-thirds full with water and bring to the boil.
2 Break an egg on to a saucer and slide carefully into the water.
3 Using a large metal spoon, gently roll the egg over two or three times to wrap the white around the yolk. Take the pan off the heat, cover and leave to stand for 3 minutes. Serve immediately.

HOW TO SCRAMBLE AN EGG

1 Allow 2 eggs per person. Beat together in a bowl with salt and pepper.
2 Melt 1 tbsp butter in a non-stick pan and pour in the eggs.
3 Cook over a very low heat, stirring constantly until the eggs start to scramble. Remove from the heat and continue stirring until the eggs are cooked but not rubbery. Serve immediately

HOW TO MAKE AN OMELETTE

1 Put 2 eggs in a jug with 1 tbsp cold water. Season with salt and pepper and whisk with a fork to combine.
2 Melt 15g (½oz) butter in an 18cm (7in) non-stick frying pan over a gentle heat. Tip the pan around so that the butter covers the entire surface.
3 Pour the egg into the hot fat. Stir gently with a wooden spatula, drawing the mixture from the sides to the centre as it sets and letting the liquid egg from the centre run to the sides. When the egg has set, stop stirring and cook for another minute until it is golden underneath and still slightly creamy on top.
4 Tilt the pan away from you slightly and use a wooden spatula to fold over a third of the omelette to the centre, then fold over the opposite third. Turn the omelette out on to a plate with folded sides underneath and tuck in straight away.

CHOP AN ONION

1 Put the onion on a board and use a sharp knife to slice the onion in half from root to tip. Peel off the skin from each half, taking the thick outer layer of onion as well

2 Put the flat sides down and make three horizontal cuts from the pointed end almost to the root.

3 Cut along its length six or seven times. Now chop across the width, from pointed end to root, to make dice. Throw away the root.

HOW TO COOK AN ONION

1 For one medium onion heat 1tbsp vegetable, sunflower or olive oil over a medium heat for 30 seconds.

2 Add the chopped onion and stir to coat in the oil for 1 minute. Turn the heat down to its lowest setting and cook for at least 15 minutes,stirring regularly to make sure they cook evenly.

3 Don't let them burn. Add a splash of water if it looks as it they're going to. The longer onions cook, the softer and more translucent they'll become.

HOW TO COOK RICE

Remember the rule double the volume of water to rice and you won't go far wrong.

1 Measure 150ml (5fl oz) long grain rice into a jug. Pour into a pan with ½ tsp salt. Pour over 300ml (10fl oz) boiling water. Cover with a tight-fitting lid and bring to the boil again, then reduce the heat to its lowest setting and simmer gently for 15 minutes.

2 Remove from the heat and lift the lid – the rice grains should be tender, all the liquid should have been absorbed, and the surface should be covered in regular holes. It won't need draining. Fork through the rice to separate out the grains.

HOW TO COOK PASTA

1 Allow around 100g (3½oz) pasta per person.

2 Bring a large pan of salted water to the boil. Add the pasta and stir briefly to stop the strands or shapes sticking together.

3 Cook for the time stated on the pack. As soon as the pasta is cooked, drain well, shake off excess water and add immediately to the saucec

FRUIT

BERRY SMOOTHIE

✋ **HANDS-ON TIME:** 10 MINUTES 🍲 **COOKING TIME:** NONE ✖ **SERVES:** 4

METHOD

Put the bananas, yogurt and spring water in a food processor and whiz until smooth. Add the frozen berries and whiz until a purée forms. Using the back of a ladle, press the mixture through a nylon sieve. Serve.

VARIATIONS

- Grab a handful of fruit and whiz up one of these anytime treats in minutes. For each recipe, chill two 300ml (10fl oz) glasses. Put all the ingredients into a blender and whiz for 1–2 minutes, then divide between the glasses and serve.
- **STRAWBERRY SMOOTHIE** 225g (8oz) strawberries; 1 medium banana, sliced; 150g carton natural yogurt; 100ml (3½fl oz) iced water
- **TROPICAL CRUSH** 425g can tropical fruit salad, drained; 300ml (10fl oz) orange, pineapple and mango fruit juice
- **MINT COOLER** 30 fresh mint leaves, roughly chopped; 2 x 150ml cartons natural yogurt; 2 tbsp honey; 300ml (10fl oz) iced water

INGREDIENTS

2 large bananas, about 450g (1lb), peeled and chopped
142ml carton natural yogurt
150ml (5fl oz) spring water
500g bag frozen summer fruits

PER SERVING (BERRY)
70 cals
trace fat (of which trace saturates)
15g carbohydrate

PER SERVING (STRAWBERRY)
60 cals
trace fat (of which trace saturates)
12g carbohydrate

PER SERVING (TROPICAL CRUSH)
70 cals
trace fat (of which trace saturates)
17g carbohydrate

PER SERVING (MINT COOLER)
60 cals
1g fat (of which trace saturates)
11g carbohydrate

SIMPLE FRUIT SALAD

✋ **HANDS-ON TIME:** 15 MINUTES 🍲 **COOKING TIME:** NONE ✖ **SERVES:** 4

METHOD

1 Combine all the ingredients in a large bowl. Leave to stand for 30 minutes to let the flavours combine.
2 Serve with a spoonful of cream or crème fraîche

INGREDIENTS

3 large oranges, peeled and cut into segments
100g (3½oz) seedless black grapes, halved
½ pineapple, peeled and cut into chunks
2 large bananas, peeled and sliced
4–5 tbsp orange juice

PER SERVING
120cals
trace fat (of which trace saturates)
30g carbohydrate

PANCAKES

🖐 **HANDS-ON TIME:** 5 MINUTES, PLUS STANDING   🍲 **COOKING TIME:** AROUND 16 MINUTES   ✕ **MAKES:** AROUND 8

INGREDIENTS

125g (4oz) plain flour
a pinch of salt
1 egg, beaten
300ml (10fl oz) milk
sunflower oil to grease

PER SERVING

90cals
2g fat (of which 1g saturates)
14g carbohydrate

METHOD

1   Sift the flour and salt into a bowl and make a well in the centre. Add the egg, then gradually beat in enough milk to make a smooth batter. Cover and leave to stand for at least 20 minutes. This helps any air bubbles to rise to the top and escape.

2   Heat 1 tsp oil in an 18cm (7in) heavy-based crepe pan or frying pan. Pour in a ladleful of batter and twist the pan so the base is thinly coated. Cook over a moderate heat for 1 minute or until the pancake is golden. Turn with a palette knife or toss – if you're feeling brave! – then cook the second side for 30 seconds– 1 minute. Don't worry if your first attempt is a bit soggy – it always takes one try to get it right.

3   Transfer to a plate and keep warm. Repeat with the remaining batter, stacking the pancakes on top of each other with a small piece of baking parchment or greaseproof paper in between each one. Keep them warm and serve as soon as all the pancakes are cooked.

VARIATIONS

Three great pancake fillings...

- Sprinkle with caster sugar and squeeze over lemon juice.
- Spread with 1 tbsp chocolate spread and top with sliced banana.
- Mix 25g (1oz) each grated cheese and chopped ham with 1 tbsp crème fraîche. Spoon on to the pancake, fold over and serve.

FLATBREADS

🖐 **HANDS-ON TIME:** 10 MINUTES   🍲 **COOKING TIME:** 2–4 MINUTES   ✕ **MAKES:** AROUND 5

INGREDIENTS

150g (5oz) strong white bread flour
½ tsp salt
½ tsp fast action yeast
75ml (3fl oz) warm water

PER SERVING

100cals
trace fat (of which trace saturates)
23g carbohydrate

METHOD

1   Sift the flour and salt into a large bowl. Stir in the yeast.

2   Add the water and mix either by hand, or in a freestanding mixer with the dough hook attachment to make a soft, smooth dough. You may need to add a further tablespoon of warm water.

3   Preheat a large, heavy-based frying pan over a medium heat. Divide the dough into five equal pieces and roll each out on a floured work surface to 3mm (⅛in) thick.

4   Toast the flatbreads in the pan for 1–2 minutes on each side until golden and cooked through.

CARROT SOUP

HANDS-ON TIME: 10 MINUTES   **COOKING TIME:** 50 MINUTES   **SERVES:** 6   V

METHOD

1 Melt the butter in a large, heavy-based pan. Add the carrots and onions and cook over a low heat for 10 minutes until softened.
2 Add the stock and bring to the boil. Reduce the heat, cover and simmer for around 40 minutes until tender.
3 Cool the soup slightly, then whiz in batches in a food processor. Return to the pan, season with salt and pepper to taste and reheat before serving.

INGREDIENTS

25g (1oz) butter
700g (1½lb) carrots, peeled and sliced
2 onions, peeled and sliced
1.1 litres (2 pints) hot vegetable stock

PER SERVING

90 cals
4g fat (of which 3g saturates)
11g carbohydrate

LEEK AND POTATO SOUP

HANDS-ON TIME: 10 MINUTES   **COOKING TIME:** 30 MINUTES   **SERVES:** 6   V

METHOD

1 Melt the butter in a large, heavy-based pan and add the onions and leeks. Stir well, then add 3 tbsp water, cover the pan and cook over a gentle heat for 10 minutes until soft.
2 Stir in the potatoes, bay leaf, stock and milk. Bring to the boil, then lower the heat and simmer for 20 minutes, covered, until the potatoes are tender.
3 Discard the bay leaf and season with salt and pepper to taste. Cool the soup slightly, then whiz in batches in a food processor. Return to the pan and reheat before serving.

INGREDIENTS

75g (3oz) butter
2 onions, peeled and sliced
450g (1lb) leeks, trimmed and sliced
175g (6oz) floury potatoes, peeled and diced
1 bay leaf
1.3l (2¼ pints) hot vegetable stock
300ml (10fl oz) milk

PER SERVING

180cals
12g fat (of which 7g saturates)
15g carbohydrate

CHERRY CHOCOLATE CHIP COOKIES

👋 **HANDS-ON TIME:** 20 MINUTES, PLUS COOLING 🍰 **COOKING TIME:** 10–12 MINUTES ✕ **MAKES:** 12–14

METHOD

1 Preheat the oven to 180°C (160°C fan oven) mark 4 and grease several baking sheets. Using an electric whisk, beat together the butter, caster sugar, muscovado sugar and vanilla essence in a large bowl until well combined. Gradually beat in the egg until the mixture is light and fluffy.

2 With a metal spoon, lightly fold in the flour, orange zest, chocolate and glacé cherries. Put tablespoonfuls of the mixture on the prepared baking sheets and bake in the oven for 10–12 minutes. The biscuits should be soft under a crisp crust. Leave the cookies to cool on a wire rack and then dust with icing sugar.

INGREDIENTS

75g (3oz) unsalted butter, softened, plus a little extra to grease
25g (1oz) caster sugar
50g (2oz) light muscovado sugar
a few drops vanilla extract
1 large egg, lightly beaten
175g (6oz) self-raising flour, sifted
finely grated zest of 1 orange
125g (4oz) white chocolate, broken
125g (4oz) glacé cherries, roughly chopped
icing sugar to dust

PER SERVING
210-189 cals
9-8g fat (of which 6-5g saturates)
31-26g carbohydrate

HONEY AND YOGURT MUFFINS

👋 **HANDS-ON TIME:** 15 MINUTES 🍰 **COOKING TIME:** 17–20 MINUTES ✕ **SERVES:** 12

METHOD

1 Preheat the oven to 200°C (180°C fan) mark 6. Line a 12-hole muffin tin with paper cases.

2 Sift the flour, baking powder, bicarbonate of soda, mixed spice, nutmeg and salt into a bowl. Stir in the oatmeal and sugar.

3 Mix the yogurt with the milk in a bowl, then beat in the egg, butter and honey. Pour on to the dry ingredients and stir in quickly until just blended – don't over-mix.

4 Divide the mixture between the paper cases and cook in the oven for 17–20 minutes until well-risen and just firm.

5 Leave to cool in the tin for 5 minutes, then transfer to a wire rack. Serve warm or cold.

INGREDIENTS

225g (8oz) plain white flour
1½ tsp baking powder
1 tsp bicarbonate of soda
½ tsp each ground mixed spice and ground nutmeg
a pinch of salt
50g (2oz) each ground oatmeal and light muscovado sugar
225g (8oz) Greek-style yogurt
125ml (4fl oz) milk
1 egg
50g (2oz) butter, melted and cooled
4 tbsp runny honey

PER SERVING
180 cals
6g fat (of which 4g saturates)
27g carbohydrate

CHEESE AND CHIVE SCONES

🖐 **HANDS-ON TIME:** 10 MINUTES   🍲 **COOKING TIME:** 30–35 MINUTES   ✕ **SERVES:** 6–8

INGREDIENTS
225g (8oz) self-raising flour, plus extra to dust
pinch of salt
75g (3oz) butter, at room temperature, cut into small cubes
100g (3½oz) Gruyère cheese, finely grated
1 tbsp chives, finely chopped
½ tsp cayenne pepper
1 tsp mustard powder
1 large egg
2–5 tbsp buttermilk or milk, plus extra to glaze

PER SERVING
300–230cals
17–13g fat (of which 11–8g saturates)
29–22g carbohydrate

METHOD
1   Preheat the oven to 200°C (180°C fan oven) mark 6.
2   Sift the flour into a bowl, add the salt and mix in. Add the butter and lightly rub in with your fingertips until the mixture looks like breadcrumbs. Add 75g (3oz) cheese, the chives, a pinch of cayenne pepper and the mustard powder.
3   Put the egg into a jug, add 2 tbsp buttermilk or milk and beat together. Make a well in the centre of the cheese mixture and add the egg mixture. Using a round-bladed knife, mix the egg gradually into the crumble. As the dough forms, bring it together with your hands; it should be soft not sticky. If it feels dry, add extra buttermilk or milk, 1 tsp at a time. Shape the dough into a rough ball, then pat into a round.
4   With a floured rolling pin, roll the dough gently into a circle at least 2.5cm (1in) thick. Mark the round into 8 wedges and brush lightly with milk. Sprinkle with the remaining cayenne pepper and cheese.
5   Cook in the oven for 30–35 minutes or until well risen and golden. Cool on a wire rack, then pull apart to eat. Good with soured cream and guacamole.

TOFFEE APPLES

🖐 **HANDS-ON TIME:** 10 MINUTES   🍲 **COOKING TIME:** 15 MINUTES   ✕ **SERVES:** 6

INGREDIENTS
575g (1 ¼lb) sugar
300ml (10fl oz) water
6 eating apples

PER SERVING
420 cals
0g fat
113g carbohydrate

METHOD
1   Gently heat the sugar and water in a heavy-based pan until the sugar dissolves.
2   Meanwhile, spear the apples with a stick or fork. Once the sugar has dissolved completely, otherwise it will crystallize, turn up the heat and let the mixture boil until it turns a caramel colour. Take the pan off the heat and immediately dip the pan in cold water to stop the caramel cooking further.
3   Quickly dip each apple into the caramel to coat, then put on non-stick baking parchment to cool. They should last for 2–3 hours before the caramel starts softening.

CHARTS

ROASTING MEAT

MEAT		Cooking time at 180°C	Internal Temperature (160°C fan oven) mark 4
Beef	Rare	20 mins per 450g (1lb), plus 20 mins	60°C
	Medium	25 mins per 450g (1lb), plus 25 mins	70°C
	Well Done	30 mins per 450g (1lb), plus 30 mins	80°C
Veal	Well Done	25 mins per 450g (1lb), plus 25 mins	70°C
Lamb	Medium	25 mins per 450g (1lb), plus 25 mins	70–75°C
	Well done	30 mins per 450g (1lb), plus 30 mins	75–80°C
Pork	Well done	35 minutes per 450g (1lb), plus 35 mins	80–85°C

TURKEY ROASTING TIMES

Oven-ready Weight	Number of Servings	Cooking time foil-wrapped
2.3–3.6kg (5–8lb)	6–10	2–3 hours
3.6–5kg (8–11lb)	10–15	3–3¼ hours
5–6.8kg (11–15lb)	15–20	31/4–4 hours
6.8–9kg (15–20lb)	20–30	4–51/2 hours

THREE-TIER CELEBRATION CAKE

Throwing a party for twenty or more? Here are the quantities to make two smaller tiers for the White Chocolate and Orange Cake. Follow the method on page 212 and make another quantity of syrup, to drizzle over the extra cakes. Assemble up to 4 hours ahead, wrap loosely and keep chilled in the fridge.

CELEBRATION CAKE – INGREDIENTS FOR TWO EXTRA TIERS

	12-PORTION MIDDLE TIER 15cm (6in) cake tin	4-PORTION TOP TIER 200g clean baked bean can
Eggs	3	1
Golden caster sugar	125g (4oz)	40g (1½oz)
Self-raising flour	75g (3oz)	25g (1oz)
Ground almonds	75g (3oz)	25g (1oz)
Orange zest	From 1 orange	1 tsp

For the ganache

White chocolate	125g (4oz)	50g (2oz)
Double cream	284ml carton	142ml carton
Strawberries	175g (6oz)	50g (2oz)
Cooking time	30–35 minutes	25–30 minutes

INDEX

ACKNOWLEDGEMENTS

PHOTOGRAPHY CREDITS

All photography by Lucinda Symons.

PUBLISHER'S ACKNOWLEDGEMENTS

Project Editor: Carly Madden
Consultant Editor: Barbara Dixon
Design Manager: Gemma Wilson
Layout: Ben Cracknell Studios
Art Direction: Abby Franklin
Senior Production Controllers: Morna McPherson and Laura Brodie
Home Economist and Stylist: Sarah Tildesley
Nutritional Analysis: Jenny McGlyne
Editorial Team: Kathy Steer, Fiona Corbridge, Michéle Clarke

ACKNOWLEDGEMENTS